BUCKING THE TREND

BUCKING THE TREND

BY CHRIS ROGERS

and DANIEL BRETTIG

hardie grant books

Published in 2016 by Hardie Grant Books, an imprint of Hardie Grant Publishing

Hardie Grant Books (Melbourne)
Building 1, 658 Church Street
Richmond, Victoria 3121
hardiegrantbooks.com.au

Hardie Grant Books (London)
5th & 6th Floors
52–54 Southwark Street
London SE1 1UN
hardiegrantbooks.co.uk

A Cataloguing-in-Publication entry is available from the catalogue of the National Library of Australia at www.nla.gov.au

Bucking the Trend

ISBN 978 1 74379 250 6

Cover design by Luke Causby/Blue Cork
Cover images courtesy of Getty Images
Statistics by Lawrie Colliver
Typeset in 12/18pt Sabon by Kirby Jones
Printed by McPherson's Printing Group, Maryborough, Victoria

The paper this book is printed on is in accordance with the rules of the Forest Stewardship Council®. The FSC® promotes environmentally responsible, socially beneficial and economically viable management of the world's forests.

To my family.
Without their support,
I'd probably have given up …

CONTENTS

FOREWORD

DURING THE BOXING Day Test, the walls of the Australian team dressing room at the MCG are adorned with key words. Patience, Persistence, Partnerships, Professionalism and Performance are five that stick out; these just so happen to neatly describe one Chris Rogers.

Patience, as they say, is a virtue and given the flow of Chris' career, it sure was necessary – not all went smoothly in those early days in Western Australia. Making it into first-class and then Australian ranks, then dealing with demotion before ultimately flourishing for his country, Chris had plenty to deal with. His resilient and determined nature helped him to get through those roadblocks in his cricketing journey.

Indeed, the gap between his initial Test selection and his second, five years later, is exceptionally rare in the history of the game. It took a special type of doggedness to keep going.

Players these days make strategic decisions to seek new challenges and environments, far more so than in the past when state loyalties overrode all. I think Chris made a great one in coming to Victoria. In a moment when the stars aligned in early 2008 our paths crossed, words were spoken and commitments made. The Baggy Blue of Victoria sat well on his head.

By now a hardened professional, Chris joined a group hungry for silverware – and with a keen eye on the Baggy Green. He did not have to prove himself to these players, but he liked what he saw and felt at home, surrounded by minds unafraid to explore the game. We Bushrangers loved the competitor who walked through the door and bonds were quickly formed with Bob Quiney, Nick Jewell, David Hussey and Brad Hodge.

The Rogers family has a proud history in cricket, with both parents providing their wandering minstrel of a son with a home base. Doubtless this aided his ability to balance the pressures of elite sport with a healthy and positive attack on life away from the game. Cricket is unique in the amount of time spent in the dressing room, and Chris distracted or cocooned himself with reading and crosswords – before sating his appetite for the rhythms of the nightclubs. A fine dancer, he must be slowing down sometime soon!

Partnerships are the lifeblood of a team's success, particularly those involving opening batters and bowlers. Thanks to the brave decision to give Chris another crack at Test level, an unlikely union with the dynamo of Australian cricket, David Warner, became a crucial cog in revitalising the national team. David had found the Jekyll to his Hyde.

Chris' annual English escapades were significant chapters in his learning curve. The variety of people, game situations and leadership opportunities rounded and confirmed his instincts on the game. Cricketers come with a wide range of emotional and intellectual intelligence, and this guy knew his craft, shirked no issue and performed with remarkable consistency. No man has matched Chris' seven consecutive Test half-centuries in 2014–15. He did it with a unique technique of his own devising, one immediately recognisable.

His recollections show what it means to be immersed in a team, playing for your country and with your mates. Chris is always happy and willing to share the knowledge gleaned over many and varied seasons. Hopefully, once the door closes on his playing career, another will open to the path of coaching.

Sportsmen crave the respect of their opponents and teammates. Chris' career has earned him that, from all those he touched, annoyed or defeated.

Greg Shipperd

CHAPTER 1

SETTING THE SCENE

Durham, 2013

'BUCK, IF YOU don't get it now you'll never get a hundred. You don't want to screw this up.'

Thanks a bunch, Matt Prior.

I'm standing out in the middle of the County Ground in Durham on 10 August 2013, four runs away from a hundred. I've made 60 of them in first-class cricket, and half of those in England – it's not like I don't know how to pass three figures. But I have not made one in a Test match. Right here, right now, I haven't the faintest idea how to get those four runs. The pressure of Graeme Swann's bowling, the match and series situation, the hubbub of an Ashes crowd, the fact I've got the Australian crest on my helmet instead of the logo of Middlesex, Victoria or others … it's all added up to one panicking left-hander, and Prior, the English wicketkeeper getting in my ear, knows it.

To think that twenty minutes before I'd consciously thought I was going to get there in the space of two balls.

I'd hit a four, a full toss outside off stump that I got enough on to beat the short cover to his right and the extra cover to his left. That got me to 96, and the next ball was short and wide. I got so excited, I thought 'this is the ball, I just need to hit this in the middle, pick a gap and it's four'. But I've always found it a bit difficult to hit a square cut or forcing shot. I tend to try to hit it with my top hand, rather than letting my bottom hand come through. You almost have to slice it a little bit, but I hit it with my top hand and tend to jam it straight down. That's exactly what happened, I bunted it into the ground, it trickled out to backward point, and I was standing there with my bat between my feet thinking 'I won't get a much better chance than that'. I was right. Swann didn't bowl another bad ball to me.

I had four lucky escapes in the next 19 balls. I got beaten outside off stump, and I tried to manufacture shots from two balls. I got a leading edge to one that lobbed up to mid-on and landed on one bounce to Stuart Broad. I looked up at the big screen and saw the replay and then the reaction of my Australian teammates on the balcony. Captain Michael Clarke was front and centre with his head in his hands. He wanted this as much as I did.

Then, stupidly, I tried to do it again and it landed on one bounce to midwicket. Shane Watson got out, caught down the leg side off Broad. We'd lost a bit of momentum and I was guilty of putting pressure on Shane in that period – neither of us could get down the other end. It was bad batting and really good bowling, particularly from Swann. Not for the first or the last time, he found another gear to tie me down completely.

As ever in international cricket, the combination of silly mid-off (Ian Bell) and wicketkeeper took every opportunity to remind me of the hole I was digging for myself. Prior and I had a good friendship from playing together for the Sydney Thunder, but he wasn't shy in talking it up. These were just about the last words I wanted to hear, and my sense of panic was mounting. Next Swann bowled me a ball that I thought was short and wide and I opened up to cut. But Swann's deception had the ball skidding through low with the arm, so I played over the top and it missed the off stump by a couple of inches. Back I went into head-bowed posture, as everyone on the field, thousands at the ground and many more through television could see how much I was struggling. The longer I spent marooned on 96, the further away that hundred seemed to get.

In some ways, this episode was a little like my whole career. As an undersized kid I'd fought my way into junior, club and state ranks before I had the power to muscle the ball as others did, and focused very much on batting as problem-solving. That method worked for me, and took me to the fringes of the Australian side in 2007, then out onto the WACA Ground as a Test debutant in January the following year. But from a position where I was so close to a career with the national side, it all slid away, to the point that in 2012 I had mentally prepared to quit the game in Australia and play in South Africa or New Zealand in between County seasons in England. Somehow I had found my way back into Test cricket, and fought my way to 96 today. But those last four runs now felt about as reachable

3

as a place in the Australian team had once been. I was consumed by doubt.

Oddly enough, doubts and insecurities have actually been quite a powerful force driving me as a cricketer. Some players are able to back themselves in, but my own doubts about my ability to pull off certain shots led me to a very pragmatic game, where I worked out the most reliable ways of surviving and scoring without taking undue risks. You often hear about the use of positive thoughts to generate good results, but I'm a big believer in finding a way to channel negative thoughts. At one point the former Cricket Australia executive Marianne Roux sat us down and said 'for every negative thought you've got to tell yourself to have five positive thoughts'. I can't say that's ever worked for me.

You spend so much of your time questioning yourself and competing against others that you need to find a way to use those doubts. To block them out successfully means kidding yourself, and how long can that last? Instead I find it best to know and own those doubts, and use them to sculpt a technique within my own limitations. By thinking my way through it, I've been able to find ways of succeeding where others have not, particularly as an Australian batsman in England. There is, perhaps, something for others to learn from that, in an age where we constantly hear so much batting bravado talk, which can lead either to rapid scoring or rapid collapsing.

Back in Durham, I've been left with a desperate kind of multiple-choice question. After a moment's contemplation I decide that I've simply become a wicket in the making for

Swann, unless I can attack him in a way he doesn't expect. It's a case of taking things on or getting out. The options in my head are to try to hit him back over his head, or play the sweep, neither shot a favourite of mine. When it came to sweeping, I'd habitually avoided the shot because I felt the chances of lbw were too high. But if I try to take him over the top I'm more than likely going to deliver a skier to one of Swann's catchers, just as Steve Smith had done when he made it to the fringes of a hundred in the previous Test at Old Trafford. Later, I find out that at about this time John Inverarity turned to his fellow selector Rod Marsh with the words 'I know what you'd do.' In unison they laugh and exclaim 'slog!'

Ultimately I decide the sweep will have to do, even if I have to fetch it from outside off stump. Funnily enough, that moment's fatalism is rewarded when Swann tosses one up on the perfect length and line for me to swat to the leg side. Looking back at the footage it appears almost as if I was expecting it – a happy coincidence – and the ball pings sweetly off the bat, over the square-leg umpire's head and into the unmanned expanses beyond him. There is a split second, just as I strike it, when I'm the first person on the ground to know I have a hundred. I yell 'YES' as in to run, but I know I've got four – and it takes a moment for everyone to recover from their shock that I'd finally managed to hit one off the square.

As I jog down the other end, a sense of exhaustion overtakes me: I can't believe it's happened. A few people told me later that they enjoyed how restrained my celebration was, but it was really a case of being too overwhelmed and overcome to do anything else. Brad Haddin comes down the wicket, puts his arm around me and said 'mate enjoy this, you deserve it'. We trade singles in the next few balls and I find myself at the non-striker's end for the following over. It is then that it all hits me, the enormousness of the moment. So many hours of so many days over so many years working up to this innings, and so much of that time playing the game without any real expectation I'd get the chance to do what I have just done. Alone in those thoughts, under the helmet and looking down at the ground, there are tears in my eyes.

We go off for bad light a few overs later. I walk up the stairs to the Australian team's collection of smiles and pats on the back, and sit down in something of a daze. That's when Darren Lehmann comes up to me and says 'mate, you can enjoy this now, you're allowed to smile', which gets me grinning. He asks me to say something about it to the guys, but I can't manage much. My mum Ros and dad John have been at the ground watching, and while the team invites them into the dressing room, I head off with the media manager Matt Cenin to speak to the press. While I'm away David Warner ushers Mum and Dad into the rooms, sits them down and offers a drink, in a warm gesture they haven't forgotten.

A lot of the media conference is a blur to me, but I've read back what I had to say and this passage sums up how I was feeling, after the Fox Sports reporter Daniel Garb asked whether it meant any more having waited so long: 'After all this time you just don't think that this opportunity is going to come up. I wanted to believe I was good enough, but never knew. To get a hundred, that's something that no one can take away from me, and I can tell my grandchildren about it now … if I have any.' That last bit gets a big laugh. The journalists seem to know a little about me.

On the way back from that chat to the media, a Durham security guard escorts me to the change room and says: 'Mate that was amazing. I've done a few games here and there and I've never, ever seen a crowd applaud an opposition player like I saw today.' That's still one of the nicest memories I have of the day, because it said something about how much of a role England had played in my story. Andrew Strauss, the former England captain, helped too by saying on Sky that you wouldn't see a better first Test hundred.

I'm meant to have dinner with an old friend Frank Biederman, who picked me up from the airport on my very first time to the UK to play, but my only thought is to share the moment with my parents and we have dinner at the team hotel to soak up the day's events. It isn't a case of big conversations or anything like that, just a nice chance for my two biggest inspirations and I to sit back and enjoy the fact I'd finally done it. They'd been there since the beginning, and been through just as much as I had along the way, right down to agonising over those 19 balls stuck on 96. We got there in the end.

CHAPTER 2

BEGINNINGS

Sydney, Perth and places in between

IN THE EARLY hours of 31 August 1977, the final throes of the fifth Ashes Test flickered into Australian living rooms. It came from the Oval in London via the television coverage provided by Kerry Packer's Channel Nine, and the broadcaster was significant. A rain-ruined match at the end of a dank tour for Greg Chappell's team had been overshadowed by the looming breakaway of World Series Cricket, orchestrated by Packer so he could broadcast cricket in the Australian summer and take for himself all the associated commercial benefits.

Australian cricket was at a moment of great change, and all had been revealed in the midst of that Ashes campaign. Riven into two groups of WSC signatories and the rest, the touring party was divided off the field and miserable on it.

Another event marked the morning of 31 August in Sydney: the birth of Christopher John Llewellyn Rogers, second son of John and Ros.

If not quite born at the batting crease, Chris certainly arrived in its vicinity. John's life had been lived in and around cricket circles.

His younger brother Derek was among the outstanding cricketers of the New South Wales Riverina, while John advanced as far as a quartet of appearances for the NSW Sheffield Shield side in the 1960s. He established himself as a stalwart of the St George first-grade side, then as captain-coach of the nascent University of NSW club, where one of his cricketing pupils was Geoff Lawson, the future Australian Test fast bowler. John's attacking captaincy rubbed off on the younger man, as he acknowledged in his autobiography *Henry*, and Lawson's captaincy of NSW in turn influenced two future Australian captains, Mark Taylor and Steve Waugh.

John's own education in the game had arrived in part through the testing experience of matching wits with Richie Benaud's leg-breaks in grade competition years before. In November 1963, John found himself batting against Benaud at the outset of the older man's final season as an Australian cricketer. John remembers well the experience of watching the master bowl in the nets and at exhibitions at Sydney's Royal Easter Show, where he would bowl blindfolded at a handkerchief placed on the pitch – and repeatedly hit it.

Their relationship broadened in later years, when Benaud employed John as an assistant at his consulting company, based in the same Coogee apartment Benaud and his wife Daphne would call home right up until his death in 2015. John helped with various elements of the business, and would watch fascinated on Thursday afternoons when Benaud pulled together his weekly newspaper column in little more than half an hour of fierce concentration. 'I think,' Benaud once told John, 'through my fingers.'

Three years after Chris was born, John was appointed general manager of the Western Australian Cricket Association. The family moved from the east coast to the west, thrusting John into the cricket politics of the time. WA players were a large chunk of the Test team, including the polarised and polarising trio of Rod Marsh, Dennis Lillee and Kim Hughes.

As well recounted in cricket annals, Hughes was the establishment's choice to stand in for and ultimately replace Greg Chappell. Marsh felt he should lead, and so too did Lillee. Their squabbles and the related aftershocks, which stood at the centre of Australian cricket for years on end, would often cross John's desk.

Arguably John's major achievement at the WACA was to co-author a report that outlined how much money the game was generating for Packer and the pitifully small dividends for the ACB. That report started a process that led to a richer television deal for Australian cricket, a fully-equipped administration and far better-paid players. Those benefits were just starting to appear as Chris found himself drawn to the game in his teens, beginning the path towards something only barely imaginable for an Australian cricketer on that late August night in 1977: the life of a full-time professional.

Watching Chris work his way through junior cricket and tennis ranks, John Rogers saw a shy, introverted son who possessed plenty of fighting qualities. These came to the fore when playing sport.

'It showed on the tennis court most. Essentially he was a little kid, battling as hard as he could. In cricket it was more that as a little kid, he was difficult to get out, made more noticeable by the fact that his talented elder brother somehow did get out much more easily.

'In the backyard against his brother and various friends, he could be very showy, but when competing against other teams,

he was much more concerned at staying in the contest. He was very shy; very conscious of his lack of height, and did not like his frizzy hair one bit! But there was a quiet self-confidence there too that showed in sport – he'd keep battling.'

Though he had experienced something like the top of the game as a first-class cricketer for New South Wales, John never pushed great expectations upon his son. He simply wanted to see him do his best. John saw plenty of young talent – some progressed, others didn't. What he saw in Chris was a player capable of working his way through situations, and a determination to keep working.

'I never ever talked to him about playing for Australia. It was only ever about doing as best as he could. The kids in older years always looked much better, as did the WA cricket team as he started doing well in grade cricket and WA youth teams. I'd seen a lot of good kids do well from my own playing days in so many different ways, and I reckoned he had something.

'When he showed he was keen on cricket, it was more a matter of me hoping he would get as much out of cricket as I had – and just as I had never really thought I was anywhere good enough to play for NSW let alone Australia, I held no such specific ambitions for him and never talked about it – it was more about doing well at the level he was at.

'Of course the personal characteristics stood out. I've seen hundreds of kids in a range of sports who have stood out clearly from the rest. Usually they are quicker than anyone else, strong and well-balanced, are very competitive, read the play much quicker, and often they have a pleasing way of doing it that

attracts attention immediately. Until he turned 15 and started to grow, Chris was always one of the smallest in his year group, lacked strength, was not a fast runner and had no particular charisma – so attracted little attention.

'For some reason even as he got stronger, that perception by outsiders continued. It was only those people who took an interest, and teammates, who noticed that he had something few others had. Essentially this was his capacity to persevere, to keep his cool, to do his own thing in his own way, to not be fussed by a situation nor by his opponents.

'It took some time even for me to realise, that for every team he was chosen for, he'd mostly start quietly, yet by the end of the season he was the most consistent performer. Mostly he'd be chosen a little reluctantly, and by season's end would have made himself a candidate for the next level – junior teams, school teams, club teams, under-age rep stuff – and then into senior teams, and eventually the WA team. The same process happened in England in all his club teams and then his county teams. And so too, eventually, the Australian team.

'Until he turned 16, I had no expectations of him other than that I thought he'd do pretty well. There were lots of times when he simply couldn't hit the ball off the square, and looked quite awkward, and even lacking in talent – if talent means the ability to hit the ball effortlessly.'

John remembers the two days of his son's 279 in 2006 for Western Australia against a Victorian side featuring Shane Warne at the WACA as the day he thought the family had an Australian Test cricketer on their hands.

'That required a lot of composure. Up to then the top players in that top Australian team seemed on a different level. His 194 against NSW [in 2002–03] with both the Waugh twins scheming to get him out, had been pretty good, but this one against Warne, even though he did little other against Warne than nurdle singles on the leg side, meant he could stand up to the best.

'There were plenty of setbacks – WA dropping him, Victoria contemplating removing him from the contract list, Middlesex rejecting him initially, and Australia regularly telling him he was on his last chance.'

SPORT WAS ALWAYS going to form a key ingredient of my childhood. Dad – or JR as he is well known – was an accomplished sportsman in his own right. He played four first-class games for New South Wales in the late 1960s, some decent rugby for St George and was a pretty good tennis player as well. He tells people he even beat Tony Roche as a child (but fails to mention he had a few years on him). His family had always been into sport, especially cricket. He tells me my great-great grandfather was the president of the Gosford Cricket Association in the 1880s, after arriving in Australia as a child from Nottingham in 1850.

Dad's love of sport was passed down in particular to his two sons. David, my older brother, tried his luck as a leg-spinner but succeeded in that department about as well as I did. He preferred rugby and still goes by the nickname of 'Dancin' Dave Rogers' at the University of Western Australia

Rugby club. Without the influence of my father and brother, I doubt I would have played first-class cricket … let alone for Australia.

I was a pretty lazy kid without a lot of motivation, but it was my competitive nature that drove me on the sporting field. Dad pushed me to train every day with the words 'If you're not doing it, you can guarantee others are'. Dave made sure his little brother had to work hard to beat him at anything, and these were two magic formulas for me. That evolved into a strong tenacious streak. I didn't like losing anything and would fight hard, not so much at training but whenever the first ball was bowled, the first whistle blown or the first serve delivered.

I have a big sister also, who left home when I was pretty young and moved from Perth to Melbourne not long after, a move that became significant later in my career. Gillian and I are close, but I probably missed her female influence when I was coming through my teens.

Last but not least is my mother Ros, who by choice I think took a slight back seat in my development, though she loved us playing sport. She'd argue that it would've been a bit hard having two parents who pushed you. However, I think I can say that the true characteristic that set me apart and enabled me to fulfil my dreams was what I inherited from her. As I worked out pretty quickly and was reinforced every time youth sides were picked without me in them, I was not viewed as being as talented as a lot of my peers. Bigger, stronger and more confident than me, I had to find another way to be better than them and as I'll talk about later in the book, it was my mental talent that gave me the career I never dreamt I would experience. As Dad would agree, it was from Mum I mostly inherited this.

Memories of renovating my first apartment with her in my early 20s are of seemingly hitting brick walls when it came to problems and Mum repeatedly working methodically through each of them while I stood by fascinated. There was never an issue that was too much for her and whenever someone talks to me about resilience, it reminds me of her. You'd have to be to be married to JR for that length of time. Dad might disagree slightly, but it seemed to me a case of she was the brains and he was the brawn.

I don't want to bore you with too many details, as childhoods in other biographies make for hard reading to me. Undoubtedly it's what shapes you into the adult you become, but many of those decisions are not the writer's choice. No doubt a fairly simplistic outlook, but then it is my book.

Born in Sydney in 1977, I lived in Chatswood for my initial two years. I'm the third of three children and have parents who at the time of writing are three years short of their 50th wedding anniversary.

Recently I spoke at the St George 50th anniversary of the 1965–66 Sydney grade cricket premiership title. I followed up on stage a panel of three members of that side, Warren Saunders, Peter Leslie and Dad. All three are club greats, particularly Warren, who captained for many years and is still involved. Anyway there was a photograph of the side lined up as cricket sides do, displayed on all the ten or so screens in the room. At the back left was a fresh-faced JR, who at the time was 22. Next morning, at breakfast with my parents, I asked if they could find me a copy of it, to which Mum replied the day that the photo was taken the very day my parents met, at a rugby club lunch straight after, as Dad was late due to this photo. Pretty cool for a child to see an image of a parent on such a fateful day.

Dad was originally a teacher but then a company secretary and a NSW cricket state selector – before moving the family to Perth in 1980 to take up his position as general manager of the Western Australia Cricket Association. What followed were seven years growing up in the south suburbs of Perth, first in Brentwood and then a year in Shelley. In December 1986, the family moved back to Gosford in the Central Coast of NSW, where Dad's family is from. This is my first memory of playing cricket. I played for the Avoca Under 11 side, which was coached by my best mate Matthew Sawyer's father, Brian.

We lived on 10 acres of bush, in a pretty remote place that overlooked Copacabana Beach, where I went to school. I'm pretty sure life would have turned out differently if we had stayed there. But a year later we were back in Perth and I was back in Brentwood Primary. The merry-go-round didn't stop and we continued to move houses, albeit in the same area – my parents realised a sure way of making money was to renovate and resell – something they were very good at. I think I moved house 17 times in the 21 years I lived at home. It never bothered me, and I do wonder if it gave me a taste for trying new places.

But a tennis court was mandatory wherever we went and by the end, even a paved area was designed as a batting net against tennis balls. I must have hit a million tennis balls out the back of our various places. Often these sessions would end in heated arguments about the best way to go. Dad would have overloaded me with his thoughts, leaving me trying to sift through what worked for me and what didn't. It was a curious development and what so many coaching manuals these days tell you not to do. Dad had so much information to impart that he felt he needed to do a lot at once. The manual says filter it in slowly and allow the student to focus on one thing at a time.

Not long ago I worked with the Australian Under 19s in Perth against their England counterparts. I was advised that the players had their own techniques and it was more important to help them with match awareness. What a load of rubbish, I thought. Technique is something that keeps developing throughout your career. At 18, very few batsmen have a technique without a weakness. If one does then he'll make it anyway because he will be another Ricky Ponting.

Dad ended up throwing so many balls his body started to fall apart. One memory was of him bending over to pick a ball up and suddenly screaming out in agony. I honestly had a split second thought someone had shot him. As he was doubled over, he had to shuffle full pace to a low wall nearby to stop himself keeling over. Turned out his back had gone, so he retreated to the living room where he lay on his stomach on a number of pillows. His request of me to walk on his back was met with a fair share of pessimism but there I was with hands on the ceiling walking up and down his back. The next day at the chiropractor, the doctor asked him what happened and then after a check up asked if anything else had happened as his back was worse than the usual spasm. When JR told him about me walking on it, you could have knocked the chiro over with a feather. He thought it was one of the funnier and more stupid things he had heard – JR was always good for a theory.

I went to high school at Wesley College in South Perth. The first time I actually was taken there to get my uniform from the club shop, I overheard the only other kid in the shop telling his Mum he needed a cricket jumper. Coincidentally that other kid, Craig Ruthven, ended up becoming my best friend for about the next 15 years. I played three junior seasons for Ardross Cricket Club, plus my first appearance for Melville Cricket Club in the Inverarity Shield, the district junior competition for Under 13s. I tried bowling, wicketkeeping and batting up and down the order, before playing for the first time as an opening bat.

I was never much of a cool kid. Bit hard when you are one of the smallest kids in the year, have a fuzzy red bouffant and terrible skin – clearly not the ladies' choice! Nor was I fan of going to house parties and listening to the likes of Nirvana, Pearl Jam and other grunge acts that were so popular at the time – I preferred old school hip-hop. Fortunately my sporting skills helped me out. Craig played cricket and ended up captaining the first's soccer side and we also attracted another sportsman to our group in Nick Phillips, who was the best rugby player in the school.

This was significant, as Nick's father ended up teaching at the school around the same time as Dad did. It can be highly embarrassing having your father teach at your school, especially if he is somewhat extravagant, but as Nick was the biggest kid in school it gave me a shield of protection against abuse. I found myself caught a bit between the nerds and the jocks. This can probably be summed up by the fact I spent time playing in school chess tournaments – as well as tennis, rugby and cricket.

Dad can be a little absent-minded and was not your usual teacher type. He'd fall asleep during class, and sometimes send people outside for punishment and then forget them. Not to mention his rather annoying choice in headwear. He'd alternate between the khaki hard hats beekeepers wear and black leather chauffeur caps that might be better suited at the mardi gras. I ended up throwing that one away.

But he had an extraordinary ability to listen and be interested in what his students would say. I still have people come up to me asking if I'm 'JR's son' and then telling me a random story about how they used to swap seats when he was writing on the board just to confuse him or something like that. I'd mention the person's name to Dad and he'd be able to recall the student and what his parents did for a living.

Perhaps my favourite story is when he took some of his older economics students to a farm in the country. Most of these kids were boarders and pretty grown up already. Somehow they'd managed to smuggle up some alcohol and were playing drinking games, which Dad stumbled upon. In true JR fashion he told them that's not how you play drinking games and proceeded to show them his own, including the one where you put your head on a stump and spin around it after drinking and then run about 20 metres which inevitably ends with a dizzy sideways stack.

The next day, with a slight hangover, Dad emerged from his digs to retrieve something from the bus he'd driven the boys down in. Head down and in blazing sun he shuffled to where the bus was left, only to lift his head and notice the bus was nowhere to be seen. The boys had managed to get in, take the handbrake off and push it round the corner of the building and out of sight.

With a brief look left and then right, JR shrugged his shoulders and returned to his bed. The boys watched the whole episode. I still get told that one. Dad maintains they were a good group of kids, so he wasn't fazed.

As for school itself I was not a bad student – just easily bored. I ended up doing the two hardest math subjects, physics, economics, English and woodwork. I inherited my mother's skill with numbers and her analytical mind – I've won every Sudoku challenge I've had in cricket and hear surprisingly only Glenn McGrath would beat me, though I'll believe it when it happens. I don't tend to think outside of the square that much, which can be a weakness, but this straightforward, problem-solving style of thinking helped me adapt to Dad's method of coaching.

I was absolutely useless at woodwork and physics though and had no idea what I was doing in either of them. I still have the odd nightmare about having to go to a physics lesson and being so far behind with so much to catch up on. I finished up doing ok in general however, and got the marks I needed to do Commerce at the University of Western

Australia. All that being said, my memories of school are on the sporting fields.

Wesley won the cricket competition in my final year where I broke school records with three centuries and an average over 100. This record was shattered a few years later by a Year 10 student by the name of Shaun Marsh and then by his brother Mitch a few years after that. It was a nice moment years later when the three of us all played for Australia together.

As memorable as the cricket was though, the rugby was just as good, and I managed to be player of the year for the first 15, which was a pretty good effort being the smallest kid on the team. I think my skill of being able to read the game and be in the right position as well as avoid danger was developing and crossing over to the cricket field. Nick, despite his size, played five-eighth, I played inside centre, and we developed a good combination. Despite winning player of the year I felt Nick was clearly the best player and I still have a memory of him carrying three players on his back as he surged over the last 10 metres to score in the corner. We didn't win a lot but we had great fun.

At school we would also play a mash-up version of AFL and rugby during lunch breaks. One day a kid called Ben Kaye lined me up for a solid hip-and-shoulder bump that put me on my backside. Later in the game I had the chance to tackle him and flung him with plenty of gusto. When he hit the ground I heard a sharp cracking sound, and the next moment he was screaming, as the others were lining up to jump on top. I took him to the infirmary, and interrupted the nurse to say 'there's something wrong here'. As the colour drained from Ben's face, she told me to hang on while she helped another student with what looked like a runny nose. This was no fun for Ben, who it turned out was now carrying a broken collarbone, much to the nurse's rather delayed dismay.

On weekends I was often on the tennis court at Blue Gum Park club, which has 14 natural grass and eight plexipave courts. As a little kid who could barely see over the net, I made a bit of a name for myself as I could out-rally the adults. I even made a state squad coaching group between the ages of 12 to 14, and my folks thought tennis might be my career. There are pictures of me as the undersized kid in junior tennis clobber, no doubt in between chasing down balls in my very own Lleyton Hewitt phase, which also featured a couple of tantrums and broken racquets. But there was something about the individual nature of tennis that I couldn't get my head around, summed up by a match at Sorrento Tennis Club.

My opponent had the backing of a small but parochial club crowd, and on one occasion served an ace that to my eye was clearly wide of the mark. I called it out, but to play up to his gallery he replied 'no that's in, that's in', and walked over to the other side of the court while I waited for a second serve. After a bit of a delay I eventually put my hand up and said 'look you can have the point, I don't care anymore'. That was really the moment where I decided to play cricket, because the selfish, individual focus of the sport wasn't for me. I enjoyed the sense of a team sport more than anything, and so finished up my tennis days. Besides, my opponents were growing bigger and more powerful and I wasn't.

My cricket was nothing special at that stage – I could hardly hit the ball off the square. Then at 15, playing for South Perth in the WACA Under 17 Saturday morning comp, I scored my first century. I'm not sure I even had a 50 before that. Dad remembers watching me grind my way to 80 before a flurry of boundaries took me to three figures, and 124 not out in the end – he reckons it was the first time he started to believe I might be a good cricketer. From there I made the WA Under 17 team and then the Under 19 team, and after a 99 against New South Wales, I found myself as one of two WA boys chosen in the Australian Under 19 team – David Hussey being the other. The humorous side of being picked in the state Under 17 side was that Huss was chosen as the off-spinner batting nine and me the leg-spinner batting 10. I bowled about 22 overs in the first game but then the wheels came off and I couldn't land them. By the end of the tournament I was batting four and not bowling.

It was then that I started to realise I was growing up and had to figure out what to do with my future. Without any real desire to find a profession I did what a lot of my friends did and what Dad thought I should do and enrolled in Commerce at UWA. Failing two subjects in my first semester and then scraping through with marks of 50, 52, 54 and 57 percentiles in second semester, I realised I wasn't cut out for sitting behind a desk dealing with numbers all day. Working in a restaurant washing dishes and having a limited social life around uni was not exactly how I envisioned life as an 18-year-old.

By this time I was playing senior cricket at Melville Cricket Club, which was being captain-coached by the ex-Hampshire and England cricketer Paul Terry. He asked if I would like to play cricket in the UK, in a remote corner of North Devon called Instow. There wasn't much of a decision to make. Keep studying something I didn't like or defer and go play cricket for another six months? More or less as he was asking the question, I was packed and ready to go.

CHAPTER 3

INTO, AND OUT OF, THE PATHWAY

Perth, Country NSW, North Devon

A YOUNG MAN starting to think seriously about playing cricket in Australia in the mid-1990s did so at a time when things were starting to get a little more complicated. The time-honoured pathway – from club cricket, state colts and second XI to Sheffield Shield competition and the Test team – had sprouted other subdivisions and elite identification streams.

Talented juniors were now pitted against one another in Under 17s and Under 19s at national and international levels, while the influence of the Australian Institute of Sport had helped encourage the foundation and growth of the Cricket Academy, run by Rod Marsh in Adelaide. The academy 'scholars' were often identified out of under-age competition and then had something like priority access to state squads and beyond: not a summer in the 1990s went by without numerous stories spruiking the strength of this system, particularly when lined up against the struggles of the English game. As if to underline the point, an Academy side beat Michael Atherton's England touring team twice in as many days at North Sydney Oval in late 1994. Before the summer was out, Atherton would be on the losing side against another group of up and comers: the Australia A side that tipped England out of the limited-overs World Series finals to leave a supposedly international tournament contested between teams led by Mark Taylor and Damien Martyn.

At the international level, Australia had plateaued in the early 1990s following the surprise World Cup victory of 1987 and the drought-breaking Ashes triumph of 1989. There was a sense that under the leadership duo of Allan Border and the coach Bob Simpson, earlier gains had been sacrificed through a lack of ambition and aggression. Marsh and others rejoiced when Mark Taylor brought a more daring streak to the team in 1994–95 following Border's retirement, and it was that as much as the emergence of Shane Warne credited for delivering the Frank Worrell Trophy to Australia in the Caribbean in 1995. The future seemed tailored towards the aggressor over the accumulator.

Marsh made that much clear when he spoke to Kerry O'Keeffe for a piece in the *1995 Wide World of Sports Cricket Yearbook*: 'Often Rod Marsh's cricketing mind is as bristling as his famous moustache. He imagines that down the line there will be no place in the game of cricket for the "sheet-anchor" batsman, those who have built their reputations on rock-like reliability.'

Marsh was right. Within a decade, a Test batting order of Matthew Hayden, Justin Langer, Ricky Ponting, Mark Waugh, Steve Waugh, Damien Martyn and Adam Gilchrist would indeed be capable of sustained acceleration unimaginable just a few short years prior. Batsmen of a more deliberate bearing – batsmen such as Chris Rogers – would indeed appear less prevalent in Australian sides. Those who did emerge, such as Simon Katich and Michael Hussey – had to face intermittent criticism for not 'getting on with it'.

Back in 1995–96, when Chris Rogers was first chosen for Australian Under 19 duty, his batting heroes just happened to be those of the kind Marsh thought to be on the way out. David Boon, Geoff Marsh, Taylor and Border had been Australia's batting engine room, and these were the men from whom he drew inspiration as an undersized youth who made up for a lack of obvious power with rare tenacity and a method weathered against the theoretical and technical testing of his father John.

In terms of size, approach and pessimism, there was an unmistakable similarity to the early cricketing forays of another left-hander, Michael Hussey. Two years older than Chris, and a graduate of the Cricket Academy, Hussey recalled in his autobiography *Underneath the Southern Cross*: 'My batting game was all about hanging in there.'

Hussey, of course, went on to a very fine career, and from solid defensive foundations he built arguably the most versatile batting method yet seen in the game. But his teenaged sense of inferiority was understandable given the Australian cricket climate of the time. It was no easy thing to be a nicker and nudger at a moment when the national team had just become the world's best. Chris' path was to prove a difficult one, leading him not to the Academy finishing school but to a more modest cricket destination on the other side of the globe.

AT 18 YEARS of age it would be fair to say I was pretty wet behind the ears. I'd only lived at home, had a couple of jobs that weren't very taxing and played a bit of cricket and rugby. Going to an all-boys school didn't help with my social life. I think I might have only kissed one girl, and that was only after dragging her down about half a dozen times on the local ice rink. Not surprisingly she didn't fancy a second date!

I had begun to play senior cricket at Melville Cricket Club, starting out in the second team but quickly progressing to the firsts after an 80 against Fremantle. My first-grade debut pitted me against England bowler Alan Mullally and I stood up and made 55. My second game wasn't quite so auspicious, as I had my off bail broken for two by the Western Australia bowler Craig Coulson, who was a genius at grade level.

My third game for the firsts was the one that stood out. Playing against a full-strength Midland Guildford team, I batted for nearly two sessions in making 77. Midland Guildford had a host of Australia players in their XI – Tom Moody, Brendon Julian, Jo Angel, Simon Katich and Tim Zoehrer, plus one or two other state players. I look back now and think that was a big moment in my career, although at the time I still didn't believe I would make it as a professional cricketer.

All I remember of that day was big Jo yelling at me time after time and even from the boundary rope while I was batting 'You lucky little bastard!' This was a great initiation for any young, aspiring batsman and I loved it. Jo became one of my favourite teammates and was always brilliant to me. It was such a privilege to play with him and what he did for his side was as good as I've ever seen. The only time I didn't enjoy him was when I'd purposely put on a bit of Enrique Iglesias music just to annoy him and he'd catch me, hold me down and dead-arm my forearm – his signature move.

Despite the attention I gained from the way I batted that day, I was still searching for motivation and reason, so when the chance to head overseas to play cricket came up I knew I had to take it.

At this stage, life as a professional cricketer was still not something I looked upon as a realistic goal. I just had no motivation for anything else and none for a working career. I look at some of the young cricketers coming through the ranks now and their awareness is off the charts. Their single-mindedness to succeed and make a living out of sport blows me away. No doubt it has a lot to do with more opportunity these days compared to when I first started, and the bigger amounts of money on offer, but also I was just too naive. I needed to grow up.

Around this time a lot of guys I knew were getting invites to go to the Cricket Academy, which at the time was in Adelaide (now Brisbane). I had blown that opportunity. David Hussey and I had been picked to play NZ Under 19s in country NSW and suburban Sydney – pretty low-key stuff, which neither Dave nor I enjoyed too much. We found ourselves competing for a No.6 batting spot much of the time, as the NSW and Victorian boys seemed to get a golden run. Brad Haddin was the wicketkeeper, while Nathan Bracken, Don Nash and Mathew Inness made for a handy bowling attack. In the third and deciding 'Test', I finally was selected at No.3 in the batting order (Dave was 12th man) and top-scored as we won the series – and then found myself as the only member of the team not to get an invite to the Cricket Academy, then run by Rod Marsh.

That was more than likely because I managed to piss off Richard Done, who happened to be Marsh's understudy at the Academy. Our argument was part of a wider experience that showed me representative cricket for Australia was not always going to be smooth sailing, particularly when a bunch of young men from different and competitive states are thrown together by the selection panel. It was a major eye-opener for a naive kid, and it wasn't long until I started to feel like I didn't want to be there.

After doing well in the preceding state competition for WA and arguably playing the innings of the tournament against NSW, who had Bracken, Nash, Jamie Heath and the off-spinner Paul Sutherland, I had been left out of the first 'Test'. I was left out with Mathew Inness and we ran drinks. Matty Inness ended up becoming teammates at the Warriors in later years and got every ounce out of himself as he forged an impressive career. After that match we played a one-day game, where I batted No.3, made a painstaking 13 or so and ran out Chris Davies, who would go on to play for South Australia and now holds a senior position at the Port Adelaide Football Club. Not a great start.

Next up was another one-dayer and I was due to bat No.4. In pursuit of quick runs, my style was not deemed useful and I started to slide down the order until I ended up batting No.9 or 10 in a losing effort. It was at this point I started to feel a little homesick and left out, which wasn't helped by some pretty shabby treatment from teammates. My low personal confidence and bad hair and skin didn't help me fit in. Sharing rooms, I was kicked out by one teammate so his girlfriend could spend time with him and when she came out at 3am and saw me asleep in the corridor outside she started to apologise, to which he responded 'don't fucking worry about him'.

However when we turned up to the second 'Test' and I was once again left out, I was devastated. When one of the players said he needed something from the change room, I put my hand up to get it for him, but instead sat in the change room for 15 minutes, near tears. I was telling myself, 'No one likes me here, I'm not getting a chance, what's the point of being here at all?' Pretty ordinary behaviour by me, I must admit.

Later that night I was called in to the coach's room. Richard Done told me how disappointed he was with my behaviour. My only question to him was 'Isn't the team meant to be rotated so everyone gets a go to show what he can do?' His response was that he was trying to play what he thought was the best side as it was an important series to win. Even now, I'm still not sure what to make of that. In some respects it is fair enough, but I also had a strong desire to call bullshit. No one can remember what happened in that series and it certainly didn't reflect who made it and who didn't. I was eventually selected in the third and final 'Test' in place of David Hussey – he and I the only two batsmen to play more than 20 first-class games and to represent Australia.

It is fair to say that until I was recalled to the Australian Test side in 2013, those few weeks had a negative effect on how I perceived the idea of playing for my country. Subsequent times around the national team or Australia didn't quite feel right, as though I was worried it was going to be a similar experience. There would be times, too, when personal or interstate rivalries and outside distractions would mean the environment was not always very welcoming. Something else that emerged in my thinking as a result was the belief that players can always improve at different speeds – a battler at 17 can grow into a far better player than those he struggles to keep up with in his teens.

But having not been able to handle that environment, I was left with the distinct impression that I needed to grow up. In hindsight, getting away and living out of home and making new friends was exactly what I needed. I never went to the Academy and I don't regret it. Some guys need to work on their game and that is a great place to do it. I needed to work on maturing as much as my game. A lot of that would take place in England.

Boarding a plane from Perth, I was accompanied by Dimitri Mascarenhas, who ended playing a lot for Hampshire and England. He was a club teammate at Melville and Paul Terry had organised for him to go over as well. I'll never forget getting off the plane to be met by two of North Devon's senior players. Frank Biederman was the vice-captain and in his late 20s, but probably three stone overweight with bad teeth. The other – Colin Payne – was 44 at the time, the opening bowler, four stone overweight and balding, with a big bushy beard and even worse teeth. I thought … Is this for real?

Unbeknown to me, they took one look at the athletic, tall, good-looking Dimitri and then the tiny, ugly, ginger, bad-skinned boy next to him and thought 'Have we got the wrong one?' It turned out to be a match made in heaven. I didn't know at the time, but these two were to become two of my closest friends in cricket.

The drive from Heathrow down the M4, M5 and then Link Road to North Devon takes a bit over three hours on a good day. For me it was like being on Mars. Everything not only looked different, but it felt different. I was dropped off at the Palmer household. Brian was then club secretary and his wife Dorrie was a tiny slip of a woman. They welcomed me into their home and were lovely to me. Aged in their mid-60s, they served up a roast dinner before offering me an aperitif of sherry. I didn't even know what sherry was and although I accepted that night, I was sure to never again.

That first month in Instow was quiet. The Palmers were lovely, but I needed to find people more my own age. I'd been given a job as groundsman at Grenville College and worked for a Welshman whom I could barely understand, but he looked after me. One of the students, Ben Moore, was 18 at the time and a member of the North Devon Cricket Club. Ben took me under his wing and took me out my first weekend. It was about early May and quite a balmy evening. I returned home around 1am and couldn't work the door. Not wanting to wake my hosts up I decided to sleep on the bench in the garden. An hour later I woke up completely wet and shivering with cold and knew I had to get inside. After some banging on the door, it was opened to astonished faces. After a brief explanation, they rushed me inside and insisted on a hot shower. They thought sleeping outside was hilarious. I clearly still had some growing up to do. Ben became a good friend as well and even invited me to stay with him and his wife in Dublin about 12 years later.

I'll never forget my first game playing for North Devon. It was a warm-up match. Keen as mustard and asked to field, I immediately headed to backward point where I hoped to show off some fielding skills. The captain, Tom Stanton, immediately asked me to head to square leg, but I replied that I was a good fielder. He said, 'Trust me, that's where you want to be.' Colin was opening the bowling and wicketkeeper Mark Overton (father of twins Jamie and Craig, who both represented Somerset) immediately stood up to the stumps. It was a 6–3 leg-side field and no slips but a short leg. I thought 'What the hell is going on here?'

Colin's first ball was delivered at about 90kph, starting well outside off stump before hooping in and striking the batsman on the thigh pad before trickling to me at square leg. I burst into laughter. He would have done the same in that first over about four times. I'd never seen anything like it. He continued to play for the first team until he was into his early 50s, and I wouldn't be surprised if he held the world record for most deliveries striking the thigh pad.

This would be helped by the fact that Devon was a holiday destination and touring teams would visit North Devon from not only all over the country, but from all over the world.

Mid-summer you could play at least six times a week and often I did – it beat working. Colin often played mid-week as well, as he owned his own fire protection company, so could do more or less as he pleased.

Not only did I enjoy the cricket, but the ground itself is spectacular. Where two rivers meet the ocean, it sits proudly in the corner with a sea wall and thatched pavilion and scoreboard. I still think it is the most picturesque ground I've played at, including Lord's.

Those early memories of playing there were as much about the characters as the cricket. I was learning my trade and my first year was hardly spectacular. Colin was larger than life and took me under his wing and treated me like another son – he already had two, Dan and Neil.

The year I first played there was the year the Devon League first played 50-over matches. Playing Bovey Tracey in the first game, the scoreboard had 25 overs up on the board in our innings. Walking around the ground Colin asked 'Is that 25 overs gone or 25 to come?' Then there was his comment when he was captain of the Sunday League side after we'd been turned over by local rivals Bideford: 'When you boys learn to hate losing, I'll teach you how to win.' He was as competitive as they come, and it was for this reason there is one other moment that resides forever in my memory.

Playing in the 16 eight-ball-over competition (the prelude to Twenty20), one of the biggest hitters in the area, Arnie Searle, played for the opposition. The sun was out this day and there wasn't much swing, so unfortunately for Colin, Arnie decided to line him up. There wasn't a local player who didn't want to take Colin down a peg or two and most couldn't. But Arnie got him this day and in one over dispatched him for six boundaries, including two maximums. It was some phenomenal hitting and we were left in awe as Arnie hit Colin where he pleased. On the last ball, a pull shot was almost valiantly stopped by a desperate boundary rider who ran 20 metres and dived, only for the ball to slip through his fingertips.

Everyone at the ground stopped to look at Colin's reaction. With hands on hips in the middle of the wicket, resembling a teapot, he bellowed 'For fuck's sake … Pick up the fielding!' His enthusiasm was infectious and rubbed off on me. In subsequent years at North Devon and even when I played elsewhere, he was like a surrogate father to me. I had problems with living arrangements the next year but he ended up letting me live at his place of work and then my following season there I stayed with him and his family.

As for living arrangements, the Palmers were lovely to me, but I ended up moving in with Lee Hart, the team off-spinner and No.4 bat. A lawyer by trade, he was a typical Brit. Witty, intelligent and dry, he would often have me in stitches. It was at this time I got myself my first girlfriend, but his good-natured pressure ribbing got to me. It was all a laugh; he did it brilliantly and still does. He reminds me of the British comedian Steve Merchant, Ricky Gervais' offsider. It helps that Lee is also tall, at about six foot five.

Lee now lives in Taunton, in Somerset, with his wife Sue and two children and while captain of that county we have been able to catch up on our friendship. Likewise with another Taunton resident, Mike Paine, who played in those days for another North Devon rival, Braunton. He is my age and about the only one around that age who would go out with me on the weekends. He lived with me in South Perth for six months too. Frank Biederman, who met me at the airport, is someone else I'm still very close to. His place was dubbed the Pig Pen; he is now married with three children. He was three stone overweight; these days he runs marathons. Who would've thought?

The one other character who will never be forgotten, despite passing away a few years back, is the legendary local vicar John Edwards. He played more cricket per week than me – a phenomenal effort considering he was in his late 70s at the time.

He had a little black book full of names who he would get to play for his mid-week sides, which is no mean feat considering there was a game just about every day. I thought Colin was slow but John would bowl genuine donkey drops … striking fear into the opposition. One wealthy side imposed a 200-pound fine on any player dismissed by him. On one occasion their West Indian import defended against him for about an over before taking an almighty swing at an Edwards delivery, only to hit it straight up and be caught. He was last seen destroying his helmet on the way off.

Vicar John batted No.11 in every game he played. He could only block and there was no point running, as he was reduced to a shuffle by this stage. This was a fact I used to take advantage of by stationing him as the only leg-side fielder when I bowled and then aiming at leg stump. He would head after it and I would jog behind him and then swoop past him at the last second to pick it up and throw it back in. It always got a laugh, and he loved the attention.

One game we needed 47 to win when he came in as last man, with me still at the crease. The opposition would have all the fielders on the boundary for me, so I would try to hit boundaries from the first three balls and then get a single fourth ball of the over for Edwards to face the last two deliveries. He wouldn't even back up and would stand two metres behind the stumps when I was on strike. On this particular day we ended up winning the game and scoring the 47 for the last wicket. John made 0 not out but was carried off while I trudged after. He was a character.

It was in these mid-week games I even batted right-handed a few times. Sometimes I'd get annoyed at the lack of sportsmanship by the opposition, who would set unrealistic targets, so I'd take the mickey and play opposite-handed. Years of batting right-handed in backyard games with my neighbour in Mount Pleasant, Josh Bolto, paid off and I managed to get a few scores doing this.

One day I made 90 right-handed and managed to play shots I couldn't even execute left-handed, as my dominant right hand was now my bottom hand. The opposition – not knowing I actually batted left-handed – were impressed and said they understood why I was in the WA squad at home. They were a little annoyed when they found out the truth.

I'm telling you all this because my first three years representing North Devon were probably three of the best I have had in the UK. Every experience was brand new and playing cricket all the time with good mates was a dream. I worked in an Irish bar for my last two years and that was brilliant. I fell in love every year, including with a girl I saw for many years, and I was starting to grow up and get some much-needed confidence. Not only that but my batting was starting to develop to the point where I had returned to Perth after a few seasons in the UK and earned the chance to represent WA. I was starting to figure things out.

CHAPTER 4

ONCE WERE WARRIORS

Perth, Sydney, Brisbane

WESTERN AUSTRALIA HAS always been a place apart, by virtue of its distance from the rest of the country. For a long time the distance itself left the state lagging behind the rest, particularly in the years after the Second World War when the state was first granted a place in Sheffield Shield competition. As Anthony J. Barker relates in his history of the WACA:

> 'In its post-war period Western Australian cricket unavoidably appeared backward in facilities as well as performance... The team had a makeshift appearance... the first WA teams took the field in a wide variety of club caps and sweaters... Western Australia in the 1940s and early 1950s was closer in lifestyle to the 1930s than to the late twentieth century.'

Yet WA always had an uncompromising attitude to sport, which became a means of identity and a way of proving the state's credentials against the rest. Following a fortunate Sheffield Shield victory in its debut season, 1947–48, when a percentage system favoured the state's restricted schedule, WA waited 20 years for another. But when the Englishman Tony Lock led an emerging side to the title in 1968 it heralded a period in which the west became Australian cricket's dominant force, lifting the Shield 14 times in 31 years. In addition, WA representation in the Test team peaked in 1981, when it provided seven of 11 players.

That level of success began with young and united teams, helmed first by Lock then the learned John Inverarity, and persisted as less-cohesive units trampled over opponents through a combination of enormous talent, self-belief and an affinity for the WACA Ground's uniquely fast surface.

After leading WA to four Shield titles, Inverarity departed midway through the summer of 1978–79 to take up a teaching position in Adelaide. His sagacious manner and understanding of human psychology was to be missed, in what became an increasingly fractious team environment over the ensuing years – which ultimately would leave its mark on Chris.

WA's aforementioned competitive streak was exacerbated by the World Series Cricket split, which in effect doubled the number of Test cricketers taking part in state and club cricket, while adding another layer to already strong rivalries. There was a combustibility to cricket in the west.

Rod Marsh and Kim Hughes wrestled for the leadership of both state and national sides. Graeme Wood was a highly skilled and single-minded batsman who led as much by example as anything else, but he lacked the communication skills of the best leaders and often left coach Daryl Foster mending the fissures he left in his wake. Geoff Marsh, a loyal Test match lieutenant to Allan Border, inherited the captaincy when Wood was sacked in 1991. But his career was already on the wane, and he retired in 1994. This is all without mentioning the brief coaching reign of the masterful swing bowler Terry Alderman, who was left bitterly angry at the WACA when removed from the job in 1993.

Wood and Marsh left in their wake an increasingly divided team, where competing egos and disconnected generations scrapped with each other as much as the opposition. The early cricket experiences for the likes of Tom Moody, Damien Martyn and Justin Langer – among others – were thus characterised as much by a need for self-preservation as a fierce commitment to the team itself. This trio were pitted against one another in the race to succeed Marsh as captain, and both Moody and Langer were left nonplussed by the appointment of the sublimely skilled but unpredictable Martyn for the summer of 1994–95. The state team's results dived almost as fast as Martyn's own batting.

Now the coach of WA, Langer has been a powerfully influential figure in Australian cricket, and has always promoted values of unity and team spirit – even if his unrelenting intensity are not for everyone – too much at times even for Chris Rogers.

Moody, meanwhile, tried to find a middle ground between disappointment and friendship with Martyn, and was rewarded for his forbearance when the younger man's leadership flamed out, leading the team to four Shield finals from 1995–99, winning the last two.

Victories achieved through a tenuous alliance between richly talented but contrasting characters left WA with an elevated sense of self-worth once more. It was into this febrile environment that Chris Rogers found himself cast.

THE SOUND AND sight of cricket at the WACA Ground is different to anywhere else in the world. At a sparsely attended Sheffield Shield game the sound of bat on ball is incredibly crisp. This comes from the pace of the ball off the wicket and the openness of the ground, resulting in an unmistakable crack when a batsman has middled one. Perth's hot and dry climate also results in seemingly endless days of clear blue skies in summer, and as a kid I remember the yellow helmets of Western Australia's batsmen standing out against this backdrop, without any moisture, smog or humidity haze to obscure them.

Once I graduated to playing for WA, I got used to the rhythms of the ground. Typically the first session would be very tough for batting, the second would be excruciating for all concerned due to the heat, and then the last would be beautiful as the breeze came in. At lunch you would be tired, at tea completely exhausted, but then the evening would bring a literal second wind to help the players and spectators enjoy the arena as shadows crept across the field.

Over my years in the west this experience would be affected by the way the pitch evolved. At first it was lightning fast, and I would often look back with trepidation at how far back the wicketkeeper and slips were standing. But around 2001 the surface slowed a touch and flattened right out, so much so that we nicknamed the seasons that followed as 'the fielding years'. We spent plenty of time batting of course, but the main memory is of spending seemingly endless hours in the field and struggling to get wickets. That, more or less, is how the square has remained to this day, as exemplified by the high-scoring drawn Test between Australia and New Zealand in the 2015–16 summer.

Batting at the WACA was a unique experience for another reason: the ability to score runs to all 360 degrees. At the MCG for example, you're trying to hit straight and not pull or cut that much because the wicket can be a little two-paced. But at the WACA it was possible to play just about every shot in the book, provided you were able to adjust to its pace. That made it an excellent place to learn the art of batting and scoring, provided you could learn to shelve some of your shots when playing elsewhere. One technical element you developed was to punch the ball into the wicket square because it was so hard, and another was to use the pace off the pitch to advantage.

Less visible but equally memorable was the hair-raising experience of batting in the WACA nets, which to this day are faster than any pitch prepared in the middle of any ground I've played at. I always hated going in for a net, from the first day I trained with the state squad. Back then all the fast bowlers in the squad were tall operators able to generate bounce – Brendon Julian, Jo Angel, Mark Atkinson, Sean Cary, Matthew Nicholson and Brad Williams to name a few – and all could leave you fending for your life in there.

I'll never forget one day I watched Adam Gilchrist batting out of his crease to these guys in training, cutting, driving and pulling the ball everywhere. I thought to myself 'oh the wickets must be a bit slow today', only to get beaten from pillar to post, bowled, nicked off, you name it. I was standing well back in my crease, but it was no use. I was left in awe of

Gilchrist, and in terror of the nets. For a while I avoided them, as did Murray Goodwin, but eventually Justin Langer pulled me aside and said, 'Mate I know you don't want to do it, none of us want to do it, but you've got to get in there. That's what makes you tough, that's what gives you courage. If you can do it in there, you can do it anywhere.' That resonated with me, and so I forced myself to get in there.

It was a tough school I came home to on my return from Devon in 1998. At the time I was feeling pretty good about life. But the list of recent inductees to the Cricket Academy reminded me of how far back I was in Australian cricket. The Academy was being written about as the world's ultimate cricket finishing school. But that one incident with Richard Done appeared to have cost me my chance. All these other young players were going to the Academy and I was left wondering if I'd been left behind. To this day I still wonder how much that cost me in later years.

That being said, it was in many ways the best thing to happen to me, because I had to go away to England. If I'd been in another cosseted little cricket environment at the Academy I don't think I would have grown up. I had to experience life and engage with people who had lives beyond the game. From what I heard, Rod Marsh at the Academy was trying to promote this by mandating the players also have jobs. I felt I needed the autonomy to work things out for myself.

Having grown up largely in Perth I needed that experience, because the capital of Western Australia was not somewhere I had to stretch myself to live beyond my comfort zone. The best word I can use to describe the lifestyle of the place is 'easy'.

To this day, having moved to Melbourne, there are places and areas there that I don't know much about, the city being so big and diverse. But in Perth it was not so hard to know everywhere, because there really isn't that much to know. If you were playing club cricket you'd jump on the freeway and never be more than 40 minutes' drive away from home.

While that was comfortable and familiar, it also had a tendency to breed a kind of insularity and even incestuousness in relationships and behaviour – everyone seemed to know everyone else, whether they liked it or not. When I was nearing the end of my teens I remember there being a club where all the cricketers went – all except me. I didn't feel comfortable in that company, and in knowing well before turning up that there would be so many familiar faces in attendance yet again. The rock music selections didn't encourage me to return either.

So I was still something of an outsider to WA cricket culture when I was first picked in the Western Australia state squad at the age of 19. This much was obvious because when I turned up no one knew me – I was starting from a long way back in terms of relationships, if not performance. That counted, because the WA team of the time was immensely strong and competitive for places.

I was among a group of batsmen around the fringes of the state team at the time. Rob Baker, an outstanding junior batsman and sound technician was one, alongside Michael Dighton, Marcus North and myself. It was to be Baker's decline – he was to battle chronic fatigue syndrome and not make his way back into the team – that gave me my first chance, and I quickly discovered that my lack of familiarity counted against me. The players loved Baker, and regarded me with looks that said 'who's this bloke?' My first innings for the state didn't help, when I was out to the modest part-timers of Mark Ramprakash just before the touring Englishmen took the second new ball.

The team's next trip was to New South Wales for a Sheffield Shield match at the SCG, in November, 1998. While it was a thrill to play at such a grand old ground for the first time, the most vivid memory is of the social dynamics of the team on tour. We were staying in Coogee and on the first afternoon we got there the group went to the Coogee Bay Hotel. I went to the bar and ordered a beer, then found myself standing next to a senior player. The following exchange took place.

'What are you doing?'

'What do you mean?'

'Don't you ever fucking stand next to me in a pub again.'

With that I put my drink down and walked straight out of the pub and back to the hotel, just about in tears, wondering what I'd done.

Looking back, it is true I was fairly loud, obnoxious and opinionated – three qualities that were never likely to go down well in a West Australian dressing room where junior players were expected to be seen and not heard. How times have changed. The cricket itself was bruising and also dramatic: the SCG match came to a swift end as we were shot out for 58 by Nathan Bracken, Gavin Robertson and Stuart MacGill on a wearing, spinning pitch, before we returned the favour in Perth. Having been sent in, the Blues were rounded up on a fast track for 56 in a mere 25.2 overs. My contribution of 20 was not enough to keep my place and I wasn't to be called into the squad again until the following summer.

It was December 1999 when I got my next chance, joining the team ahead of their meeting with Queensland in Brisbane. The previous leg in a two-week tour had been in Sydney, and all I heard once I arrived were stories of how much fun the boys had enjoyed around that trip. The Gabba was no cakewalk however, with Andy Bichel, Adam Dale, Scott Muller and a young Andrew Symonds all capable of making the ball talk on a well-grassed pitch. Sent in we were out cheaply on day one, before Symonds clattered us to all parts as the Bulls built up an imposing lead. Batting again on the second evening I was again out quickly, and as it appeared the game was heading only one way I found myself heading out late that evening.

One factor in this was that I managed to get talking to a girl, which was still pretty rare for me at that stage. But the other was the stories of various hijinks enjoyed by the team in Sydney, leaving me to think that having effectively ended my part in the match I had some sort of licence. The team was staying in sets of two-bedroom apartments, and the following morning my roommate Michael Dighton's alarm went off just in time for him to get to the ground on time. He knocked on my door but I was still some way from being able to think straight. Another 30 minutes or so passed before I was able to get out of the room and head for the ground, which I reached as warm-ups were halfway through.

This decidedly unprofessional behaviour was met sternly by the coach Wayne Clark, who said simply: 'Go back to the hotel and pack your bags, you're on the next flight home.' As it turned out, the debutant Darren Wates was able to fight it out for long enough to take us into a tiny lead, and we had to go field again. The Queensland players were soon asking where I was, and the response that I'd been sent home early for getting out on the gas did not help my reputation beyond WA.

Back at the hotel, I looked in the mirror and told myself 'well that's the last time you'll play for WA'. The journey home was an afternoon's worth of considerable embarrassment, and I couldn't bring myself to speak to Dad about it. At the next WA training session, the state captain Tom Moody pulled Michael Dighton and I aside to say: 'Guys what's your problem? Do you actually want to play for WA?' After I replied with an apology and an affirmation of my desire to contribute, he turned back and said 'as for you, you're a fucking disgrace' before launching into the biggest rocket I've ever received – thoroughly deserved too.

A few days later, Dad could tell something was up and so we discussed it. I relayed events with trepidation, worrying about how he was going to react. I'd well and truly braced for another dressing down when he more or less shrugged his shoulders and said 'son, everyone makes mistakes, don't worry about it, you'll learn from it'. After my relief at avoiding more abuse, the lesson stayed with me, as did Dad's perspective. No cricketer, past or present, has gone through their career without making a mistake. I made lots, but over time you begin to learn from them, and start to make better decisions with the benefit of those experiences. You can't be young and naive forever.

The WA side that had been so strong for so many years was actually about to go into decline. The talent coming through from the next generation was not as good, and there was the ascension of a few senior players to the national side and Simon Katich going interstate – but the culture of the team at the time was not one that helped the newer generation perform. As coach, Clark had been excellent in managing the egos and personalities of a richly talented bunch, but all of a sudden he was left with a younger and more needy group, and it took him a while to adjust.

In club land I had moved from Melville to University, and though I made plenty of runs, there was a common view in WA that the club's home ground at James Oval was simply too friendly a batting surface to fully trust the runs gathered there. After my first few Shield matches, Clark sat me down and told me 'you probably need to leave University because James Oval is just too flat and it's not going to teach you good habits'. These were wise words, reinforced by the experience of being beaten for pace in an early encounter with one of the Lee brothers at the WACA Ground. It was widely known Brett Lee was quick, but to face his older brother Shane and be unable to cope with his pace and bounce was a sure sign I needed a tougher batting environment to learn in.

I was sad to leave University, particularly as the players there tended to be more worldly and outward looking than the single-minded and occasionally limited horizons in the state squad. But while many of the university players were the smartest blokes I ever played with, they were also some of the dumbest cricketers, over-theorising and forgetting how to equip themselves with thoughts and actions you can remember under pressure. So for my next club I moved to South Perth, known for a faster and tougher home pitch. At the start I struggled to find my feet.

A season in which I averaged around 25 in club cricket and did not get near the state team had a couple of choice memories. One afternoon I faced up to Dennis Lillee's son Adam – a serviceable medium-pacer – and simply missed a straight one. Another day we played against Mount Lawley and I was subject to some pretty unrelenting sledges from Mike Veletta, who just happened to be the man set to replace Clark as WA coach the following year. My hopes of making it as a professional cricketer were ebbing away, and I'd started thinking about returning to study and even working with my Mum's embroidery business.

These thoughts were at the forefront of my mind when towards the summer's end, an optometrist, Helen Venturato, was asked to test the state squad players' eyes. It wasn't something I'd ever thought about before, but the visit to Helen's practice was a turning point in my life. The deterioration of my vision had happened slowly, and I wasn't really aware of how much I had lost until I first wore the testing lenses and thought 'oh my God'. I realised this was why I was missing straight balls, because my eyes were simply not capable of the focus required. Combined with the colour blindness/deficiency I suffered from, it became clear that simply seeing the ball had become problematic, which had added to my batting woes.

I'm often asked about being colour-blind and sometimes the misconception is that I can't see colour at all, but that isn't the case. To my understanding, I see a dulled-down version of what most people see. Sometimes I describe it as seeing what others do when they have sunglasses on. The problem in cricket though is the dark red ball can sometimes merge in with dark backgrounds and become difficult to pick up. Getting out to a full-toss from Graeme Swann in the 2013 Ashes was simply because the unusually high trajectory of his delivery meant the ball actually went above the line of the sightscreen and merged in with the supporters sitting above it. I lost sight of the ball until it was half way down the wicket. The dismissal was no less embarrassing for that though. In the past it has been an issue but like with most difficulties, over time they can be overcome.

Being told that I actually had quite poor vision and needed contact lenses or glasses gave me a different angle on my recent struggles, and in the final two games of the season a couple of scores in the 60s began an upward trend towards consistent run-making that vaulted me from South Perth back into the state side the next summer.

After finishing a two-week second XI tour as captain in Adelaide and Brisbane and having the obligatory last night celebrations, I was woken by the phone around 7.30am to be told Murray Goodwin was pulling out of the Shield side due to the impending birth of his child and that I would replace him to play the next day in Sydney and to get myself to the airport ASAP. I made 53 in my only innings but it wasn't enough to keep my spot. With the return of Murray I missed the next two games and wasn't selected again until two months later in the return fixture against NSW.

Against a very good attack, I battled early before Stuart Clark had me absolutely plumb on 33, only for the umpire to deny his appeal. I still think it was a turning point in my career. Whether I would've been dropped after this game who knows, but I scraped to 96 that day before hooking Clark into the safe hands of Michael Bevan at fine leg. I've always wondered what the hell was he doing there.

Two games later I scored twin unbeaten centuries against South Australia, all the while copping some rather colourful criticism from Greg Blewett and Paul 'Blocker' Wilson, who found my style of playing and missing and edging down to third man for a boundary rather frustrating. It was a fantastic lesson and experience, and I'll never forget Blocker sticking his head into our change room after we declared to ask 'Where's Buck?' I was completely unsure what he was going to say and wondered if he hadn't finished with me before he continued, 'Well done mate, that was fantastic.'

Blocker has since become a great friend and it was a great moment seeing him get married on the foreshore of South Perth years later after he had joined the Warriors. The blooming of that friendship was a great example of how performance also helped alleviate a lot of my earlier anxiety and my outsider status, because the currency of runs compels teammates and opponents alike to find value where previously they might not have. I look back now and think what might have happened without the eye test. Not much in the game of cricket, that's for sure.

CHAPTER 5

FROM CLUB TO COUNTY

Devon, Lytham, Derby, Leicester

IN THE PETITE shape of the Ashes urn, Australia's cricket rivalry with England has one clear and enduring symbol. But there is another tale that speaks equally of the cultural differences between the game's two oldest powers – the winding, oscillating story of Australian cricketers making the long journey across the globe to play professionally in the land of their nation's origin.

That story has a beginning in 1931, when it appeared that a steady wage with Accrington in the Lancashire League held more appeal for a young Don Bradman than further feats in the Baggy Green. He ultimately rebuffed the approach, after Kerry Packer's grandfather, Robert Clyde Packer, fixed up a deal.

It was Bradman the administrator who was behind the harsh treatment meted out to many who chose to accept money for League and County contracts. Leg-spinner Cec Pepper, who went to England as a professional after being omitted from the 1948 touring party, was one, another was NSW all-rounder Bill Alley, who became a legendary figure at Somerset and, like Pepper, a highly respected umpire. Upon his return to Australia in the summer of 1951–52 he found himself not only ineligible for selection but physically barred from entry to the SCG – where he had proudly represented NSW – without a public ticket. 'That incident just shows the bitterness and scars left by the exodus of talent to Lancashire and Yorkshire,' Alley wrote in his autobiography, saying he was labelled a traitor for his actions. A handful of players, such as Ray Lindwall, and later Graham McKenzie, did manage to walk the tightrope between Test duty and League contracts, but for most it was a case of choosing club or country.

But there remained a certain reticence among Australians to make the journey, for reasons Allan Border summarised in 1986. For one, he felt that few Australians actually looked upon themselves as full-time players until after World Series Cricket. Secondly, he felt that post-season beach and golf days appealed far more than grim April days in England. As he wrote in *A Peep at the Poms*: 'Oh God, what am I doing here', I thought to myself. I could have been lying in the sun, enjoying a few cool beers and lapping up the good weather.

The staleness Border spoke of was a large reason why Bradman and others were implacably opposed to the development of workaday cricket attitudes seeping into the Australian game. Yet within the space of a few weeks with Essex, Border's early reticence had been replaced with a rather different view. England could be exactly the kind of finishing school a young Australian cricketer needed. At a time when the rebel tours to South Africa had stripped the nation's talent stocks close to bare, Border envisaged County competition as a way to hasten the education of the young men he was now leading in a hesitant Test side.

*'There is no better grounding for a young player than to go
over to England. I realise that now – I've seen it at first hand.
When I get back to Australia, I'll be talking to guys like Greg
Ritchie and young Steve Waugh, telling them to think about
going to England. It would help them a hell of a lot. In this
environment, you've got to become a better, more mature player.
You learn how to play the game under different conditions and
in various circumstances. After a few years in County cricket,
your education is all but complete. Looking at it through purely
Australian eyes, I believe that if we could somehow get the top
20 Australian cricketers playing County cricket, I think that within
two or three years, Australian cricket would be a real force in
the world game.'*

Steve Waugh did indeed go, to Somerset in 1988, and Border
encouraged Essex to recruit his twin Mark in 1990. As *Wisden* stated:

*'Australian cricket has two nurseries for its finest young players.
One is in the verdant grounds of Adelaide's glorious Oval,
where the Australian Cricket Academy prepares a balanced
squad of 14 teenage prospects every year. The other is 12,000
miles away, in a country small enough to slip into Australia's
back pocket, but where the opportunities for cricketers are big:
England, of course, where the beer is warm, the climate cold
and the Poms live.'*

Chris Rogers ultimately was to miss out on the Academy nursery,
but would complete his cricket education first in English Leagues
cricket, then the County game.

MY FIRST YEAR at North Devon had been memorable, and as the relationship grew I found myself totally immersed in the place. Apart from the cricket, I worked numerous jobs in clubs and bars, and found myself getting into my first serious relationships. That brought its own complications in my second year, as several host families did not take kindly to me bringing company back home for the night. One father went as far as to dismiss me with a new nickname – 'the bonking barman'. Almost a book title, that one.

After spending 1998 at home trying university for a second time, my final year at North Devon came in 1999 and coincided with the World Cup. The whole team watched the Edgbaston semi-final between Australia and South Africa, spellbound as Steve Waugh, Michael Bevan, Allan Donald and Shane Warne all took turns grabbing the match before that extraordinary last over had Damien Fleming somehow finding a way to deny Lance Klusener the winning run. Having watched that finish I was absolutely adamant I would be watching Sunday's final, against Pakistan at Lord's.

Trouble was, we had a game scheduled that day at Westward Ho! (yes it is really called that) The ground was on a steeper slope than Lord's, and if you stood at fine leg you couldn't actually see the feet of the batsmen. The venue did not enhance my enthusiasm, and I found myself debating the necessity of my playing with the captain, Colin Payne. He kept telling me 'you've got to play, it's a big rivalry' to which my response was something like 'mate I couldn't give a shit, I want to see the World Cup final'. In the end, we compromised. He promised to bring a television along with an extension cord, they'd plug it in and I could watch the game when I wasn't batting.

Come the Sunday morning, we get to Westward Ho!, only to find that there is no power point anywhere! I was furious, saying all sorts about provincial cricket grounds and what was I doing here. But as the day went on, score updates filtered through to let me know I wasn't missing much – Australia won the final easily, with hours to spare. The entree had turned out to be the main course.

For 2000 I decided it was time for a change, so I moved a short distance south-east to Exeter, a bigger town. The idea had been to go somewhere a little more lively, but I was accommodated at the university and found that to be more isolated than the community I'd enjoyed in North Devon. I once again made some very good friends and the Lammonby family – Glenn, Jill and a very talented two-year-old son Tom – continue to keep in touch. I've since played a second XI game with Tom for Somerset, just to remind me how old I am still playing this game.

Exeter, however, was very much a family club and lacked many in my age group. Careful what you wish for I guess. This experience had me moving again for 2001, well beyond the boundaries of Devon to Lytham near Liverpool. Competition-wise it was a step up, and I was proud to help the team finish fourth in the division that year.

Lytham seemed like a lovely place but the club itself slightly disappointed. The chairman took the game too seriously perhaps and the players themselves didn't completely buy into the concept of team spirit. A couple of occasions batting second I'd watch as batting partners were dismissed only to retreat to the sheds, shower and put on the dancing clobber for a night out in Blackpool even before the game had finished. As soon as the game was over off they'd pop and the pavilion would only be left with the hardcore members.

Blackpool was certainly a trap, as one story details. Pushing the wheeled covers off, a teammate and I accidentally rammed one into a teammate, Beef, who was pushing another. He went down in agony clutching his leg. Beef tried playing but couldn't manage and we played one short. After the game he had a few bevvies and eventually decided he could join in on the venture into Blackpool. He was the life of the party that night and was happily showing off all and sundry his dance moves. Next day he woke up and couldn't move, so visited the doctor, only to find out he had a broken leg!

The best thing out of playing for Lytham was I became very good friends with Phil Watkinson who played for the club and coached juniors in the area. Roughly my age, we trained hard together and he even nicknamed our exercise course on the foreshore of Lytham as the Rogers Regurgitator. Phil ended up relocating to Perth to live with me for a few years and worked hard enough to first attain his professional residency and then his Australian citizenship. In the meantime he'd been on a rugby tour of the United States and met a Canadian woman, Melissa, who he married and followed only months after obtaining his citizenship. He didn't expect that to happen.

Another winter at home in 2002 gave me time to think about where to go next, and I wound up at Wellington

Cricket Club in Shropshire, a team promoted to the top division of the Birmingham League the year before. It was also the first time the club had engaged an overseas pro, so I was somewhat of a novelty.

In many ways this would be one of my fondest years, helped in no small part by the fact we won the competition. I didn't have the greatest summer personally, and we were not the most fancied of teams, but we were able to get onto a roll in the second half of the summer, winning seven games in a row to take the title. It was the first time I'd really felt enormous confidence walking out onto the field, looking around me and knowing all my teammates felt the same about winning the game not even being an issue. That confidence bred some great displays, including a handful of the best catches I've ever seen taken. The belief we had in that team was something I won't forget.

Not only was the cricket fantastic but the social side was equally so. I had found another set of surrogate parents in the club president Terry O'Connor and his wife, Sharon. They've since become exceptionally close to my parents and have even hosted each other's ventures to the other side of the world on numerous occasions.

Adam Byram and his pregnant wife at the time, Fiona, housed me at the beginning of the summer before I moved in with club coach Chris Dirkin. But it was the fantastic nights out in Shrewsbury, the largest town in the area, with a number of teammates all around the same age that brought us together. The likes of Anthony O'Connor (Terry and Sharon's son), Steve Moules, Adam and his brother Gavin, Chris

Martin, Mark Downes, Gareth Howell, Anthony Gower and Greg Johnson and not forgetting the unforgettable but older David Street who introduced me to the drink, Kermits, all made it a brilliant summer. I'm just glad no photos have surfaced of the naked run Greg and I did to the scorebox and back from the pavilion two hours after we won the title.

I would have been very happy to go back to Wellington for 2004, but it was around this time that my improving displays for WA meant there was a little bit of County interest in securing my services. The moment arrived when Michael Di Venuto was ruled out of the summer due to a back injury, and after a move for Marcus North fell through, the Derbyshire coach Dave Houghton signed me up. Though I took shoulder and hamstring niggles with me to the club, the year began very well; I enjoyed the team and Derby, while the higher standard of play kept me on my toes.

Entering into June it seemed a fruitful summer was in the offing, but I was soon to find myself in all sorts of bother courtesy of a short ball from Mark Cleary, a fellow Australian. We were playing Leicestershire at Oakham School. Out grounds are a common point of irritation for County players, as they make the adjustment from first-class venues to dicier surrounds on lively wickets, often with minimal sightscreens and plenty of other visual distractions from watching the ball down the pitch. First innings of this match I was lbw first ball and barely saw it. Second innings, batting No.3, Mark, or 'Ice' as we knew him, was bowling seriously fast.

Pretty quickly I knew I was likely to be in trouble, because his pace combined with the low sightscreens and trees behind them meant I was really struggling to pick up the ball. I've seen pictures of myself batting that year and it's staggering to think now how low many of us allowed our helmet grilles to be – far too much room for the ball to get through. When a bouncer came down I was nowhere near ready for it. It flicked my glove and hit me flush in the right eye socket. I went down, undoubtedly concussed, and panicking at what damage had been done. My hand moved instinctively to my face. I couldn't see a thing out of my right eye.

Mark came running down the wicket and when he got to me he yelled 'push it back in, push it back in'. For a moment I thought my eye had popped out. In fact, I had a really bad and deep cut above the eye, along the brow, and the flesh was flopping down over the eye itself. I can still remember the queries of next batsman Hassan Adnan, saying 'Buck, ok? Buck, ok?' in his broken English as the support staff walked me from the field. I ended up sitting in a chair in the pavilion with a towel to my face while they tried to find a medical centre open on a Sunday. In a confused state, I tried to process the information as Hassan was once again asking about me in the pavilion shortly after.

Poor Hassan had actually gone in to bat immediately after me, looked down and seen a pool of blood on the batting crease, backed away to the square-leg umpire only to edge a catch behind and just about run off the field to see how I was!

It was ultimately decided to take me home to Derby hospital. On the ride home as I covered my eye with a towel I noticed we were passing Loughborough University, well known for its sporting endeavours. I noticed all sorts of fit-looking people running around the campus. It was at this stage my thumb started to throb I remember.

I needed eight stitches across my right eye, which by now was completely closed over, and the thumb that took the glancing blow before my face turned out to be broken as well. The black eye took a couple of weeks to subside, and for a time I had problems with the pupil not dilating when I ventured outside. One optometrist told me it was possible my eye had been so badly damaged that this wouldn't heal – citing the example of several squash players who had been struck in a similar spot by the ball.

That revelation knocked me sideways. I said to him 'but if it doesn't heal, I won't be able to play cricket'. Came the matter-of-fact reply: 'probably not'. I left the checkup that day in tears, and needed reassurance over the next few hours and days that this was only the worst-case scenario. The need for rest had me catching up on the aforementioned shoulder and hamstring problems, with the decision made to send me home to Perth for the rest of the season, where I underwent shoulder surgery. By the time my shoulder was out of a sling it was time for surgery on my hamstring, which happened to be on my birthday, and it was a pretty glum winter waiting to get everything right away. That was probably the closest I've been to feeling depressed.

Even after I came out of that funk, it took time for me to get over the blow to the face. I was extremely jumpy about facing Mark again, and the whole concept of batting itself was not something that filled me with enormous anticipation for a while there. When I did face Mark again in state ranks, it was clear the incident had affected him too, because he didn't bowl me a single bouncer. But after getting through that innings, I found myself feeling more comfortable again. Mark and I became good friends, particularly when he later moved from South Australia to Victoria.

What the episode left me with was an appreciation of how much responsibility lies with the batsman to make sure you are protecting yourself properly. Short bowling is a legitimate tactic for a fast bowler, and they need to feel secure that they can do that without undue risk of causing serious injury or worse. I think it should be compulsory for batsmen to wear as much safety gear as possible, because it's not just about them and their comfort. If you take the short ball out of the game for safety reasons you create a one-dimensional game, as we sometimes see in limited-overs formats. Intimidation is part of a fast bowler's armoury, and as batsmen we are responsible for making sure that's all it is.

A year on and I returned to England in League cricket, this time with South Wiltshire in Salisbury, near Southampton. Early in the season a call came from Leicestershire, as their overseas player Dinesh Mongia had been called up for duty with India. I was grateful for the call because I had not actually been playing very well down south, partly through difficult wickets, but also because I was using a round rather than oval bat handle – a round handle tends to allow my bottom hand to take over and stop me from playing straight, a little like Graeme Smith. After my first game with Leicestershire against Somerset, I went to see my bat-maker Paul Bradbury, who happened to be in Taunton and did the necessary sanding down of my bats so I would have better feel. A fortunate turn of events!

'Braddles' had played for Fremantle and had watched on as University overseas player Mark Ramprakash and I put on 230 unbeaten for the second wicket. Next day he signed me up. His bats were widely recognised at the time as some of the best going around and there were many players using his bats with their own sponsor's stickers on them. Fortunately I got on very well with his wife Sally, who is the brains behind the operation and we have stayed friends since.

On the bus back from Taunton to Leicester, I got talking with wicketkeeper Paul Nixon about the next match, a tour fixture against the Australian Ashes tourists. We had a few days before the game, and as we arrived home, he said to me: 'Bud, you and I are going to do work every day before this match, and you're going to get runs against Australia.' Again this was great timing, because it was almost as if Paul had seen how significant this game could be for me – much more so than I had. So each day we did two-hour batting sessions, during which he would throw balls at me for all but 10 minutes. A few times I asked him if he wanted me to even up the balance a bit, but he kept rebuffing me, saying how important this game could be.

Importantly, this was just about the first time someone had worked with me to help me develop a more 'English' technique, where my feet and weight were moving more in the direction of mid-on. Paul had seen that I was conscious of getting across the crease and in line with the ball. That was useful in Australia, but in England it tends to be better to stay leg side of the line, keep your pad out of the way and play the ball alongside your front leg rather than out in front of it. Waiting to play the ball later is something you hear Australian players say constantly about playing in England, but it takes time and effort to make the adjustment properly. I'll always be grateful to Paul for directing me this way.

We worked hard for three days and his constant message was try to get my weight to go to mid-on. Growing up on bouncy Perth wickets I'd learnt to get across and in line with the ball, but that style was getting me in trouble in the UK, where the ball would often dart at you off the wicket and hit the pad in front of the stumps. I'd realised the best tactic was to stay leg side of the ball and try make sure the ball didn't hit pad as well as allowing me to play later; I just didn't understand how.

Paul wanted me to look at the mid-on fielder as the bowler was running in to bowl and put my weight on my heels, which goes against a lot of coaching manuals, which say be on the balls of your feet. When I did that though you could push me from behind and I'd almost fall flat on my face, telling me my weight was only going to go in one direction when trying to play a shot ... and that was to the point fielder.

By looking at mid-on and sitting back and having a more centred balance I ended up getting my head to move up and down the line of the stumps, which improved me significantly. The two innings that followed and in fact the next three weeks were brilliant and that method is still almost the first thing I think about after I haven't batted in England a while.

Duly equipped, I found myself batting first on day one, and facing up to some white-hot pace from Brett Lee. He bowled a five-over spell with the new ball that had to have been around 150kph. Even though it was a flat wicket, getting through that spell helped my confidence no end, and I was reasonably chuffed to have made 56 before Lee eventually dismissed me. We lasted just over 55 overs before facing up to a long stint of leather chasing. Justin Langer, Ricky Ponting and Damien Martyn all peeled off hundreds, putting them in good touch ahead of the first Ashes Test at Lord's.

An overnight declaration left us with the final day to bat. The night was a Saturday, and I remember basically not being able to sleep because there was a noisy wedding reception in the hotel I was staying at and the walls were seemingly as thin as paper. Still a bit groggy the next morning, I had to contend with another lightning spell from Lee that quickly woke me up. They were clearly keen to knock us over quickly and head down to London as quickly as possible. I fended a couple of these deliveries off my hip around the corner, so Ponting posted a leg gully. Lee however wasn't able to get his line right, and I took advantage of some space behind square on the off side to cut a pair of boundaries. In response, Ponting shifted the leg gully back to traditional gully, and he was still moving as Lee came in to bowl.

Naturally I pulled away, and as Lee followed through, ball still in hand, I let out a 'sorry mate', to which he replied after following through all the way to me 'you sure will be!' Next ball was quite possibly the quickest bouncer I ever faced, leaving me motionless as it skimmed past my helmet grille. I heard the swoosh of the ball passing and my heart skipped a beat as I realized how lucky I had been. But once that initial spell was through, Lee dialled back down a gear or two, content all was working as it should be for the Tests. As the overs ticked by I became more fluent, helped admittedly by a very dead wicket. I reached my hundred in mid-afternoon, at which point Matthew Hayden quipped 'ok mate, you've had your time but you can get out now, thanks'. I actually remember thinking 'fair enough', but that's not how it turned out.

I started swinging for the fences, scooping a few over gully and square leg. Amid this passage of play I nicked one behind off Jason Gillespie but was reprieved by a no-ball – Dizzy would struggle for rhythm throughout the Ashes and lose his spot by the end of the series. That escape left me feeling very relaxed, basically without a care in the world. Only a few times in my career have I felt more or less invincible out there, like I simply can't get out. This was one of those periods, until the realisation hit that I might be able to get to 200. I hit three sixes off Stuart MacGill, rare indulgences for me, and rolled along to a most unexpected 209 from, believe it or not, 219 balls. My dismissal on that tally brought the game to a close, and drew plenty of generous handshakes from the Australians.

Leicestershire's coach, James Whitaker, greeted me with a couple of messages: first that I was needed for interviews, and secondly that he didn't want me to celebrate too much as there was a Twenty20 match the following night. The first message got through, not so much the second. My comments caused a bit of a stir when I mentioned Hayden's request for me to get out. 'I would not expect them to do it, so I wasn't going to do it. No way.' A little bit cheeky perhaps, but also rather misinterpreted. Hayden was only having a light-hearted moment with me and I thought it would be nice to share a moment I'd had out there with some of the legends of the game. The media felt it was the best line of the interview and I've constantly had people asking me about the 'sledge' since, but it was all in jest. Dinner that night with the Leicester boys, including future Australian Test player Jason Krejza and West Indian Ottis Gibson, was warming up nicely when Whitaker called again to make sure I was keeping things under control. He also told me an Australian radio station wanted another interview. After a fun chat with David Schwarz, a one-time AFL player, I ended up having a pretty solid night out with Jason, and was far from energised at a training session and team meeting the next morning.

It was the first team meeting we had and when one of the leading players said within the space of five minutes that if we are bowling and they score a single, we win the contest and then contradicted himself unknowingly that if we score a single from a delivery we win the contest again I almost groaned in frustration.

It's one of the banes of a cricketer's lot to have to sit through some of these meetings talking about plans for opposition players. Each individual opposition batsman will be analysed and critiqued for a lengthy while, only for nine times out of 10 the plan to be 'top of off stump with the odd bouncer!'

After a 45-minute meeting and finally a much-needed nap, we played our T20 quarter-final in the evening, and

I kept my run going by top-scoring in a win that took the club through to the lucrative Finals Day. The scenes on the balcony at Grace Road were brilliant but also a bit comical for me – I mean, who pops champagne corks and sprays the crowd for winning a quarter-final? That being said, given the two days I'd had, the taste was pretty sweet. Those runs against Australia meant I'd graduated from club pro to County professional.

CHAPTER 6

A TEST IN THE WEST

Coffs Harbour, Perth

WHEN THE 2005 Ashes series ended in Australian defeat, there was a lot of talk about sackings and changes. Ricky Ponting faced the first serious questioning of his captaincy, and others at Cricket Australia, from the coach John Buchanan up to the chief executive James Sutherland, faced similar censure. Numerous speculative teams were chosen for the next Ashes series in 2006–07, or the next tour to England in 2009. By dint of his double century against the touring team, Chris was named at the top of the order by many – the other man to pass 200 against the Australians in the tour, a young Alastair Cook for Essex, would soon be a Test man himself.

However the players who gave up the Ashes in a memorable encounter with England had no such thoughts of regeneration. United in the belief that they had to regain the urn before letting the curtain fall, many chose to stay on longer than they might have otherwise done. This was certainly true of Shane Warne, who may well have retired there and then on day five at the Oval had he managed to conjure a last-gasp victory to tie the series. More telling for Chris and others was Justin Langer's determination to hang onto his spot and his partnership with Matthew Hayden, even after a series of heavy knocks to the head began to affect him. Most vividly, he had to be barred from going out to bat at Johannesburg in 2006, a Test match win on the line, when still concussed. Chris and others would have to wait their turn.

As it was, those Australians whitewashed England 5–0 in the return bout in 2006–07, which coincided with Chris' breakout Shield season. He racked up 1202 runs for Western Australia in addition to a mighty back end of the 2006 English summer for another new club, Northamptonshire. Langer retired at the end of the series, and Chris was now in competition for his spot with another left-hander who had first made his name in England: Phil Jaques. Initially a fringe player in the difficult New South Wales school, Jaques had risen to prominence with prolific scoring for Northamptonshire in 2003 and 2004. By 2004–05 he was a fixture in the NSW side and, helped by a similarly strong record in limited-overs matches, an occasional ODI player for Australia. That avenue meant he was able to get into 'the system', familiar to teammates and selectors, and on his way to Test selection as an injury replacement for Langer on Boxing Day 2005 against South Africa.

Jaques was well liked in the Australian dressing room – a nickname of 'Pro' sums up his reputation – and also happened to be a couple of years younger than Chris. Over the period leading into and away from Langer's retirement, from 2005 to 2008, Jaques made 22 first-class centuries, including his first for Australia. In the same period, Chris notched 13, and none when he and

Jaques figured in the same game, either for Australia A or when WA took on NSW.

When Langer retired at the end of that triumphant 2006–07 Ashes series, Jaques got the nod. Jaques' admirable scoring was accompanied by another more hidden narrative – the creeping advance of back trouble that was to cut him down in what should have been his prime. By the time he went to the West Indies in mid-2008 and made his second Test hundred in Jamaica, he was often struggling to move. A break after that series helped, but the trip to India for four Tests in September and October put more pressure on, and this time Jaques was rendered just about immobile, resorting to 5am physio sessions to limber up and a punishing cycle of anti-inflammatory drugs that can be as bad for the lining of the stomach as they are useful to alleviate back pain.

But rather than have Chris on the West Indies or India tours as a back-up batsman, Andrew Hilditch's panel had elected to choose Simon Katich, Chris's former teammate, who had been a casualty of the 2005 Ashes defeat, but had fought his way back into contention. In the end, it was Matthew Hayden's stretched hamstring that opened a vacancy in the Test team for the third Test against India, at the WACA in January 2008 – a vacancy that Chris was to fill.

A TEST MATCH debut should be an experience to cherish. But in my case it was the catalyst for a lot of reflection, and ultimately the end of my time in Western Australia. In fact it's fair to say that the high of receiving my Baggy Green cap almost immediately turned into perhaps the lowest I had felt as a cricketer barely a week later.

By January 2008 I was fit and firing, and when the Australian side ventured to Perth for the third Test against India it was time for injury to smile on me instead. Matthew Hayden was struggling with a hamstring issue and I was called into the squad, initially as cover. As soon as I walked into the change room I could tell the players had plenty of things on their minds. The dramatic win over India in Sydney in the second Test had caused all kinds of spot fires to break out: the racial abuse charge against Harbhajan Singh for what he said to Andrew Symonds, another sledging case involving Brad Hogg and Sourav Ganguly and the general tone of the Australian team's behaviour. We didn't actually have a team meeting before the match that addressed the cricket itself.

Instead I was a wide-eyed participant in a mini-conference that tackled issues around the image of the team and the way many, columnist Peter Roebuck above all, had portrayed them. I remember seeing the likes of the ACB director and former captain Mark Taylor and the Australian Cricketers' Association boss Paul Marsh in the room, and most of the players putting across the view that they didn't feel they were being backed by Cricket Australia. But to be honest a lot of the discussion went way over my head. The dominant emotion was a sense of 'what am I doing here', as I was still battling somewhat with doubts over my own ability. The topics we went over felt like they had little to do with me, and as a new face in the team the last thing I was thinking about was how I was going to sledge the Indians! So while the team was preoccupied by 'Monkeygate', I was preoccupied by nerves.

More vivid in my memory is the fielding session preceding the match, the first time I'd been part of an Australian team preparing with the high intensity they were famed for. There can be no doubting of Ricky Ponting's leadership in this sense, for he threw himself around with a manic level of energy the others did their best to emulate. If off-field issues were affecting the team's focus, they did their best to put it out of the picture while chasing high balls and ground balls on the WACA outfield, and when India won the toss and chose to bat on match morning I knew I had to be up for that.

The wicket for the game was a strange one, fairly flat and very slow but offering some swing and seam as well. Australia's team selection clearly anticipated a different surface, as Shaun Tait joined Brett Lee, Stuart Clark and Mitchell Johnson in an all-pace attack. Shaun had a hamstring niggle and his rhythm was all over the place as India's score mounted. Off the field he didn't give much away about his state of mind, but the struggles we saw in his run-up, no-balls and general control compounded, so much so that after the match he took a break from the game. I spent a lot of a sweltering afternoon chasing balls to the point and cover boundaries, and left the field at stumps feeling very drained.

Amid all the adrenaline of a Test debut I hadn't noticed that my Baggy Green cap did not actually fit me very well. It was much too tight, and when I pulled it on before play on the second morning, I instantly felt a horrible throbbing headache. This wasn't the first time I'd struggled to find a cap the right size, and I knew from experience it was possible to stretch the head band with strategic use of scissors. Whether it was nerves or the headache, I did not get it right this time, and the attempt to stretch the cap left it badly ripped and just about in pieces. Whoops!

Phil Jaques was now my opening partner and the nearest bloke to me in the dressing room. At the sight of my ruined Baggy Green, he offered a somewhat terrified whisper: 'What have you done?' Next thing I knew, Adam Gilchrist had wandered over and let out a massive laugh at this sad sight. I was the new kid, I'd just wrecked my cap, and at a time when the Baggy Green aura was still strong I wondered briefly whether this was a sackable offence. Fortunately Adam's reaction was shared by others, and I was swiftly told 'don't worry, we'll get you another one'. 'Hoggy' was 12th man, so I wore his cap until a new one could be found. Disaster averted, I walked onto the field with the team, and heard a spectator yell 'I bet you slept in that cap last night!' Little did he know that my cap was in pieces in the rooms…

For a few years of course, I doubted I'd ever wear the cap again. I've spoken to a few guys who only played one Test, the umpire Paul Wilson being one, about the mixed feeling that brings. While it's fantastic to have the cap, because it looks so new and untouched it is almost as if you haven't earned it – a feeling of 'did I really wear that' can set in. For the next six years I didn't have the cap on any sort of display, putting it in the cupboard and trying not to think about it. This was mainly because when I did see it I could catch myself thinking 'I haven't earned that'. One of the more cathartic elements of getting another chance and going on to play 25 Tests was the fact that the cap now looks a little more battered and lived in, with beer and sweat stains telling me the story of those matches.

A bit like the rest of the game, my first Test innings was something of a blur. I got off the mark with a boundary, but was then struck on the pad by an Irfan Pathan delivery heading in the general direction of leg stump. Asad Rauf's finger went up and I found myself trudging off for that lone boundary. Hawkeye projections on TV in the dressing room seemed to suggest it was hitting, but after we'd been bowled out cheaply I found myself standing next to Asad at square leg.

'I shouldn't have given you out,' he said.

'But the replays showed it was hitting,' I replied.

'I'm not sure those things are always right.'

Not exactly what I wanted to hear.

Out or not, I spent some time thinking about the dismissal and decided I had fallen across to the off side. Once India were bowled out, we found ourselves in a difficult fourth-innings chase, and I got pretty smartly to 15, making sure I didn't get too far across. But then, just as I felt I was getting in, I got near enough to the perfect ball from Pathan. Angled in, then shaping away and on just the right length and line. On another day you play and miss, but this time I edged one through to MS Dhoni and my match was over.

We failed in our chase. Ricky Ponting had missed the chance to lead the team to a record 17 successive wins, and it was the first Test loss in Perth to a subcontinental side. The guys who played in that match will be first to admit the Australian side had been distracted that week I'd imagine, and it showed in the performance.

At the time I had wanted to keep the experience as similar to a Sheffield Shield match as possible, so I declined the offer to stay at the team hotel and remained at home: a big mistake, but one I made as Adam Gilchrist and Brad Hogg were both staying at home and I assumed this is what home state players did. It was a huge opportunity missed to get to know my Aussie teammates better and for them to know me – this is absolutely crucial for new players and I regret it.

I left that environment not really feeling as though I knew it any better than before. A sense of disconnection and unease lasted all the way through the week, and once the game was over and the caravan moved on I was left with a sense that it didn't quite seem real to me.

After the game, Mike Hussey told me that people who thought first-class cricket was as hard as Tests had rocks in their head, and I was inclined to agree. There's so much more going on beyond the boundary, meaning you need to be so much more focused when you do get out there.

You work so hard to get there, to fulfil your dream, and you find yourself there for a fleeting moment. If you're then discarded, at the age of 30, and the circus goes on, you are left thinking, 'Oh well, that was it, I'll never get another chance, or if I do I have to start again from square one.' Everything that had been achieved up until that point and the countless hours put in felt like it was erased in a heartbeat. There's a heaviness about that feeling; it settles on you and takes some serious shaking off. In the meantime you lose perspective about how lucky you are to be playing cricket for a living, because essentially you feel like a failure. That doesn't just apply to you, but also to all the people – family, friends, teammates and coaches – who supported you to get there. That was how I found myself after making my Test debut.

Then it got worse.

The Test match finished with India's victory on the Sunday afternoon, and the team went out together for drinks that night. Next morning I awoke to the news that I had been dropped from Western Australia's one-day side, meaning I was only required for squad training but not the sessions for the selected side. In the space of a week I had gone from playing Test cricket to not even being in the state squad to train for a domestic match.

By this stage I was not on great terms with either Tom Moody, who was now the coach, or Graeme Wood, now the chief executive. That was it – I was leaving Western Australia.

The Warriors played the one-day game on the Friday and Saturday I had a club game for South Perth at Joondalup. That day I woke up around the time the guys would have been doing warm-ups, got my gear together, drove out to the ground and arrived just as the first ball was being bowled – thoroughly depressed at the whole state of affairs.

The captain, Darren Wates, took one look at me and said, 'Mate you're batting No.7, go and take care of yourself and be ready for later in the day.' So I went to sit in the change room, feeling shaky and miserable and not really sure where I was at. After a few minutes passed I started to become very emotional, and called for my Dad to come see me. Looking back it was amazing to think I hit rock bottom only a week after my Test debut, but it summed up the fine edge on which I had been performing in the harsh environment of WA cricket.

Not long after that, South Perth had slipped to 5–70, and I went out to bat 15 minutes before lunch. Initially my thoughts were so clouded I could barely see the ball, and reverted to the most basic technique, covering my stumps, letting wide ones go and almost playing a sort of French cricket. After the interval I felt better for a meal and a moment to think, and went back out in a much better frame of mind. By day's end I had made 170-odd, and followed up with another hundred in the semi-final of the district one-day competition. We would win the title, after the club coach decided not to suspend me for my late arrival. The runs I made were another example of being able to play hard and work hard, but I had reached a point where I needed to move on. It was all too much.

STARTING OUT IN WA cricket, I had been given a hard time by the likes of Kade Harvey, Rob Baker and Ryan Campbell, not to mention the big boys. They ended up becoming huge supporters of me and we still keep in touch now. But at the time they made life difficult. I remember Harvey sledging me in a club game, saying 'you've got a fucking long way to go in life mate', and Campbell was tough on me too. This was all a product of the competitiveness for spots – at the time, trying to break into the WA side seemed almost as hard as breaking into the Australian sides led by Mark Taylor and Steve Waugh. Playing cricket was one thing, but it also meant fitting in as a young man.

Damien Martyn, Justin Langer, Brendon Julian, Tom Moody – they were all big fish. Everyone knew who they were. Whereas I was a ginger kid who just wasn't cool. I lacked confidence around women, I was verging on socially inept, and had to grow up, much as Harvey had said to me. My best chance to find my niche was to earn respect through performance on the field, and I had begun to do it in the summer of 2001–02. This elevation in status was both good and bad for me.

We had played a one-day game in Adelaide where I roomed with Justin Langer for the first time. The game was on the Sunday and we arrived on the Friday. As was customary, we got there and went out drinking that night, before sweating it off at training the next day, having a quiet night in, playing the game and then going out again. Next we flew to Coffs Harbour to play a full-strength New South Wales and I roomed with Langer again. The pattern was the same – big night out, training, game day, another night out.

The first night in Coffs we were at a bar and I told the guys around 8pm 'I'm rooming with Justin, I better go home'. Harvey's response was to say, 'Mate, are you having a good time?' When I replied in the affirmative he declared, 'Well stay then, enjoy yourself.' This was the sort of validation and inclusion I'd been hoping for, really the first time I had felt a respected part of the team. I mentioned going home again around 10pm, and was told 'No you're staying!' So 10pm became 11, then 12, then 1. Finally I crept back into the room, trying to keep quiet but understandably feeling the effects of the drinks. Trying to go to the bathroom, I walked noisily into the cupboard. Justin didn't say a word, but must have heard me, as I discovered later.

When the game came around, we thrashed this strong Blues side and earned a double bonus point by chasing down a modest target inside 25 overs. Amid our celebrations afterwards, Justin asked the support staff to leave the dressing room, and proceeded to go to town on us in no uncertain terms. We were called a disgrace, always out on the gas, the reason WA cricket had stopped winning trophies, the works. I'll always remember he then exclaimed 'I'm not going to name names, but Buck! I've roomed with you for five nights, you've been pissed for three, what are you doing?' I look back now and remember the message, because I use it myself when dealing with younger players.

At the time I was enjoying this new social dynamic but also scoring runs. The lifestyle did not impede my performance. And because the big runs were coming I felt I was bulletproof. But unbeknown to me I was really giving off the wrong message to lots of people above me. What I've learnt and try to tell the young guys these days, is if you need to let off steam to succeed go and do it, but you have to pick your moments, and you have to put your career ahead of your social life. What was clear to me was I had to have the right balance for me and that was enjoying the lifestyle cricket offered. I loved doing everything with maximum intensity mixed in with times where I could completely switch off. There was no middle ground – fifth gear or stop. That would mean training, playing, interacting with others before heading home and shutting down.

As it was, the problem was I suffered from a lack of forward thinking, and a lack of self-belief that I would actually get my chance to play for Australia. Even at times when I was scoring as prolifically as anyone in the country, I did not think about much other than those runs. Plus I was enjoying playing for WA and being successful professionally for the first time.

However the message being sent down the line was that while I could make runs, I was lacking focus and my heart wasn't completely on representing the national side – which I vehemently disagree with. I just didn't see how that sort of approach would help me and in fact I firmly believe it would have ruined any chance of higher selection.

The fact I was also hitting hundreds of balls every day with Dad and at training trying desperately to improve because of my competitive spirit didn't seem to matter. The stigma was I didn't take cricket seriously enough. To be fair to Wayne Clark, during his second stint of coaching WA, he actively supported what I brought to the group. He liked people enjoying themselves but fighting with everything they had out on the field.

One of my best attributes as a cricketer is that I can pick up quite quickly when things aren't working for me. The consistency I've enjoyed over years in first-class cricket comes from not being afraid to tinker and change if I feel out of sync. That extended to times when I knew I had to pull back on socialising to focus on what was ahead of me. Even moments when I needed to get away and let my hair down during times when cricket was getting the better of me and I was trying too hard. But what I saw with numerous younger players was that they struggled to see the moment at which their cricket was suffering. Instead of saying 'I've got to do things differently now', they would keep doing the same things until they found themselves out of the picture.

This is not to say that cricket teams perform at their best when there is a puritanical vibe running through the room – far from it. I still maintain that the best sides are those who socialise together, because it helps build an amazing sense of closeness that you take out onto the field.

All of these issues were in the background in 2006 when I was playing in Northamptonshire. Halfway through the season I was called home to play for the Australia A side in the Northern Territory. At the time I had lost some enjoyment in cricket and was playing very poorly. After joining up with the A team I was immediately told by the chairman of selectors, Andrew Hilditch, I wouldn't be playing in any of the white-ball cricket but instead only the two four-day games. This hit me hard and straight away I was annoyed. I wasn't enjoying Northampton hugely but I'd seen signs I was coming out of my trot and I desperately wanted to prove to Kepler Wessels, the coach there, that I could play. I'd been forced to pay for my own airfare back to Australia only to play eight days of cricket basically against kids as both India and Pakistan had sent very youthful teams. In Northampton I would've been playing at least twice that amount of very competitive cricket.

There was definitely a hierarchy system in the A side as well. Some players were closer to national selection than others and they took centre stage. I remember waiting at the end of a net for my turn to face the invited net bowlers, but a couple of batsmen stayed in for so long that when my turn came the bowlers were exhausted. I've lost count of the amount of times I've called close to a net before I wanted to as another batsman is waiting patiently for his turn. It's what you do in a team but to see a couple of players completely ignore their teammates for their own purpose once again reaffirmed my belief that I wasn't ruthless enough for an Australian spot.

Ben Hilfenhaus and I were both surplus to requirements during the short-form cricket so we took the chance to enjoy ourselves in what seemed very friendly cities of Darwin and Cairns. Cricket wasn't overly enjoyable and it was a chance to relax. I was still frustrated at the lack of game time. It came back to haunt me though when I was required to field due to an injury and put down a couple of catches.

I wasn't hungover – Ben and I weren't silly enough to do anything stupid – and just made a couple of fielding errors, but it was enough for a few of the more senior players to accuse me of enjoying myself too much. Tim Nielsen was the coach at the time and I have no doubt he shared the view as this was what he was led to believe about me so I don't blame him. Equally I don't regret it. Everyone has their off switch and I needed to breathe again, to start enjoying cricket and life once more.

Eventually the four-day games came along and in the first game I struggled. Also I was privately aghast at some of the players telling our bowlers to 'hit him in the head' and 'kill 'em' when we were fielding. When Phil Jaques and I went out to open the innings we had irate opposition running at us and swearing at us and we both kept repeating it wasn't us saying these ridiculous things.

Before the second game arrived, I decided to seek out David Boon who had replaced Hilditch as selector on duty for the second leg and told him how difficult I was finding cricket. I'll never forget his answer. He told me the selectors saw me as a batsman who batted all day. How simple it seems, but it completely changed my outlook. Out of form, I had almost been trying to get runs too quickly, thinking I'll get the bowlers before they got me.

The final game I scored two 60s while Phil scored two centuries. He pulled ahead in our private battle, but I was happy for him and for me. I felt something had clicked and returned to Northampton reinvigorated for the second half of the season. It was in this period that I made the two highest scores of my life – 319 for Northamptonshire against Gloucestershire and later 279 for WA against a Victorian side that included Shane Warne. In both matches the pitch favoured the batsmen, but it was still an extraordinary feeling to get into that kind of a batting groove, where everything seems so simple.

The score against Warney was exceptionally satisfying. I'd first came up against him in 2004 playing for Derby when he was captaining Hampshire. He dismissed me early and almost didn't celebrate because it had been too easy for him. In the second innings in Arctic-like conditions I managed to get around 80 and managed his unbelievable skill a bit better in tough conditions for him.

Then in the first Shield game of the 2006–07 season it was known he was going to play and Victoria would have a very good bowling side featuring Shane Harwood, Mick Lewis, Gerard Denton, Andrew McDonald and of course Warney. After learning so much on the spinning wicket of Wantage Road and Northampton, I was desperate to see off the quicks and test myself against the best.

It was a desperately batter-friendly wicket and quickly we had the upper hand. Eventually Marcus North was to join me and we put on a record 459, together eclipsing record after record. We weren't told that the highest ever first-class partnership in Australia is 464 by the Waugh twins. I was duly caught on the boundary rope and missed the chance of a lifetime – but it was the battle with Warne that I loved. He kept attacking me all day and even had no fielders on the boundary to entice a sweep but I held firm and instead kept picking him off and waiting for the bad ball.

After the innings and in the lunch room Warne approached me to say how well I batted and I asked if I could talk to him about playing spin after the game, to which he agreed. Following the match, which was a draw, the WA players relocated into the Victorian change room for a chat and a well-deserved drink. Speaking to Dave Hussey, I suddenly heard Warney calling my name, saying he was talking to 'Northy' about playing spin if I was interested. After venturing over, he was brilliant and exceptionally giving in his advice, which was fantastic.

I kept up the standard for most of the rest of the season, and finished the 2006–07 Shield season with 1202 runs at the end of a summer in which Justin Langer, Damien Martyn, Shane Warne and Glenn McGrath had all retired from the Test side. There was a genuine opening there, something I joked about with Adam Voges via the catchphrase '1202, get in the queue' – for a while it was my number, a bit like Jason Gillespie will always have his 201! That season earned me a spot in the Australia A team to tour Pakistan later in 2007, and it was widely felt that I was duelling with Phil Jaques for the Test opener's spot opposite Matthew Hayden. I had Kookaburra in my corner at least, as they signed me up to a major contract over four years in expectation that I'd be the man for the job.

The Pakistan tour was the last time an Australian side ventured to the country. I can remember our security advice was all based on the idea that we would be safe on the premise that extremist groups would not attack a cricket side because the outrage would cause them to lose a lot of their support. That was the thinking we followed, sadly to be disproved when the Sri Lanka team and match officials buses were attacked in Lahore in early 2009. Our security measures looked impressive on paper, but I can remember the cordon around the team bus being quite porous, and also that our convoy had to stop at traffic lights.

It was a transitional group, featuring the likes of Jason Gillespie and Stuart MacGill, both very near the end of their careers, but also the young spin bowlers Dan Cullen and Cullen Bailey. I was rooming with James Hopes, and we worked our way through several seasons of *Entourage* together. The cricket was high scoring: Pakistan A won the three limited-overs games chasing down totals each time, before we won the first 'Test' by an innings and then fought out a draw in the second. I made a hundred in the third limited-overs match, scoring at a good rate without smashing the ball all over the place. I had to laugh when the wicketkeeper Sarfraz Ahmed remarked from behind the stumps 'well batted, but no sixes!'

That innings aside, the Jaques-Rogers duel was a conclusive win for the New South Welshman, and I knew I had to make a strong start to the home 2007–08 summer to be any chance of squeezing into the Test side. We were playing NSW at the WACA in the opening game, and after Phil removed all doubt about the selectors' order of preference by cracking 167 in the second innings, I found myself waylaid by appendicitis and ending the match in hospital with a two-week recovery plan after surgery that ruled me out of the last Shield game before the Gabba Test. The irony of all this was that Phil's runs obscured a developing back problem that would force him out of Test cricket within a year – my appendix issue did not harm me for any longer than those two weeks. And it was someone else's injury – Matthew Hayden's – that would get me into the Test team. Then I was out. And soon enough out of WA. Feeling like a failure.

CHAPTER 7

THE VICTORIAN AGE

Melbourne

'DON'T WORRY MATE, this sort of stuff happens all the time in Victoria.' With those words, Andrew McDonald assured Simon Katich he shouldn't worry about his infamous confrontation with Michael Clarke in the SCG dressing room in January 2009. In many ways, that sentence also summed up the fractious nature of Victorian cricket, and how a new generation had learned to succeed despite it.

In 1991, on an MCG yet to see the erection of the Great Southern Stand, Victoria won their first Sheffield Shield since 1980. It was a young team, featuring the likes of Darren Berry, Darren Lehmann, Jamie Siddons, Simon O'Donnell, Tony Dodemaide, Paul Reiffel and Damien Fleming. Standing to one side of the team victory photo was a bashful 12th man called James Sutherland, who of course would later head the ACB. Shane Warne had made his debut for the state that season, while Dean Jones and Merv Hughes were away with the national team in the West Indies. Lehmann remarked in his autobiography *Worth the Wait* that

Victoria had more than enough talent to win several more titles quickly. It would be another 13 years until their next one.

Egos and reputations dominated the Victorian dressing room. Jones and O'Donnell duelled frequently, while Berry and Siddons were hardly shrinking violets. The biographies of players who took part in that period invariably include a chapter or two on the internal battles played out at Victoria, and their varying opinions of how the team and the coach, Les Stillman, handled it all.

Under Jones, the newly christened 'Bushrangers' captured the domestic limited-overs title in 1995, resplendent in navy shorts. But things deteriorated the following year, amid a dispute that saw Berry briefly replaced as wicketkeeper by Peter Roach. Some years later, Berry wrote in *Keeping It Real*.

> 'There wasn't one player in that Victorian team who did not respect Jones as a player and the way he prepared himself to play cricket. He was in another league to most of us. What we didn't like was the way he treated people. He treated us like second-rate citizens sometimes. Jones thought he was a great leader of people but he alienated the players and turned them against him. Deano lost the plot in the summer of 1995–96, with ramifications for all of us. He was starting to talk like a dictator.'

The path towards a more cohesive environment was tracked by the man who replaced Stillman as coach in 1996, John Scholes. Accomplished enough to play in three Shield-winning teams for Victoria, Scholes was also noted as a team man, selfless enough to hold the state record for most appearances as 12th man. Scholes was always keen to instil the game's traditions and virtues in players, and loved to chat about the game to all-comers. The unity Scholes worked to foster was vital in securing a pair of Shield final appearances for the Bushrangers during his tenure, even if highly talented Queensland combinations stopped them short of claiming the title itself. Scholes stepped down in 2001 for personal reasons, and all of Victorian cricket mourned his death two years later.

By then, a strong group of players was emerging to vie for domestic honours. They were to be guided by David Hookes, the former Test batsman and South Australia captain known for his derring-do with the bat and outspoken opinions off the field. They were well on the way to that elusive Shield title in January 2004, when Hookes died after a punch from a bouncer outside a St Kilda pub caused him to fall and hit his head on the road. Amid their grief and anger at events, the Bushrangers rallied round Cameron White and Hookes' assistant Greg Shipperd, who would help guide the team to the Shield and so begin a long tenure as head coach. While disputes did occasionally crop up between players during Shipperd's time, nothing would ever be allowed to bloom into the sorts of scenes witnessed in 1995–96. Nevertheless, a ruthless streak ran through Victorian cricket that could affect relationships between teammates as well as civility with opponents. And this was the place where Chris Rogers came in late 2008 to escape the politics of WA cricket.

FOR MOST OF my time with Western Australia, I didn't have an agent. My first contract with WA was a one-year deal for $5000 and it rose steadily from there. But the longer I spent in Perth the more conscious I became that doing my own contract negotiations wasn't necessarily a good thing in terms of relationships with the association. I argued numerous times with the operations manager Rob Langer over terms, and would find myself pushing back when he appealed to my honour at representing the state and brought up the memories of previous generations that played for next to nothing.

I have to admit that sort of talk frustrated me, particularly as my mode of playing was so obviously dedicated towards the long form of the game and doing my best for state and country. The game was changing around us anyway, with the IPL Twenty 20 version about to blast cricket to another financial level that put many a state or county contract in the shade. I've always accepted that those riches were never going to be for me, and tried to look at the game's grassroots for reminders of how lucky I am rather than worrying about how much cash is being pulled in by the T20 stars. I've also never seen much point in arguing about a contract once you've signed it – a deal is a deal, the time to improve your lot is when it is near to expiring, not before then.

Even so, over time I realised that agents were, for lack of a better term, a necessary evil. Rather than being mercenary, they took you out of the hard negotiations that had so much potential to curdle relationships. Player and cricket association are both aware that the agent is doing his best to get a good deal, and that's what he's paid for. So by 2008 I had signed on to be managed by the former Essendon footballer Rick Olarenshaw, who remained my friend even after he left that management firm and was unfortunately no longer my agent.

It was to be a call from him that set me on the path across the continent to a new home in Victoria.

Changing states in Australian cricket is far from a simple decision. Rather than moving around the corner to another company or a couple hours' drive away to another county, you're required to uproot yourself totally and move more or less to the other side of the continent. This has historically put the states in a powerful bargaining position.

I came to the realisation it was time to leave WA over the course of a trip to Adelaide late in the summer of 2007–08. It was by then the quietest dressing room I'd ever been in and too reliant on two players – Marcus North and Adam Voges, both fantastic leaders but slightly reserved characters at the time. My relationship with coach Tom Moody had become strained and it quickly became apparent I was becoming surplus to requirements. After we finished a four-day game a day early against South Australia and had to stay for the one-day game, Tom organised a trip to the Barossa Valley, which was a highly enjoyable day where we ended in a bar winding down.

Teammate Ben Edmondson was going through a slight blip in form and was a little down on confidence. I was worried he was becoming too meek and letting people walk over him, so over a beer I told him so. I said words to the effect that if he didn't stand up for himself, his teammates, his coach, his wife and his friends and family would take advantage of him. Ben and I have a fantastic relationship and he looked like he needed a little help from a friend. We had positioned ourselves away from the group for the deep and meaningful and I then excused myself to go to the toilet. Unbeknown to me Tom noticed, came over to Ben and told him that I shouldn't be talking to him like that – basically the same thing I was saying to him!

I returned to face an angry Ben who started yelling at me that I had no right to be talking about his wife and family, which was fair enough. I started yelling back that I was only trying to help and tempers flared. Tom quickly came over to ask me what right I had to talk to him like that and I lost it and basically yelled at him to piss off – I'd never spoken to a coach like that before. I stormed out of the pub, completely confused as to what had just taken place. When I left Ben for the toilet he was in complete agreement with me.

Close to tears, I found another establishment to sit by myself to try to comprehend where my life was heading and I finally realised it was time to look elsewhere. My presence in the change room was becoming an issue as I was trying too hard to drive the banter and make it fun, as everyone seemed to be withdrawing into themselves. For years we had ribbed each other affectionately – my red hair providing an easy target for teammates – but it was starting to get too much for some.

'Vogesy' did come to check on me that night and I voiced my concerns to him that perhaps it would be better for the team if I left. He disagreed and tried to talk me out of it, as did a few others, such as Ben and Steve Magoffin, but it was clear to me. Too much water had gone under the bridge at the time and I couldn't see how Tom and I could mend our fractured relationship, which was a shame because we since have. For a number of years I resented having to leave family and friends, but it was one of the best things that happened to me and I no longer feel any bitterness.

When it became apparent that I was looking to leave WA, South Australia and Queensland were the first states to get in touch. I flew to Adelaide to meet with Rod Marsh, still a little hesitant about things due to what had happened in my teens. But we hit it off well and I found myself looking at an attractive financial offer that also included the honour of leading South Australia. That was appealing, though I was worried by the fact my arrival would have coincided with the departure of Ryan Harris.

Having faced him in the summer of 2007–08 I was aware he had gone up a notch in pace and confidence, and was surprised to see the SACA unfussed by his move to Queensland after they failed to match the offer of a three-year contract. As troubling was the fact I was told they would be replacing Harris with Grant Lambert, a steady all-rounder from NSW who was not of the same class as a bowler – as 'Rhino's' subsequent Test career would underline! From my time captaining Derbyshire in England I realised that a captain is only as good as his bowlers. You can set a field all you want, but if your bowlers don't put the ball in the right areas you will be made to look a poor captain. In the end neither Lambert nor myself joined the Redbacks, and Graham Manou became captain.

Those issues were still in the back of my mind when I flew up to Brisbane and met with the late Graham Dixon, then chief executive of Queensland Cricket. Our conversation went well enough, and it was followed up with an evening's drinks with numerous members of the squad. I already knew James Hopes and Chris Hartley quite well, and had a lot of respect for the Bulls as a team. That being said, I had serious reservations about playing half my season as an opening batsman at the Gabba. The WACA's pitch had already started to get lively again, a surging Tasmania were leaving plenty of grass on the wicket at Bellerive and even the SCG had changed character. But nowhere was more testing than a seaming pitch in Brisbane, with the extra bounce and pace on offer – very rarely did domestic surfaces resemble the relatively benign Test strip.

As I pondered that possibility I ventured down to the Gold Coast for a day with my girlfriend Kate at the time, and had a call from Rick to say that Victoria's coach Greg Shipperd wanted to speak with me. Curious, I booked a flight down to Melbourne to meet Greg and the cricket operations manager Shaun Graf. Their message was simple: Jason Arnberger had reached the end of the road and they were eager to find another strong opening batsman. There were other helpful circumstances also: Damien Wright, who I knew well, was moving up from Tasmania, and my old juniors teammate David Hussey had established himself as one of the leading lights of the Bushrangers' middle order. My sister lived in Melbourne, and my growing admiration for London had me thinking it might be nice to live in a bigger Australian city. It wasn't long after I walked out of the meeting with Greg and Shaun that my mind was made up. The response to my interest was a three-year contract.

Queensland were understandably disappointed to hear I'd committed to the Bushrangers, and I felt somewhat bad about giving the impression of wanting a move there to Graham Dixon in particular – it was a big loss to cricket when he died of cancer in 2013. South Australia took the news as well as could be expected, and the conversations I had with Rod Marsh around that time were the start of a decent relationship. Some years later when I dealt with him as selection chairman for Australia we got along nicely, and that rapport began with talks about my state future in 2008.

After choosing Victoria, I didn't really give the move interstate much more thought, until I got a message from a guy called Charlie Burke. We'd crossed paths a few times when he worked at the WACA, but were no more than acquaintances when he sent me a Facebook message asking if I'd like to move in with him in Prahran, just south of the Melbourne CBD. I can admit now that in WA I'd struggled to remember Charlie's name, but this generous offer came at the right time. When I touched down in Melbourne for the first time later in the year, he picked me up from the airport and took me out for a drink and a look around. He's become one of my best friends, and is now doing terrific work as coach of the Hong Kong men's and women's teams. After a short stint with Essendon, I also ended up playing club cricket for Prahran through Charlie. He helped a lot in getting me settled in.

My introduction to the Bushrangers squad had come through a pre-season camp in Mooloolaba on the Sunshine Coast in Queensland. I was assigned to a three-bed apartment with Brad Hodge and Andrew McDonald, two very senior members of the squad and close mates. Initially there was a bit of distance, not helped by the fact I had a bedroom to myself while they shared the other one – their choice! 'Huss' was initially quite busy and Damien had settled quickly into the group, having joined them a few weeks before I got back from England. For a couple of days I started to question whether the move had been the right one, particularly when one evening Brad and Andrew went off for dinner without me. It didn't feel like my team.

A few minutes after their departure I mustered the courage to message Andrew, who quickly replied that they'd just assumed I was asleep – the red-eye flight I had caught to meet the team from Perth and the return from the UK were still wreaking havoc on my sleeping habits. So I joined the pair for dinner and from that point the ice was broken. We had a team night out at the end of the camp where I mixed with the rest of the guys, and on our return to Melbourne I did not take long to get into the swing of the town through Charlie's help. Victoria's first away trip was to Adelaide, and some first-innings runs that game helped build respect for me within the room.

The greater catalyst for finding a good place in the Victorian team was how 'Hodgey' warmed to me. I had worried whether he would feel threatened, as the team's premier batsman, by having another top-order type arrive. But within the space of a few games he could see how a strong opening partnership between Nick Jewell and myself meant that he was now coming in to bat when opposing bowlers were getting into second and even third spells and the shine was off the ball. There was a healthy respect for the way I went about my batting and my bow-legged running, even if Hodgey's way of showing it was to mimic my technique with hilarious accuracy! He is without a doubt one of the funniest blokes in cricket.

Seeing how Hodgey and I were getting along, other members of the team started to open up to me, and that went hand in hand with scoring a lot of runs. An aggregate of 1195 runs went a long way towards taking the Bushrangers to a victorious Shield season, and five hundreds was a new mark for me in any first-class season, including three centuries against WA and a first-innings hundred in the Shield final against Queensland when we had first use of a sticky seamer on day one.

As satisfying personally was to play all Victoria's one-day games and win the limited-overs player of the year award for the competition – a bit of a riposte to WA's selectors, who hadn't thought I was suited to the format.

Returning to Perth as a Bushranger was a particularly memorable week. First we played a one-day game for which I scooped man of the match, before the Shield game revealed a certain level of tension about my move interstate. Marcus North made a hundred on day one, and when he reached the milestone made a point of kissing the WA badge while glaring in my direction. Our relationship had fractured somewhat over my departure. At the time I was enjoying a rare stint in the slips, and I remember Huss exclaiming, 'Mate, he just looked at you and kissed the badge!'

'Yeah he did, didn't he?'

Batting second, I found a fluent vein of form and made one of my better Shield hundreds, 115 from 132 balls out of 188 while I was at the crease. It was an innings where everything clicked for me and in tough conditions I played about as well as I ever had or ever would. It seemed destined for some reason. The game of one-upmanship was now well and truly on, and when Marcus got going again in the second innings, I said to Huss as a joke, 'If he gets a hundred and kisses the badge again, if I get a hundred in the last innings I'm going to kiss the badge!' Sure enough, Marcus looked straight at me again and kissed the badge for his second hundred of the match. 'You've got to do it now,' said Huss, as I realised it had been a stupid comment to make.

We needed 321 to win on the last day, and I anchored our chase with help from Huss and 'Ronnie' McDonald. When three figures rolled around I did as promised, and it all kicked off in the middle – the WA guys didn't like it one bit. Adam Voges, who had been one of the guys who tried hardest to get me to stay, sledged the shit out of me, and the gesture was widely reported on. A sweeter moment arrived when I swept the winning runs, then stood, bat raised skywards, while looking towards my family sitting on one of the WACA's grass banks. It was an extraordinary week, quite emotional, my innings clearly inspired by the turmoil that had taken me to Melbourne and then back to Perth as an opponent. But I've never kissed the badge since.

That season is the most dominant one of which I've been a part. We had an extraordinarily strong group of players, just about every base covered, and also a good, strong and professional dynamic among the team. This applied especially to their ability to play strongly for each other despite various ructions between guys off the field. Even during that first trip to Adelaide we'd had to have two team meetings about a dispute going on between a couple of the players. In the middle of the second meeting Simon Helmot, the assistant coach, looked across the room at me with a wry grin and a bit of a chuckle, as if to say 'welcome to Victoria'.

It gave me a fast introduction to the way things worked. Basically, the Bushrangers played cricket as though it was AFL. They were all connected to that culture, which was all about playing an incredibly intense and hard style of the game, verbally merciless on opponents and all about securing the win, whatever it took. But the other side to it was that you didn't have to be best mates off the field to do that. So from the same dressing room where I saw some spectacular infighting, I also watched numerous guys who might be at each other's throats pull together brilliantly to perform as a unit on the field. They are a breed apart.

An example of that came during one of my early club games for Essendon, playing alongside Clint McKay. At the end of a day's play he said to me: 'Mate do you actually enjoy playing here with us? It doesn't really look like you do.' We talked about that and I came to realise that my way of playing the game, partly from doing so full-time in England, was a lot more reserved than the Victorians were used to. I was managing my emotions and getting through games without resorting to sledging and aggression all the time, whereas they played it right on the edge, like footy.

Around that time there was some criticism of Victoria from other parts of the country for being a great Shield set-up that did not pull enough weight in terms of producing Australian players. I did notice a certain imbalance in the coaching staff, in that apart from Greg and Simon, most of the other development and skills coaches came from bowling backgrounds, which didn't necessarily help in developing young batsmen in the system. It did feel at times as though they felt junior and club cricket would turn up batsmen, while the real work had to be done in shaping an attack to bowl out opponents. But to an extent I could understand this: Victoria had gone a long time without winning the Shield after 1991, and there was a strong desire to keep challenging year in, year out.

Cameron White was captain, and projected a very confident persona on the field. A very direct communicator, he was a leader the rest of the side were prepared to follow in the belief that he knew best. Sometimes in cricket that quality is more important than whether or not you're actually making the right tactical calls all the time – loyalty and willingness to follow instructions go a long way, particularly in a talented side. I didn't always agree with Cam's ideas, but I respected how the team fell in behind him. He could be a hard man with teammates and opponents alike, but that was the approach Victoria needed, rather than anything softly softly. With Australia I would later see similar qualities in Darren Lehmann as coach, and perhaps it's no coincidence that both men were shaped a lot by the mentoring of the late David Hookes.

One of the effects of such a strong and results-oriented culture was that I was able to find my own niche within it. I wasn't a sledger or ranter like some of the other guys, but they respected me for the runs I made and the role I played. Amid all these big personalities, I could actually sit back quietly and be a contributor without having to take centre stage. That was useful whenever there were squabbles inside the team, because I wasn't aligned to any particular camp or looking to build alliances. In many ways it was a simpler time for me than anything I experienced in WA, and a clean break from some of the negativity than had built up within me and around me.

Despite scoring significantly, higher recognition seemed as far away as ever. A brilliant new star in Phil Hughes had emerged and Simon Katich was proving one of the most reliable batsmen in the national side – those two looked like they had sewn up the opening slots. Cricket for me once again became about enjoyment, with the feeling that perhaps my only opportunity had slipped away for good.

Even when Phil was unceremoniously dumped during the 2009 UK Ashes and I was nearby playing for Derbyshire in County cricket, my brief flicker of hope was extinguished before it even properly took flame when Shane Watson was elevated to replace Phil.

The writing was clearly on the wall – too old and not the right fit. I was gutted, as I wanted to show the Aussie players I was not who I was made out to be.

After another good County season where I scored more than 1400 runs at 73 was followed by another victorious season for Victoria averaging just shy of 50, which was in the middle of a period of my career where I scored the most runs in first-class cricket in the world five years out of nine from 2006.

But despite Australian chairman of selectors Andrew Hilditch's advice to go away and score runs when he phoned me to say I was no longer to be nationally contracted at the end of the 2007–08 season, his argument didn't seem to carry weight, even as Australia enjoyed a slightly tumultuous time.

Frustrated, I still admired the players I was trying to oust but my aim was just to be the best I could and try to prove the selectors wrong.

In 2010 though, it was clear I was very much on the outer. When Usman Khawaja was selected for the series against Pakistan in England, John Morris, the coach of Derbyshire at the time, said he firmly believed I was the better player at the time. No doubt a push had been made for youth and Ussie's talent was beyond question, but his credentials were yet to be proven, having tasted success albeit briefly in state land.

A chronic knee injury caused my 2010 County performances to tail off and after some advice I went under the knife and missed a chunk of the state season, as I had to have my meniscus cartilage stitched back down in my knee after I had ripped it off the bone.

In the end, I was available for only four matches that season for Victoria. My return of runs was poor and there was talk of me being left out of the last match for a younger player.

I was as far away from playing for Australia as I had been at any point in my professional career. I still hadn't given up hope, but these had become the lost years.

Was it time to face reality and admit defeat?

CHAPTER 8

MIDDLESEX MAKEOVER

Derby, London, Melbourne

WHAT DOES A county look for in an overseas player? Runs and wickets of course, but there's more to it than that. As Middlesex's director of cricket, Angus Fraser is the man on the lookout for someone who can flourish at Lord's as a cricketer, a leader and a teammate. Fraser, who played 46 Tests for his country, took on the role at Middlesex in late 2008, with the club in the second division. Among his first moves was to ink a short-term deal with the late Phillip Hughes, who clattered no fewer than 574 runs in three matches before he was seconded for that year's Ashes.

By the time 2011 rolled around, Fraser knew what he wanted: an overseas opening batsman prepared to commit, who would make Middlesex hard to beat. As he tells it:

'I'd been aware obviously of Chris' performances in County cricket, he'd scored runs against us for Derbyshire, and the fact he'd scored a lot of runs for Victoria in Australia. Performances on the field indicated he was used to English conditions and

had success here, and we wanted a top-order batsman to score consistently and get us off to a good start. Nick Compton had moved on to Somerset, Sam Robson was coming through, but we hadn't found the opener we needed with some experience.

'I went up to see Chris at a pub near Derby. We had a good chat, I liked what I saw, liked what I heard. I spoke to a number of people in Australia and some were questioning whether that was quite the path to go down, but we thought it was right and he did outstandingly well for us.

'The image from the outside is of a gnarled, old Aussie figure, not the most aesthetic batsman you'll see, but someone who got stuck in and was hard to get out. In person he's different, because he's quite a lively bloke, enjoys an evening out and a bit of fun. The way he plays his cricket is a bit different to the way he is in real life, but he was a really positive influence in our dressing room. There's an energy there, it gets a bit up and down at times, a bit frustrated when guys didn't perform or weren't producing what he wanted them to, but as far as giving us a bit more steel and leadership on and off the field, he was very, very good.'

Fraser notes that Chris's determination to succeed, even on the secondary grounds often used in the County Championship second tier, provided the ideal example for the team.

'It was a good fit. He was what we needed at that point in time, a good experienced pro, a good example in the way he went about his work, trained hard, very competitive on the field, and certainly gave us some direction. He'd played in second *division and … he'd obviously played at a higher level than that. Perhaps some overseas players might have struggled to get motivated on some of the grounds we played in second division because they're not the Test grounds. But he was always motivated.*

'He made 14 hundreds for us, and I know that of his first 10 none of them resulted in a win. But the effect he had was saving us games that we'd have previously lost, so they were very important, because I think the first step you need to take to become a good side is to be a hard side to beat. The first hundred he got that won us a game was the 200 against Yorkshire [in 2014] when we chased down 480. That was one of the best innings I've ever seen by a Middlesex player. You have this image of him being a bit of a crab-like batsman, but when he opened up he could hit the ball hard and he was pretty destructive that day.'

There is something different about playing the county game out of London, with its big-city travails and melting-pot sensations. Uniqueness abounds at Lord's also, the home of cricket providing an environment steeped in history 'that humbles you' according to Fraser, and tradition that can be equal parts overbearing and inspiring – like London itself, which has challenged other overseas players. Fraser knows that this atmosphere can help shape an international cricketer, offering a little more of the pressure and sense of occasion than other parts of the country.

'He deserved to have his name on the honours board at Lord's for the hundred in the Ashes in 2015, and he's on the Middlesex

honours board here as a Middlesex captain. So the fact he's got a presence in both rooms is something he can rightly be very proud of.'

'BOYS, DON'T WORRY about this game. We can't win it, so let's go out and forget about the result. All I want to see is "fight". That's all we are going to think about.' There are wins in a sporting career that stay with you. Titles of course, but sometimes just winning a game when you're up against it can make a season. A 2014 victory by Middlesex over Yorkshire was one of those.

Yorkshire hadn't been beaten for two seasons and were sweeping everything before them, winning match after match. A team full of international representatives such as Joe Root, Kane Williamson, Ryan Sidebottom, Liam Plunkett, Gary Ballance, Adil Rashid and Adam Lyth formed the nucleus of an incredibly dominant side.

Middlesex had a few good players though – Steve Finn, Eoin Morgan, Tim Murtagh and Sam Robson – but we knew we were up against it.

Winning the toss, I put Yorkshire in and somehow we knocked their star-studded line-up over for 180. But then our turn came and something must have been up. We were rolled for 123 in a poor performance and then watched helplessly as Yorkshire, through Root, Ballance and Williamson, piled on the runs, setting us 470.

It can be hard as a captain to stand up in front of your team and look them in the eye and ask for performance if you haven't done it yourself – and I'd been found wanting in the first innings, making just the one run. So the pressure was on when it came to our second innings. I'd had time to think about it and recalled something Justin Langer had said to me all those years ago, and the words that the Middlesex psychologist Steven Sylvester said to me before my first Test in the UK had stuck with me (more on them later), which was what I drew upon when I talked to my team.

The negative thoughts about the result will surprise many, but the attempt to negate pressure was the priority. And as Langer had instilled in me, fight is the most precious commodity when your back is against the wall. Clichéd perhaps, but too many times I've seen cricketers take the easy way out in these moments.

What followed is one of the greatest games I've been a part of. Batting at Lord's in the first innings can be hazardous because of the movement from the slope, but come second innings it can be the best place to bat in the world. Evenly paced and with little movement, all of a sudden the slope provides a blessing as angles can be created and scoring areas open up.

Sam Robson and I got off to a flier. When he was out the score was 181 and the game had changed. The next two, Dawid Malan and Eoin Morgan, gave steady support with 30s, but it was Neil Dexter who came in and contributed 70 not out that helped win the game. I was playing a blinder, one of those few innings in a career where everything clicked and it almost felt like it was impossible to get out. I wanted the win. I wanted to show the guys how to fight, and I wanted to beat Yorkshire, who were the best.

I'd scored many centuries for Middlesex in the previous three seasons, but this one was the first in a winning game. Surprisingly, I was proud of that statistic. I was making centuries when we had to fight against the odds and under pressure – and that was what I prided myself on. As a leader, I wanted my teammates to do the same.

A special moment was to discover that the room attendant filmed the change room when Neil hit the winning runs as I stood unconquered at the other end of the pitch with 241. The pure elation of the Middlesex guys was clear to see. That's why we play the game. We hadn't won the title, but we had achieved something very special. This is why County cricket was such a lure. Playing professional cricket 12 months of the year doesn't excite everyone, but I loved it.

Derbyshire was my home county in England from 2008 to 2010. It was an enjoyable time, scoring runs and eventually captaining one of the smaller second-division clubs while learning quite a lot about leadership and maturing as a cricketer. Rikki Clarke had initially been captain, but performance and personal issues had forced him to take a step to one side, leaving me in charge. I worked well with the coach John Morris and took the club close to promotion in 2009. We were in it until the penultimate round of games, then in our final match my final-day declaration resulted in a successful chase for Essex and their elevation to the top tier by a single point – much to the annoyance of Northants!

But the most indelible memory of that period was another brief encounter with the Australian side, this time for a tour match in 2010 during their visit to England for a series against Pakistan, who could no longer host series after that terror attack mentioned earlier. At the time, the whole affair infuriated me.

This match was not even a first-class fixture, but a two-day affair to be played in the lead-up to the first Test at Lord's. The club had sold out Derby's County Ground several months in advance through a strong marketing effort (my girlfriend at the time, Kerry, even using her considerable marketing skills to approach local businesses), and we were all looking forward to seeing Ricky Ponting's team up close.

Around 8pm the night before the game coach John called me to say the Australians wanted to bring the match forward half an hour to a 10.30 start. It was much too late to inform all the club's members and match-ticket holders about this, so a lot of spectators arrived on the first morning to find that play had already begun. Half an hour after the first call, John was back on the line to say that now they wanted to play 12-a-side, with provision for an extra bowler – Peter George. Given the match wasn't first-class I was happy enough to wave that change through, but it would take on significance later in the game.

On match morning I did the conventional thing in these games and quietly gave up bat-first rights to the touring team, the coin actually came down my way but I gestured to Ricky he had won it. Mark Footitt and Atif Sheikh used the new ball nicely and we had them three down inside the first 10 overs. We then had a close lbw appeal against Ricky turned down, and then missed a chance to run out Mike Hussey for a duck. From that point Australia took control of the day and pushed on to a solid total, with Tim Paine and a young Steve Smith also getting some runs down the order. Bowled out right on stumps, they left us with day two to bat.

Wayne Madsen and I had formed a decent opening partnership for Derbyshire, and we were able to fight our way through the new ball, past lunch and well into the afternoon on a friendly pitch. The longer our partnership went on, the more we could sense the frustration of an Australian team who, perhaps rightly, expected to knock us over quickly. Into the 80s, I gloved a ball down the leg side off Mitchell Johnson, watched it dip into Tim's gloves and then turned around to see the umpire giving me out. About five metres into my walk off the ground, Mike called out 'Buck, you're not out mate, he didn't catch it'. Resuming my innings, I then copped a mouthful from Michael Clarke, then Ricky's vice-captain, for not walking immediately. While I understood his point, I found it a little bit odd he expected me to walk when I was still fighting for runs and my own international chance. Like Derbyshire as a club, I had to scrap for everything I was getting at that stage.

In Mitch's next over he found my outside edge to deny me a hundred. From the viewing area I got a different perspective on the day, how the crowd were enjoying our fight against an international team, and how the Aussie guys were starting to look more frequently at the clock. We were still only five down with a little more than an hour of the day to go when our wicketkeeper Lee Goddard started slogging. I remember exclaiming 'what's going on here?' before the reason became clear. Ten minutes before the start of the final hour, the tourists are shaking hands with our batsmen and beating a quick exit from the field.

Sitting next to me, John Morris jumped out of his seat yelling 'what the hell is going on?' as he knew we still had a capacity crowd in who would have happily stayed for another hour or more. Of course the Australians felt they had got all they could from the day and wanted to pack up, get on the team bus and head back to London. But my mind flashed back to the night before the game when they had asked for the extra bowler in the team. Why not use this time to get a few more overs into Peter George, Ben Hilfenhaus or Doug Bollinger?

Over the next few days the club got absolutely hammered with complaints, about the early start and the early finish. Plenty of email and letter writers said they'd never pay to watch cricket again, and that they blamed Derbyshire for wrapping things up early. In that environment it was difficult for anyone to explain that if you want touring sides to come back and play at your ground you need to play ball with their requests. The whole episode re-affirmed to me that I was very much a smalltime concern in the world of cricket: Australia's players had bigger fish to fry, and I was little more than a speed bump.

Within three years, of course, I would be in an Ashes squad and using these same matches to prepare for Tests. From that angle it made sense to think primarily about getting yourself ready and not worrying too much about the match as a whole. But I still feel it is important for touring teams to acknowledge that the world of cricket is about much more than just the Test level. As much as it can be hard because there is so much cricket, there are still paying customers desperate to come watch them play, children eager for autographs and domestic teams trying to do their best on the fine margins of the County circuit. The whole week left me feeling quite steamed up at the time, but now, having played more international cricket, I can also see the perspective of a touring team with other goals in mind. Even so, it is a good example of the class structures that exist in County cricket, as domestic sides try to feed off scraps from international tours.

Perhaps that week helped get me thinking about a move to a bigger County club. By the end of 2010 I had become eager to live closer to London, which was increasingly the place I enjoyed spending time, more than just about anywhere else. One night in particular I remember watching Australia against Japan in soccer's World Cup in a pub with some friends and a whole lot of Aussie expats, and after that decided I would call my agent to say if there was any chance of going to a London county, let me know. But before I could make that call, he rang me to ask how I would like to play for Middlesex. Good timing.

I met with the Middlesex director of cricket, Angus Fraser, at a pub near Leicester. He told me he'd spoken to Justin Langer, who had enjoyed a productive stint at Lord's in the recent past, and had been told that while my batting would be top notch, he would have to decide whether I was the right off-field fit for the team. It was about this time that I was wising up to how to be around a team and striking a far better balance between work and play. Captaincy had helped that, and my rougher years with WA had long receded into the background. So there I was, signing on to play at the home of cricket for 2011.

Once again, I was joining a club with some problems in terms of performance and leadership. Middlesex was a very different deal to Derbyshire, Middlesex played at Lord's, had a tremendous history and offered the enviable opportunity to live in London. But at the same time there were similarities, as the club had slipped towards the bottom of second division and had a captain, Neil Dexter, who was battling his own personal demons. Within about three months of my arrival I found myself taking over the captaincy, and we were quite quickly able to turn things around with the help of some other recruits.

West Indian Corey Collymore, also in his first year, was absolutely outstanding as a seam bowler and a leader around the team, and in Tim Murtagh he had the perfect off-sider. Tim is a terrific bloke, who plays the game in the very best way – business on the field but ready to enjoy himself and not take life too seriously off it. Corey meanwhile was the epitome of West Indian cool, languid and effortlessly hilarious. Importantly, he was also a hugely dedicated trainer and a selfless bowler, showing the sort of ethic I imagine was the case when Caribbean sides were the world's best. Having that pair of highly skilled operators at my command was a huge help in allowing us to top division two in 2011, rising up from second-last the season before, and build up the club in terms of confidence and expectation.

The other factor in how we were able to improve was the way we were able to gel socially, to the extent that it quickly became the best environment I'd been around at first-class level. I'd got the impression that Angus wanted a leader who could be a social organiser as well, which I was only too eager to provide. We would invariably have a drink together after games at the Tavern next door to Lord's or in West Hampstead near my lodgings. All the players' wives and partners would come along, and we'd spend a lot of time out together. For 2011 and 2012 that atmosphere was sustained, and as captain but also a single man I was able to enjoy the company of the younger guys as much as those of my own generation.

I saw a lot of cricketers get into relationships early because they wanted that safety blanket. You're in such a competitive environment, particularly when you're young, and some of the banter among players can be really hard to get used to – it's pretty ruthless. A lot of the time you can leave the team environment feeling really self-conscious, lacking self-confidence. Sometimes you restore that via your family or your partner, who will be there to tell you they love you, particularly when you're away on tour or playing overseas. For a while there I needed that as well. I had numerous long-term relationships because it was just nice to have someone there to reassure you of your place in their lives, and in the world.

Over time, however, I realised that it actually suited me to not have that tie. The flip side of a relationship is the emotional difficulty of thinking about it while you're in the game, whether at home or away. A lot of players do it really well, but I ultimately concluded that while I was playing it just wasn't for me. Part of my thinking came from seeing guys I played alongside who were struggling with things going on at home. It is so vital as a professional cricketer to be able to turn up each day with a smile on your face and to bring positive energy to the team. If you're not giving to the environment, you're taking away. That might sound harsh, but it was the way I came to view things with the benefit of experience. And to do that is doubly hard if there is trouble going on at home. If your personal life is falling apart, it's bloody hard.

This is not to say that I never wanted to be in relationships, or didn't find someone I connected with. There have been several times in my life where I am happy to admit I fell in love, and did see a long future ahead with those women. But ultimately I found myself choosing my cricket before them, and breaking up. To sustain the roaming lifestyle you need to find someone who is enormously understanding, and also someone who can deal with long stretches of time apart. In a few cases I've found myself living with a girlfriend within weeks of meeting them, largely because if you don't push things it will be time to fly to the other side of the world before you know it. In turn that could lead to me wanting my own space again, because we were living in each other's pockets before we'd really had time to let the relationship grow.

All this led me to where I am now, playing and living as a single man. Whether that changes when cricket is done remains to be seen, but at Middlesex it worked well for the group. Sam Robson was one young player who I was able to build a very strong relationship with, as opening partners but also friends. That was helped by the realisation that I was playing a very important role in how these guys grew as cricketers and young men. That meant finding the middle ground between educating them on the game but also helping them to enjoy themselves at the right times, and not get so intense as to make the whole experience more draining than exhilarating. Dawid Malan, a hugely talented batsman and sometime leg-spinner, was one guy who I tried to help get the game in perspective, finding a positive outlook so you're adding more energy to the dressing room than you're taking away. The wicketkeeper John Simpson was another.

I learned a lot about the process of captaincy and leadership through dealing with Steven Crook, a talented all-rounder from South Australia who played at Middlesex before moving on to a successful career with Northamptonshire. 'Crooky' is one of the best blokes I've met in the game, but he could frustrate me at times by drifting off from a strong focus on the field – epitomised by a two-year hiatus from cricket, instead writing and performing music for his band Juliet and the Sun. He did have one hit that was played on Radio One in the UK, but he could never convince me his taste in music was anything but junk. I kept telling him, 'grunge is dead mate!'

For a long time I felt that the best thing I could do as a captain was let players work things out for themselves, setting fields and bowling in the way they knew best to succeed. But in the case of Crooky I realised in conversation with our team psychologist Steve Sylvester that he needed a different approach.

'You should tell him,' Steve said once, 'exactly what field he should have and tell him every ball what he should do.'

'How is he going to learn to think for himself then?'

'Because he'll be listening to everything you say and start to develop his own patterns.'

That made a lot of sense, and influenced how I worked with others too.

From winning promotion in 2011, we contended for the Championship for much of 2012, before slipping back towards the end. We had the bye in the last round, and in our last game we played a relegation-threatened Lancashire, who needed to win outright. While I knew they would go for anything, I was also aware our bowlers were cooked at the end of a long season. This sparked a debate with the coach Richard Scott over our potential finishing position. If we drew the match we would finish fifth in our promotion year: not bad. If we lost, we could finish as low as seventh: not so good. But if we won we could finish as high as second, with the top four teams all winning prize money. I was saying 'let's declare', while the coaching staff preferred not to risk it. To that I replied 'I don't care, it's the last day of the season'. We agreed ultimately that I'd put it to the bowlers and make a call from there.

Crooky was adamant we should go for it; Corey and Toby Roland-Jones said they were exhausted but would give it a go. I got to Gareth Berg, our plain-speaking South African all-rounder, who was less than enchanted with the idea. In the end I walked out on to the Lord's balcony to declare, setting Lancashire a target of 294 from 40 overs. At that moment the coaching staff threw their heads back in dismay, thinking I'd let Lancs back into the game. When they got to 2–107 after 16 overs I shared some of their trepidation, but Crooky came through with a brilliant spell of reverse swing, and the left-arm spinner Ravi Patel was equally good. 'Bergy' took the last catch, and we carried on like Championship winners.

That day brought about a good discussion with Richard and the rest of the support staff about who was responsible for what. I always believed a declaration was my decision, and the chat we had afterwards clarified that it always would be. During the last round, we all followed the scores to see where we would finish. Nottinghamshire did us a favour by holding out against Warwickshire for a draw to leave us third. Not only was that a great achievement by a promoted team, it was a handy extra pay day for all of us – including Bergy, who even texted me to let me know how much he would be taxed on his bonus! Bergy was a latecomer to professional cricket, starting at the ripe old age of 27, and has since gone on to 10 years of first-class cricket despite being told his career was over after a serious shoulder injury. He defied medical assessment and has proved his worth over and over at new club Hampshire.

Just as things were working out to my satisfaction in England, the landscape shifted in Australia.

My second year with the Bushrangers, 2009–10, had seen the introduction of the Futures League, which compelled states to play as few as three players over the age of 23 in the second XI competition, Not surprisingly, this had drastically thinned out the stocks of mature players. Pressure was exerted by Cricket Australia to have states looking for youth, most obviously in 2010–11 when a network of state talent managers were recruited, all reporting back to the national talent manager Greg Chappell, a big advocate for flushing older players out of the system in the name of finding young players for the Test side.

Victoria's talent manager was Andrew Lynch, and he was eager to do something similar with the Bushrangers. As you know, in 2010–11 I had brought a knee injury home from Derbyshire that limited my availability in the Sheffield Shield – and my contract had expired at the end of the season. Rob Quiney had emerged as a run-maker at the top of the order, and with Andrew McDonald, Cameron White and Dave Hussey all settled, there was a move on to open up a spot in the team. As the oldest of these guys, a non-Victorian and a player who was thought to be out of Test calculations, I soon discovered I was getting pretty close to having an 'expendable' sign on my forehead.

That was certainly the message I got in mid-2011, when the selection chairman John McWhirter visited London and invited me out for breakfast. Amid the eggs and coffee he dropped this bomb: 'Mate, we're not going to be able to offer you a contract. We know you're still doing a good job, but there's a lot of pressure on us to get the young guys coming through and we feel this is the way to go.' I left that meal in a state of shock, wondering how on earth I'd gone from a top state contract to losing it altogether.

Over the next few weeks I made serious efforts to look at playing elsewhere in the Australian summer. John

Morris, my Derbyshire coach, called up and said there was interest from Dolphins in South Africa, and I also made some enquiries about New Zealand. In Australia, Rick Olarenshaw had been looking around the states too, and told me that Tasmania may be able to table an offer. In the midst of the search, Victoria got back to me and said they would be able to offer me a spot after all – a one-year minimum contract. Compensation for not being part of the inaugural Big Bash League, I also received an additional $10,000 from the Australian Cricketers Association.

The downgrade left me feeling fairly sore about it all, and the feeling of disconnection came out after I made a hundred at the SCG against New South Wales. After play I gave a pretty outspoken interview about my treatment from Andrew Hilditch's Australian selection panel. 'The last time I rang somebody he never called me back, so that was pretty disappointing,' I said. 'I topped the first-class aggregate in the world for the next two years but still didn't hear much from them. I think they probably didn't see me in their plans, but I think you want to know where you stand.' To add to the sense of injustice, Simon Katich followed up the next day with his own hundred and some choice words about his omission from the CA contracts list for the summer.

To an extent my own concerns about a state contract had allowed the wider events of the year to pass me by. After losing the Ashes at home in 2010–11, CA had set up Don Argus to review the national team's performance, and as part of his findings the selection panel had been dismantled and replaced by a completely new set-up. Among the new selectors was

Rod Marsh, who had sought me out for South Australia a few years before. The chairman was John Inverarity, who had seen me bat as far back as junior days in Western Australia, and also when he was a successful coach of Warwickshire. At the moment when I felt about as far from calculations as possible, my stocks were actually on the rise: in Middlesex and, unbeknown to me, in Australia too.

CHAPTER 9

TWENTY20 HINDSIGHT

Sydney

WHILE THE ARGUS Review was changing Australia cricket off the field, a major change was taking place on it. It started as far back as 12 January 2005, when Western Australia played Victoria in the first domestic Twenty20 match played on Australian soil. Two things of significance about the early-evening encounter: the match attracted a sell-out crowd of 20,071, unheard of in Sheffield Shield or 50-over cricket – and Chris did not make the WA squad for the night.

The gates had been shut half an hour after play began, with the squeeze so tight that one woman, trying to return to the ground and her family after parking her car, was denied entry. WA won, scoring at the then astonishing rate of 11 an over. Within a couple of days, another crowd of similar dimensions had watched Australia A play Pakistan at Adelaide Oval.

T20 was first glimpsed in England, taking hold through its simplicity and canny advertising where other 'third generation' formats like Sixes, Super Eights and Martin Crowe's Cricket Max had not. It was first coined as a professional venture in 2001 by

Stuart Robertson, then head of marketing of England's cricket board, and was first played by the counties two years later. As Robertson explained to the *Daily Mail*:

> '*I commissioned massive consumer research into what we should do. We spent £200,000, which was considered to be a lot of money for something like this. We tried to identify who was coming to cricket matches but, more importantly, who wasn't and why. There was a significant decline in attendances across the board and we had to do something about it. We came up with something that we hoped would appeal to people who were cash-rich but time-poor.*'

Initially, T20 was used as Robertson had first intended, as a value-add for cash-strapped domestic teams in England and then Australia. Though matches were competitive, there was an element of vaudeville to it all: Australia and New Zealand donned retro kits for the first T20 international, at Auckland's Eden Park in 2005, while NSW signed up rugby league's Andrew Johns as a celebrity member of the state T20 team.

The combination of a first World T20 tournament, played in South Africa in 2007, a surprise victory by India in the final, and the entrepreneurial bent of then BCCI vice-president Lalit Modi – who had first toyed with a franchise-based Indian limited-overs competition a decade before – pushed T20 into more serious commercial territory. Once the subcontinent woke up to its virtues, so too did broadcasters, and within a year Sony and ESPNStar had paid near enough to US$2 billion for rights to the Indian Premier League and its multi-national Champions League offshoot.

Where the possibility of a more accessible game had first swayed fans, now this flood of money served to shift the priorities of players, administrators and sponsors. The IPL offered the chance to swell the wages of players yet to play for their country beyond all imaginable boundaries, while the Champions League T20 offered prize money to dwarf anything on offer in Australia. By 2010, when Cricket Australia announced the launch of its own club-based T20 competition, the Big Bash League, for 2011–12, all players were grappling with this change to their livelihoods.

Ironically, given its origins, T20 grew more in India and Australia than it did in England, due to the move from traditional teams to new T20-only entities, marketed to new audiences. The BBL provided CA with a second major television-rights revenue stream, while drawing a growing and increasingly diverse set of fans to the game. Robertson had long since left the ECB, who were mired in battles with the Counties over launching a city-based competition featuring fewer teams.

DAY ONE OF the first Test between South Africa and Australia at Centurion in 2014 was also the day of that year's IPL auction. We batted that first day, and the sense of two competing forces in the game was illustrated pretty bluntly. I was out early, and spent most of the day in the viewing area and dressing rooms watching guys wandering around as they tried to keep up to date with what was going on at the auction in Bangalore.

Mitchell Johnson was sold to Kings XI Punjab for $1 million, David Warner to Sunrisers Hyderabad for a little less than that, Shane Watson was already at Rajasthan Royals for a similar amount, and Steve Smith went to the same team for near enough to $700,000. We were in the middle of a Test match – which we won handsomely, I might add – but I couldn't forget how bizarre it felt to have these parallel worlds going on. How could these guys concentrate I wondered, as they processed the news they'd been purchased for such amounts? Maybe it helped in the case of Mitch, because I'd never seen him bowl faster than he did that week. The money and the hype were very different to the cricket I knew.

Twenty20 is a part of the game I've been at the fringes of throughout, with the exception of one season in which I was thrown into the deep end. The game first cropped up in England in 2003, and I played my first match with Leicestershire in 2005. Instinctively almost, selectors both there and in Australia decided I wasn't really suited to the format, and so my appearances were fleeting. In 2009 Victoria called me into the team for my first T20 as a Bushranger in the Big Bash final, against NSW at Sydney Olympic Stadium. I have to say my display was of the sort many feared, scraping together four off eight balls and not being able to make head or tail of slower balls delivered by Aaron Bird. That little contribution didn't look too good when Ben Rohrer belted the Blues to victory off the last ball.

In England there were a couple of better days, and even the occasional six, but for the most part I watched the way the game unfolded with a combination of awe and puzzlement. The intensity of the thing, from batting to fielding, really stretched me, and I was never able to get my head around the concept of doing anything other than selling my wicket dearly. Luke Wright, an English teammate, once said that batting in T20 is all about taking calculated gambles, being prepared to fail, and accepting the fact when you do because there will be another innings around the corner. I simply hated getting out, and that held me back from the sort of freedom the game demands. As it was, my fringe status in T20 teams meant 'another innings' wasn't always around the corner anyway. At Northamptonshire I was used almost as a 'pinch-blocker', sent in if early wickets fell but otherwise sliding right down the order.

Undoubtedly the advent of the game and its financial opportunities brought big changes to the way guys prepared and prioritised. In the first year of the Big Bash League, 2011–12, it felt as though the vast majority of the Victorian guys' conversations were about T20. All the talk was of the Stars and the Renegades, and even if the banter was friendly, I could feel a definite loss of focus on the Sheffield Shield. Over the next year or so I watched as the changes played out at training. When a spinner would bowl in the nets, most of the Bushrangers batsmen would swing for the fences basically every ball.

That worried me, because although it was fine for T20, it was no preparation for Shield or Test cricket, scenarios where you needed to defend effectively or rotate the strike. This got to the stage that I saw Shield games in which guys were all at sea trying to defend against spin. Perhaps it is no coincidence that Australia's struggles in India in 2013 took place after the first two years of the BBL? I brought the issue up in a

Bushrangers team meeting, saying I felt the batsmen were letting our preparation get out of balance by trying to slog every ball in training. Things did improve from there, and you now see a more nuanced approach to facing spin bowling even within the confines of a T20 match.

The other big change I witnessed was among players who, like me for a time, didn't believe they were in contention to represent Australia. In the first few years after the IPL came in, the Champions League was there and the BBL followed, most players diverted their energy to being as good as possible in T20. Things have swung back a little bit the other way in the last couple of years, as opportunities have opened up to play for the national team. Cricket Australia is fortunate to be able to pay premium contracts that can still outstrip anything earned in the BBL, meaning that apart from the IPL most players are happy to make the Test and national one-day teams their priority.

In the first year of the BBL I wasn't in calculations, as much out of my own reticence as that of the eight new teams. But I found during that season the gaping hole in the middle of the summer devoted to the BBL left me thinking I should find a way to get involved. I can remember spending time with other non-BBL guys like Ryan Carters in a real vacuum, with coaching staff employed elsewhere and even our right to train at the MCG affected by the Stars getting priority. So towards the end of the contracting period for 2012–13 I found myself signing on with the Sydney Thunder on near enough to a minimum contract deal. The dollar figure had me thinking I was destined to go along, play one or two games and be around the competition without being right in the thick of it – wrong!

Around ten days before the tournament I arrived in Sydney for a little pre-tournament camp. One of our exercises was a spot of paintball shooting. Usman Khawaja was an absolute dead-eye shot, which says something about his hand-eye coordination. Another exercise was a 'get to know you' session where we were all paired off with guys from different states. In the middle of this I looked around the room and noticed how young everyone was: I felt I'd played more first-class cricket than the rest of the squad combined. Michael Clarke was nominally the captain, but he was only going to be around for one game and in the end pulled out of that too due to back trouble. Our marquee player Chris Gayle, meanwhile, had not yet arrived. Slowly it dawned on me that, shit, I was about to wind up as captain.

We played a practice match in Sutherland Shire, south of Sydney, and sure enough the coach Shane Duff came up to me and asked if I'd be captain. I made a few runs, Michael pulled out of the first game, and I was captain of the team. The general manager John Dyson was going through some personal problems and was not around the team all that much, so it was mainly Shane and I working together. Shane is a tremendous human being, and gave absolutely everything he had to the job, but he had never managed a major team before, and there were times when neither of us had a handle on tactics. As if to remind us of where we sat, the last event before the tournament was a joint launch with the Sydney Sixers, bristling with talent and fresh from winning the BBL/

Champions League double. With respect to our guys, it felt like they were NSW and we were the second XI.

That feeling was underlined by a thumping defeat to the Sixers in game one at the SCG, where I quickly felt myself to be out of touch with the format. When I'd first seen T20 it had been viewed largely as a bit of fun, but in the years since the start of the IPL it had already grown quite advanced in its tactics, magnified by the speed of the game that turned every ball into its own chess match. We started out with New Zealander Martin Guptill at the top of the order, because Gayle was yet to arrive, while our other overseas player, Azhar Mahmood, who has represented Pakistan and is now an English citizen, had arrived but was not yet fit to play. Usman partnered Guptill, and I was due in at No.3.

One of the points I had debated with Shane was around balancing right and left-handers through the order, so that in the event of a short boundary or spin bowler we had the right options to hit to the most accessible side of the ground. We also had South Australian Mark Cosgrove in the squad, and I thought he was a decent option to balance our right-handers. However Shane disagreed and preferred another right-hander, which left the Sri Lankan leggie Jeevan Mendis to bowl with impunity at the end of the innings with the short boundary on the off side. Later in the night our left-arm spinner Luke Doran would see numerous balls sail over that same fence, ramming home the fact our tactics weren't exactly watertight.

There were a few times when I struggled to keep up in the field. One day we walked off at the end of an innings and

I turned to see Azhar walking along next to me. 'Oh shit,' I exclaimed. When he asked what was up, I apologised for forgetting to bowl him, using only two of his allotted four overs. This demonstrated the folly of making me captain, because I simply hadn't played the volume of games, particularly as a leader, to have the right rhythm for decision-making. Someone who may have done better was Cameron Borgas, signed onto a three-year deal with a history of playing some decent T20 cricket already in the Big Bash and the Champions League. But while Cam hardly played, I led our motley bunch to loss after loss. Planning was in short supply.

It was clear to management that Cricket Australia wanted the Thunder to be the club for western Sydney. This was true to the point that when we were all assigned grade clubs, I was ruled out of playing with St George, where my Dad had spent many years, because John Dyson had decided I was going to Blacktown, further west. But any sense of getting the team itself together was undermined by the decision to allow our biggest-name overseas players to be accommodated in hotels in the centre of town, while the rest of us stayed at Parramatta. Chris Gayle was in the city, Matt Prior was in the city, the NSW guys were at home, and a handful of us were left out west, isolated by distance – and also lack of transport.

Initially we had no cars whatsoever, and were told to catch public transport or car pool with the NSW players. Having enjoyed the benefit of a sponsor car even when playing League cricket in England, this was difficult to understand. Eventually the media manager Tony Peters was able to secure a Jeep for us to share, but it was still a long way short of what we were all used to. Mainly it meant that between games the team spent virtually no time together, something that only worsened our ability to deal with other issues, whether on the field or in training. The nets at Blacktown were uneven and dangerous, and we were refused a request to train in Sixers territory at the SCG.

No one had any great affection for our home ground, the cavernous Sydney Olympic Stadium. Apart from the ground's odd dimensions, its drop-in pitches were not of a good standard, making batting difficult but also limiting the types of bowling that worked well there. A lot of the time it played similarly to a seaming, tennis-ball bouncing day-one drop-in at the MCG, which meant I'd tend to bowl Dirk Nannes right through his four overs at the start, because he knew how to use those conditions. The biggest loser on these pitches was probably Gayle, our best-paid player by a mile. It simply did not make sense to recruit him on the money that we did and then produce wickets on which it was almost impossible to hit through the line of the ball, and equally challenging to pull or cut. We were impeding our greatest strength, which hardly encouraged him to spend time training or around the team.

Another guy who had to battle with these same problems was Usman, who made for a pretty fascinating study through the tournament. His frustration at the state of our training facilities was very evident at times, to a point where in one session he threw down his bat and made it clear to everyone he expected better. It was around this time, when he'd moved from NSW to Queensland for a fresh start in the Shield, that numerous people were questioning his attitude, and whether he was too laid back to succeed at the top level. But that reaction stayed with me as evidence of how much he wanted to do well, and in a couple of innings he showed glimpses of the sort of stuff he can now produce more consistently.

Our performances deteriorated after that inauspicious start against the Sixers. Towards the end of the competition I started to feel quite down, through the sheer embarrassment of the experience. In terms of dark days, they were up there with my shoulder and leg surgeries in 2004, or the week of turmoil I spiralled into after my Test debut. We were a losing side, embarrassingly so, and as the captain I had neither the technical nor the tactical tools at my disposal to do anything about it. Most of the games felt like they had been decided inside the first 10 overs of either innings, and we certainly didn't provide much reason for the crowds to venture out to see us.

In the end I'll admit to actually hoping I would get injured. The team and I were so humiliated by it all, and there was precious little enjoyment to be found amongst it all. A broken finger before our trip to Perth meant my fairly morose wish was granted, and Gayle led the side in the final two games. Some closing drinks in Melbourne after the last match passed for our breakup party, and there was nothing so much as a debrief before we all went our separate ways. John Dyson and Shane Duff were soon out of their jobs, and there were changes higher up at Cricket NSW also. It wasn't until months later that I got a call from the new NSW chief executive Andrew Jones to thank me for taking on a difficult job – but there was no question of a contract renewal.

From that rock bottom season, the Thunder did start to get themselves together. They recruited Mike Hussey as captain, worked at building a more even squad, and in Nick Cummins they hired a very capable general manager who ultimately brought Paddy Upton in as coach. When they emerged to win the BBL in 2016, I was particularly happy for Usman, having remembered the struggles he went through alongside the rest of us three seasons before. The BBL itself has gone from strength to strength, helped by terrific television coverage from Ten, and with a city-based model that keeps the competition tight and interesting throughout.

I've long lost track of the county-based model in England, where there just seems to be too many games. Whether they shrink that down to an Australian-style model remains to be seen. But I do believe pretty strongly that T20 is at its best as a standalone competition away from the first-class teams. Fresh team identities, freedom of movement for players, fewer competing sides and matches mean that every night can be a big event, both at the grounds and on television. CA's view is very similar, but I have run into plenty of strong opposition whenever I've mentioned this in England, particularly at Somerset. I'm aware that county clubs can make as much money from one T20 match than they can make from a whole first-class season. That means the onus is on the ECB to not just reshape the competition, but to get the financial model right as well.

Either side of the Thunder experience I knuckled down with the Bushrangers and put together a solid Shield season. Three hundreds and 742 runs meant I was only behind the now-retired Ricky Ponting on the Shield home-and-away aggregates for the season, ahead of numerous younger players who the selectors had hoped to see more from. Ever supportive, Dad made sure I was aware of how it all looked entering into 2013, the year of an Ashes tour. But for the most part I refused to allow myself the thought that it might be my time.

CHAPTER 10

A SECOND CHANCE

Taunton, London, Manchester

AUSTRALIA'S ASHES SQUAD announcement for 2013 took place on 24 April, all of two months and 16 days before the first ball of the series was to be bowled at Trent Bridge. For the first time in his life, Chris Rogers was in that group as a fully-fledged member, not the last-moment injury replacement he had been in Perth in 2008.

Two months and 16 days is a long time to think about finally achieving all you've ever wanted. It is an eternity for trying to get your head around the idea that the Australian dressing room – a place where you did not exactly feel wanted the last time around – would now be your home for at least three months. And then there are the thoughts of possible failure to deal with, of having your game exposed in front of enormous crowds and still larger television audiences. Will you be seen as a fraud, or a Test cricketer?

Chris was playing at Middlesex, and its director of cricket, Angus Fraser, was first to see that all this was weighing fairly heavily upon his charge. Fraser's response was to alert Steve Sylvester, the club's psychologist, and a former Middlesex player himself. As Fraser put it: 'Chris does have a sensitive side, and he worries at times.' This was something of a surprise for Sylvester, who had worked with Chris since his arrival in 2011. As he tells it, their relationship:

> '... was quite cool at the start, because he had a dim view of psychologists in terms of them trying to provide solutions to hardened, experience professional cricketers like himself. He'd played Test cricket, been around the block, already had over 50 first-class hundreds, had been to a number of counties, done it all. So it was "what do I need you for?" that was his mentality. From there it went to him seeing the influence I was having on players, and his view of a player is helpful to me. So we then started to talk about how you manage certain people in the team, and there was a growing awareness of a different lens to look at players. He didn't need too much help with what he was doing, at least not in County cricket.'

That changed in the weeks after the Ashes announcement. While Chris sought to keep his worries close, Fraser noticed, and suggested Sylvester go see him. An annual sponsors day at John Paul Getty's ground in Buckinghamshire offered the chance for some downtime, and after some cajoling, Sylvester took Chris for a walk around the boundary, in conditions close enough to freezing.

Sylvester's work is centred upon the ego of the athlete, to the extent that he has written a book called *Detox Your Ego*. As he and Chris made their laps of the boundary, they unpacked all the anxieties and fears related to playing Ashes cricket after such a long wait. Sylvester recalls:

'Here's you, with all this expertise as a professional batsman,
and yet you sound like you've never played the game before.
Like you're starting to get into the Under 10s local school team.
The contrast with other psychologists is they wouldn't have said
"well basically you're struggling here". That was the moment
where he could relax and actually talk.

'The acknowledgement that it's ok to be struggling with it,
and to talk about that is really important. We walked around
the boundary talking about all his deep-seated fears about
the whole structure of Australian cricket and the fact he'd
played one Test six years ago, and what it meant to play in
the biggest series of his life years later. The skill was to provide
some sort of bridge in conversation, terms to connect his
expertise to his emotions ...'

Something Chris had to reconcile was how to be both a new man in the team and a senior player all at once, utilising all his years of experience in England while also getting used to an unfamiliar environment. In acknowledging that leadership was as much a part of his role as run-making, Chris grew to feel more comfortable in the side.

Parents John and Ros made the trip to watch their son. Thanks to various dramas around a missing purse, they missed seeing him walk out to bat in the first innings of the series at Trent Bridge, but were on hand for his maiden Test century at Durham. As John tells it:

'Suddenly I see a desperate sweep and an "Oh, No" I think –
and it's so dark, I don't know what's happened, immediately
think he'd be lbw – and then I see them looking square,

and there it was, careering to the fence. The crowd roar. I'm gutted, drained – even a little tear. I couldn't even stand up like everyone else. Gave Ros a hug when she sat down – completely spent, riding every near-miss, so many appeals. In the next over after the hundred, I suddenly saw him leaning on his bat looking at the ground, the realisation dawning, and he said later he had a little tear, too.'

'YOU'RE SCARED, aren't you?'

Middlesex's psychologist Steven Sylvester had almost stalked me at a charity match at Wormsley in the John Paul Getty Estate in Buckinghamshire – and here he was accusing me of being scared. He'd heard the news of my selection in the Australian squad for the 2013 Ashes and insisted on talking to me about it. I'd never been overly keen on psychologists for cricket teams, as mostly they sit back and wait for you to say something and then try to say something wise. The problem was, he was right. I'd recognised it myself, even said so in a conversation the day before to my father back home.

My first inkling that the Australian selectors had my name in mind for England 2013 came via Victoria's coach Greg Shipperd, a few days before I was due to leave for another winter with Middlesex. We met for a coffee in March, around the time the Test team were being beaten badly in India and the team was being riven by 'Homeworkgate' – four players suspended for not completing a written assignment. Amid conversation about those dramas, 'Shippy' stopped me with these words: 'Mate, I think you should take your Baggy Green with you this time.' Via the talent management system that linked the state selection panels to Cricket Australia, the coaches were speaking a lot more to the national selectors, and so this felt a lot more significant than it might have been in the past.

I wasn't taking anything for granted. I knew that Shippy had always been a passionate advocate for Victorian players being promoted to the national side, and his encouragement had not always led to selection. But on the strength of that advice, I took the cap out of a cupboard at home and took it to my parents' house, thinking that if the call did come, they would be on their way over to see it all happen.

After travelling back to London and reconnecting with Middlesex and Lord's, I became aware that there seemed a lot more media buzz than usual about my chances of being chosen. That was when I started to think 'ok, I'm more than likely going to be in here'. Late April rolled around and the announcement of the team was coming up. One morning I was doing a fitness session at the Finchley indoor centre, and was a little puffed after a beep test. Looking at my phone, I noticed a missed call. The voicemail was from John Inverarity, asking me to call back.

Within a few minutes I was outside and on the phone, hearing John say the words, 'Yes Chris you're in, we've chosen you for your skills over there and you'll be a really good chance to play. Keep doing what you're doing.' He assured me I didn't have to do much different, simply to keep playing with Middlesex and warming into the domestic season. Then he added a warning to keep it out of the press before the announcement was made. I made a quick call to Mum and Dad, to tell him it was all happening, and walked back inside with a smile on my face. Someone else had noticed the name John Inverarity on my phone, so by the time I came back the rest of the squad were crowded round saying, 'Tell us, tell us!' I might have voiced the words 'oh I'm not allowed to say what that was about', but everyone knew. The grin was the big giveaway.

What followed was a mental journey I'd never been on before. My last brief experience of Test cricket had been sudden and fleeting, all over before I'd realised it was happening. This time there was an initial high about being picked for Australia, but with all the extra time for it to sink in there came a much more sobering realisation – I was fearful about how this might turn out. The negative thoughts built up from Under 19s, Australia A, my one Test match and the lack of follow-up chances all compounded. My head became clouded with questions. Am I going to be good enough? Am I going to find out that I'm actually not good enough and never was? How am I going to fit into this team?

Most of these thoughts were kept to myself, and with Middlesex I kept playing well enough. But there must have been enough evidence of my nerves to others. As a club we went to take part in a festival match at Wormsley, and I got a call from Steve Sylvester about catching up for a chat during the day. At the time everyone was saying the same things to me, along the lines of 'you must be so happy to be in the side', and to all this I was responding with a typical 'yeah I feel so good about it'. But underneath, mixed in with the excitement was a serious case of nerves and fear. I was so nervous and so scared about what lay ahead. My mind was churning it over most hours of each day – as was my stomach.

My meeting with Steve was about three weeks after the squad was announced. He's an exceptionally enthusiastic character, full of life and energy that can't help but rub off on you. He'd say 'watching you bat is better than sex, just the way you do it, putting the ball in gaps and managing your game!' and I'd reply 'well you can't be doing it right ...' In that way he was different from just about any psychologist I'd worked with, as most were more taciturn, listening types. Since he'd joined Middlesex in 2010 he'd had a good effect on the squad, although I probably still retained a bit of reserve, as I did with most guys brought in to manage my state of mind.

This day at Wormsley was horrendously cold in the way only an early English spring day can be, to the point that we were playing in beanies. But Steve in his bouncy way said 'let's go for a lap of the ground!' and coaxed me out of the change room. We walked around past the marquee, out of earshot of anyone else, and he said 'go on mate, how do you feel about being selected?' As I'd done with everyone else I gave him the standard response about feeling excited and really good about it all. At this point the only person I'd really spoken to about my anxieties was Dad.

To my surprise, Steve retorted, 'That's just bullshit. You're scared, aren't you?' I stared back at him, wide-eyed, and almost instantly a burden lifted, because I knew I could speak to him about it. I laughed and said, 'What do you mean?'

'Mate, don't give me that shit that you're all excited and stuff like that. You're scared about how this is going to go, aren't you?'

'I can't believe you just said that. That's exactly what I said to Dad a few hours ago.'

'That's ok. Everyone would be scared. That's the right reaction.'

'So how are we going to deal with this?'

'You've got to go into this series thinking you're going to get a duck every innings.'

'What?'

'It doesn't matter. What's the worst that can happen? You make a duck every innings. So be it. Anything above that is a bonus.'

This might not sound like it makes a heap of sense, but that was exactly what I needed to hear at that moment. I desperately needed to take the pressure off myself – and setting a low standard for what I expected served the purpose of doing that. We ended up doing about three laps of this freezing oval as I tried to soak up this new attitude from Steve.

What he helped me realise was that because I'd played County cricket in England and Sheffield Shield in Australia for so many years, I'd got myself into a position where I knew I was good enough. If you have that sense it doesn't necessarily matter if you fail in one or two innings, because you know it will come around. Added to that I hadn't faced a run of outs for a long time, and I wasn't really getting nervous at the crease. But all of a sudden all these new feelings had emerged to shake me out of that comfort zone. To hear that was how I was meant to feel was a great help.

From there on with Middlesex I tried to get myself keyed up for my innings, revving myself up to feel edgier at the batting crease. For one thing, I'd learnt early in my career not to drink coffee before I batted, as it lifted my heart rate, which caused me to play rash, instinctive shots rather than in the calm, methodical manner I preferred to bat (Dean Jones avoided sugar apparently for the same reason). But here I was sculling coffee as I tried to get the adrenaline going before I batted. That was my mindset when the Australian players arrived in England, in three groups, as there was an Australia A tour going on in addition to the ODI Champions Trophy going on at the same time.

So six or seven of us had training sessions at Hampstead Cricket Club, coincidentally about 200 metres from my Middlesex home. The group included Michael Clarke, Shane Watson, Davey Warner, Mitchell Starc, Phillip Hughes and James Faulkner. A lot of these guys didn't know me particularly well, and so it was a bit of an exercise in getting a little more familiar. A little like my first Test, I was still staying at home rather than in the team hotel at Kensington, and so I still felt somewhat on the outer.

At one session I batted next to Davey and could sense him struggling with the conditions. On my side I was much more comfortable, dealing well with a challenging practice wicket. When I emerged from the nets Mickey Arthur came up to me and said, 'Do you know your back swing goes down towards fine leg?' I was a bit puzzled at this and so asked him, 'Where is it when the bowler is in delivery stride?' to which he replied it had straightened up by then. The impression I got was that he wasn't overly familiar with how I batted, which was intriguing given he was a selector.

However from there we developed quite a good rapport, to the extent that a few days later he told me I would be opening in the first Test. Mickey went on to say that when the team got down to Taunton, in Somerset, for the first tour game, 'I'll take you out to dinner and pick your brains about England, really enjoy talking to you.' That felt good to hear from the coach. Mickey had said it a few days before the team was due to assemble in Bristol before heading to Somerset. So imagine my surprise when I started to hear rumours that he was about to be sacked. The rumours turned out to be accurate.

Just my luck, I thought. Finally in an Australian squad, getting along well with the coach and they've fired him. For a while I thought I was back to square one. Mickey's replacement was Darren Lehmann, and I had no real sense of how he viewed me. For all I knew, he would think I was surplus to requirements and keep me on the fringes once more.

These were strange hours and days, as the team and Cricket Australia seemed extremely tense about what lay ahead. On the bus from London to Bristol, a senior Cricket Australia figure delivered a speech I couldn't make much sense of. In explaining Mickey's sacking he said CA felt they had to 'move forward'. He then offered this: 'To be honest, we don't expect you guys to win this series. If we could keep it to a draw that would be fantastic, and then we'll get them in Australia.' It felt strange that a CA representative was basically giving up the series before it had even been played.

These words were still ringing in my ears when the group got together in Bristol, so for the first time I found myself speaking up in an Australian team meeting. 'I don't want to be going into this series,' I said, 'with an attitude that we can't win this, because we can.' I got a sense of a few eye-rolls and blokes thinking 'who does he think he is', but it was an important moment for me because I felt I couldn't just be a junior member of the side. So in amongst a team that I could tell was still feeling uneasy and split into a couple of camps, here I was trying to assert myself. We had an awful long way to go.

Next we were told that Mickey was still at the hotel, in a room waiting to say goodbye to us. Not all the players went to see him, which said a lot about where the group was at. I followed the guys who did, shook Mickey's hand and offered him my best wishes. It was quite a raw meeting, as some members of the team were clearly very shaken by what had happened, and there was a tear or two shed. That was the last time we saw Mickey before jumping on the bus to Somerset with the new man, Darren 'Boof' Lehmann.

Our hotel in Somerset was The Castle, and I had been assigned a room on the top floor. Out of habit I opened up my bags and threw a bunch of gear on the bed in preparation for hanging it up. That moment I got a knock on the door: it was Boof. Preparing myself for the worst, I welcomed him in amid my partly unpacked bags. For whatever reason we had never really spoken much in Shield or County cricket. That distance led me to think that he didn't have much time for me as a cricketer or a bloke, and his first words didn't help.

'So you're messy are you?'

'Sometimes, not usually.'

'Ok, I just want to speak to you for a bit.'

At this point my heart sank – he was about to tell me that Mickey's assurance about opening the batting no longer applied. He continued: 'You're not going to play in the first tour game at Taunton …' That only enhanced my feelings of dread. For a few seconds.

'… but you're going to open at Trent Bridge.' Gobsmacked doesn't do my feelings justice. I was in! Through all that drama, all the change at the top and the turmoil around the team, I was going to be in the Test side. The look on my face must have been something else, because even now Darren still talks about it. Recently he sent me a card that read: 'To Bucky, still one of my best moments I've had in coaching was in that room in Taunton to say you weren't playing in the tour game but you were playing in the Test. Your face was priceless!'

An hour or so later we had another team meeting, Darren's first as coach. The first thing he said to us was, 'No meeting of mine will ever go for more than half an hour, and if it does you can walk out.' He then laid out in fairly basic terms what he wanted and expected from us, before asking how much time was left. At a reply of 'three minutes', he looked straight at Davey and said, 'This is your last chance. Don't fuck up again.' Everyone looked at Davey – who had got himself into trouble via a bar-room altercation with England's Joe Root –

and he replied with a simple 'ok', and that was that. There had been a lot of talk about lines in the sand in India, but this was the one for us and Darren. There was no bullshit, no complexity, just a simple instruction. Everyone took that on board, because it was just so clear.

With that, Darren said, 'All right boys, we're going over the road to the pub, and it's the captain's buy.' We walked to the pub directly opposite the hotel in some kind of a daze. I'll never forget it. I had come from so many cricket environments where having a drink together was second nature. But these guys were having a beer and looking suspiciously at each other like they didn't know how to behave. Their faces seemed to say: 'What's going on here, is this a test?' At the same time I was looking at them thinking how bizarre this all was, how far removed from regular cricket reality the team culture had become. As I've said and shown, drinking can be a problem, but socialising is necessary, which Boof believed too.

Things improved quickly, even while we were in Taunton. The team doctor Peter Brukner ran a quiz night one evening, won by the unlikely pair – though they might have disagreed – of Michael Clarke and Phillip Hughes. It was a really laid back, funny night, where guys were relaxed and enjoyed each other's company. You could sense they were starting to come out of their shells for the first time in quite a while. We won the tour match, too. That night we arrived in Worcester, and the team ventured together to a club called Bushwackers, perhaps the best-known night spot in County cricket circles. Another great evening was had by all; another step towards togetherness.

Something else Darren decided was to allow families to join the players as soon as possible – by the end of the week many had convened from the houses they had been staying in around the UK. Among the values he had outlined to us in that very first meeting, 'family' was right at the top of the list. Once again, this helped to put players at ease, because Darren was stripping back a whole range of rules and regulations. In their place was simple common sense, trust and enjoyment: exactly as it should be.

After deciding on having me open the batting, Boof had also settled on moving Shane Watson up the order to accompany me. He was a player I needed to get to know, having only spent time with him briefly with Australia A in 2006 when, as mentioned earlier, I didn't do myself too many favours. As well I'd heard that Shane had become a bit of a closed book to a lot of people, not trusting the advice of many and further alienated from others by the Homeworkgate events of India earlier in the year. When other players or coaches tried to speak to him, his walls would go up.

We first walked out together in the tour game at Worcester, and soon Shane was pinging boundaries everywhere. For the most part the pitch was flat and easy-paced, but it had distinctive corrugated lines running down its length. Most of Shane's runs were coming through cover drives or forcing shots through point, and he was accelerating all the time. Towards the end of the morning session a hundred before lunch looked possible, and I walked down the wicket to him to say 'you're playing so well here, but just look out for the pull shot – I reckon the odd ball might pop off this wicket'.

At that moment he looked at me defensively, as if to say 'why are you saying this to me?'

The very next ball was short – it stopped in the wicket and popped up higher than expected. Shaping first to play the pull shot, Shane dropped his hands and swayed out of the way. Walking back down the pitch between balls, he looked up at me with wide eyes and a smile on his face. Next came a small nod of acknowledgement. It was a great example of the trust that could be built up between batsmen in the space of a single ball. It was a pivotal moment, as from then on we got along well; Shane felt that he now had a partner who could offer him some guidance along the way. For all his prodigious talent, Shane benefited greatly from having someone at the other end who could help with little cues like that, in-game knowledge and tips to keep him mentally sharp. Once he opened up to me, others noticed the forming of a relationship that few had been able to cultivate.

There were still a few reasons for tension, related largely to the balance of a squad and support staff that Darren hadn't been involved in selecting. Between Shane, myself, David Warner, Ed Cowan, 'Hughesy' and even Usman Khawaja, there were an awful lot of squad members happiest at the top of the order. Ed only got one Test match before he was out of the side, and hasn't had another opportunity since. Hughesy was shuffled down to No.6 then dropped after the second Test, at Lord's, despite playing one of his very best innings in the first Test at Trent Bridge. Usman got two Tests before also losing his place, and Davey, who started the series suspended after the Joe Root incident, came into the middle order and was opening with me by the end of the series.

Darren's tactical sense was that the line-up contained too many left-handers for off-spinner Graeme Swann to target, and by the time of the return Ashes series in Australia, a top six with potentially as many as five lefties, had been cut back to two – Davey and me. The biggest winner out of all this was actually Steve Smith, included in the squad at the last minute after an Australia A tour, then straight into the batting order as a right-hander who could handle spin. He's barely looked back, and Darren's call was ultimately proven right, despite the differences of opinion several squad members had at the time.

Overall though, the majority feeling was that we were now heading in the right direction, and Boof was the right man to lead us. He spoke to us with so much conviction abut the way he wanted us to play, and how it linked back to how the great Australian sides had done it, that it was hard to disagree. Particularly given there was so little time before the series itself (and the home series that followed immediately), that sort of clarity and direction was extremely welcome.

One prominent figure around the Australian rooms that series was Shane Warne. He would become a part of the support staff in South Africa the following year, but for the moment he looked to be there as a useful link between Darren and Michael Clarke. It's so important to have your coach and captain on the same page, and I could see Boof making their mutual friend welcome to try to bring the best out of 'Pup'. It was fascinating to watch Michael in action on and off the field, and I have to say we got along well.

Trent Bridge was a fantastic Test match as it swung to and fro, plus the most amazing debut ever by Ashton Agar and then a quite amazing finish as Brad Haddin and James Pattinson almost won it from nowhere. At the time, people were saying it was one of the best Test matches ever – in fact only the Boxing Day Test got near it in terms of drama over my three Ashes series. So much happened in that first Test in England that it was almost a blur – but what a match.

A lot was made of Stuart Broad not walking at a key moment in the second innings, but the wider feeling was that we were actually a lot closer to England than many people thought we were. I made a couple of starts, and just as importantly felt I worked out a way of how to deal with James Anderson, even though he got me out in both innings. In fact, at 0–84 in the second innings chasing just over 300, the usually boisterous Nottingham crowd had turned very silent and we had a strong feeling we could run the total down. Unfortunately Shane was dismissed for 46 and then Ed and I departed in quick succession and the momentum swung back to England.

Next was Lord's and the significance of it hit me in a few ways, even though I had played there for three years with Middlesex. Whether it was meeting the Queen on the first morning, or seeing all the celebrities who filed through our dressing room over the few days – Hugh Jackman, Russell Crowe, the guys from Powderfinger, Steve Waugh, Adam Gilchrist, Lucas Neill and former PM (and cricket tragic) John Howard among them. More vivid was the fact that it turned into a horrific match for both the team and myself. To be dismissed by a Swann full-toss that basically hit me on the box was incredibly embarrassing, and it was not much better when I let one go and was bowled in the second innings. Our innings defeat set lots of tongues wagging, and exposed me for the first time to the public savagery of Ashes failure.

I'd been given a few days off after that match, staying in London rather than venturing south for the team's next tour game. A former Northamptonshire teammate and friend Stephen Peters was having his benefit year, and held a dinner at the Oval. The dinner panel included Alec Stewart, Alastair Cook and Jeff Thomson, who gave the impression he had no idea who I was. Jeff delivered a few great anecdotes about his shenanigans with Dennis Lillee in the 1970s, before the MC asked each man what the final Ashes scoreline would be. Stewart said '5–0', Cook deflected it as you'd expect, then 'Thommo' took his turn. 'I don't know, but I'm pretty worried. To be honest, I'm embarrassed about our top order,' before launching into a fair roasting of the top six. Through this I remember virtually everyone in the room just staring at me, while at the same time not knowing where to look.

Allan Border had earlier kicked it off after the game by stating the following in a column I read. 'I could honestly say the nine, 10 and jack [No.11] looked more competent than our one, two and three,' he wrote. 'If that was me in the top three I'd be embarrassed.' Shane and I spoke about it at a training session, and he explained how many former players felt obliged to speak as frankly as that in their roles as paid commentators – I've since learned in radio work that this is true. Not long after that I sourced AB's mobile number and contacted him to express my irritation, but added that if he felt he had any advice I would be happy to have a chat. He let me know he was simply very disappointed with the way the match had panned out, and just urged me to keep fighting it out.

This was all an eye-opener to me, because you never really cop that sort of criticism in domestic cricket. Having just been through the Lord's Test and still new to it all, I was pretty sensitive to these attacks. With the benefit of more experience you learn to shrug it off, and to throw out the criticism while hanging onto anything you might find useful. If you're going to play at that level, and accept all the advantages, financial and otherwise, that arise, you've got to be prepared to take on the criticism. Ultimately I was grateful to go through that episode, wiser after a painful few days.

When rejoining the team for Old Trafford, I was quite unsure whether I'd still be in the side. But the selectors chose to drop Hughesy for the return of Davey down the order, and I went out to bat again with 'Watto' alongside me. While it was a sunny morning and the best pitch of the series so far, I had no intention of playing the way I actually did. Some days, despite your own best intentions, you find yourself batting with unexpected momentum, and so it was. The ball was coming onto the bat beautifully, Stuart Broad was having an off day, and while Anderson bowled well initially, his offering of numerous full balls gave me the chance to pierce the off side. In the space of 49 balls I had 50.

No one had seen me play like this at international level, but it was reminiscent of numerous days I'd had with Middlesex, dictating terms with good placement and timing. For a fleeting moment I actually thought a hundred before lunch was plausible, but when an excellent diving stop by Kevin Pietersen was closely followed by Shane's wicket I settled back down. Swann came on and slowed my momentum, before he had Usman given out caught behind, in a decision I still cannot believe. Standing up the other end, I could see daylight between bat and ball, and there was uproar when his decision review was turned down.

Michael approached the crease wide-eyed and bamboozled, not quite sure what he had just witnessed. I urged him to focus and get through to lunch, even offering to take the whole last over even if a single was on offer. He declined and did his job, setting the basis for his best innings on the series.

After lunch, on the outskirts of a hundred, I was stopped by the distraction of movement up behind the bowler's arm. Unknown to me it was my Melbourne district-club teammate Dan Salpietro causing the commotion, as I waved for an unaffected line of sight. In truth the incident was no excuse for my subsequent dismissal, playing around a straight one from Swann, but it soon got weird. After I came off the field I saw replays of it all, including the sight of someone waving at me from the pavilion. I exclaimed, 'That's Dan Salpietro. My teammate from Prahran.' Soon it was going around the world, and he was getting interviewed as 'the guy who stopped Chris Rogers' hundred'. That night he sent me a message of apology. After stringing him along for a while I said it didn't actually make any difference.

It was a watershed moment – and one I'm perhaps as proud of as any in my time wearing the Baggy Green. The side had been down and out and mocked by everyone after Lord's. Yet after an hour in the first session of the next Test, I had 59 off 54 balls and had Australia on the front foot, our spirits lifted. As I'd said in so many captain speeches over the years, these are the times when you need players to stand up and be counted – and Michael's 187 rightly earned him man of the match.

From there we outplayed England over five days, held up only by rain in our pursuit of a surprise victory. While the draw meant England had retained the Ashes, we felt much better for how we had performed, and felt that it was another step closing the gap between the teams. Next up we got to Durham, on a pitch that looked like it would be the most helpful one for the seamers all series. At a moment when everyone was pondering a low-scoring game, Darren came up to me and said, 'You're getting 150 in this game.' To say I looked surprised would be an understatement, but it steeled my resolve to make a hundred, knowing he was in my corner. If I fell short of that mark, the three figures I scored were sweet enough – especially after those excruciating 19 balls on 96.

Apart from getting the century and helping us to a first-innings lead, there was one other very satisfying aspect. I'd been picked for England because of my knowledge of English conditions. The first three Tests had been on dry pitches, but way up in England's north-east, Durham was a typical green seamer. I'd shown in the last Test I could play shots on a good pitch, now here was a chance to show I could play in English conditions.

Stuart Broad is a wonderful bowler in such conditions, and battling him, Jimmy Anderson and Tim Bresnan was as tough an assignment as I have ever had. Yes, I had some luck go my way. I was given out twice on the same delivery and reprieved twice – the third umpire overruled a caught behind decision, but then ruled me out lbw only to have the on-field umpire overrule him under the (since-changed) law that there could only be one appeal per delivery. Amazing stuff! But as I'd hoped and dreamed of doing, there I was holding the fort for Australia, as wickets tumbled around me.

A most satisfying comment came from Steve Waugh, who was quoted as saying words like 'Rogers getting from 15 to 50 should be a text book for every young aspiring cricketer of how to bat in difficult conditions'. And at season's end, former England captain Michael Atherton, now widely regarded as England's finest commentator and writer, voted it the best innings of the series.

Alongside Michael's century at Old Trafford, I felt proud that innings helped to open a door for everyone in the batting order. At The Oval Shane and Steve followed up with big hundreds of their own, and suddenly we had some momentum as a batting group. Even though a second-innings collapse at Durham was briefly traumatic, we'd shown we could make hundreds against these guys. That sense moved through the dressing room, that England's bowlers weren't as invincible as either we or they had thought they were. At the same time Ryan Harris had delivered a series of clinics on how to bowl to their top order, and they did not reach 400 in any of the Tests. By the end of the last Test we felt strongly that if we could get enough runs at home, our bowlers would do the job. In short, we did not feel like 3–0 losers.

My battle with James Anderson was giving me more and more confidence. He'd dismissed me twice in the First Test and even signalled to the change room after a slower ball had caused my downfall. Naturally he was the bowler most feared, as his skill with the new ball is incredible but what I started to notice was he was almost too perfect. He would obtain copious amounts of swing, but I'd started to read which way he was going. Not only were there small indicators in his different actions for the in- and outswinger, but his seam was always in a beautifully pronounced and consistent position. If it was swinging in to me, I could see the seam directed at a leg slip and the other way, at second slip.

I found Stuart Broad harder to read because his wobble-seam deliveries would often have the ball 'nipping' in a different direction to the swing. With Anderson it just became a test of holding my stance in a neutral position long enough to adapt to which direction the ball was swinging.

I loved the battles with Anderson. In his conditions, he can be the best and to say I had the better of our battles is such a privilege, as few openers do.

Over the course of the series there was a mounting sense of just how much we really wanted to beat England. We'd copped a lot of sledging from them in the middle, which only increased our appetite. There was a merciless streak about that team, whether it was in targeting us verbally or the bowlers remonstrating with their own fielders in the event of a dropped catch. More than once one of us uttered the words 'these guys need to be put in their place'. I'd been sledged quite a bit by Anderson, who made a habit of calling me an old so and so, before he gave up on it midway through the series. I asked him after the fifth Test at The Oval why that was, and he smiled and said he wasn't witty enough to call me anything else. This crystallised how I'd gained some English respect, but like the others I was desperate to be an Ashes winner.

Perhaps this was also to do with my relative civility. Something Darren and Michael had stressed to us before the series was that they didn't want to see us conversing with the opposition. Most of the guys followed that to the letter, not offering greetings, let alone small talk. But a bit like when I couldn't withstand the intensity of a Justin Langer, I couldn't keep up the cold war charade. So I continued to say hello and speak to guys here and there. While this was against the management's view, it didn't stop me going out and fighting tooth and nail. No doubt it works for some guys, but to be honest I was too old for all that.

CHAPTER 11

DANCING DAYS

Brisbane, Melbourne, Sydney, Port Elizabeth

PERCEPTION CAN MEAN a lot in cricket, either adding to a player's success or detracting from it. For Chris, his long-delayed entry into the Australian side came with a few perceptions to defy. To countless observers at cricket grounds and their press boxes, he was seen as a battler, a nicker and nudger. To a generation of Australian cricketers, he had acquired a reputation as something of a waster, someone not making the most of his talent. When Shane Watson first laid eyes on Chris at training before the series in England began, he held that very view.

> 'My take on Chris before I started playing with him in 2013 was from being on an Australia A tour with him in 2006. I was 25 and very single-minded with what I wanted to do. I'd played for Australia for a bit, my whole focus was to play for Australia. Chris wasn't playing so he certainly enjoyed himself off the field and that was my take, that he didn't really want to be there, he didn't want to make the most of the opportunity the way I did.

*The times I played against him he was always very effective at
scoring runs, no doubt about that. He's always known no matter
what conditions, no matter who's bowling, how to score runs. I
always appreciated that he was able to do that but I looked at
him as someone who was happiest enjoying the social scene.'*

Watson had found in 2006 that others shared his view. A
sweeping judgment appeared to have been cast after Chris' one
previous Test in 2008.

*'He wasn't your stereotypical Australian cricketer, and that
was why also I think he rubbed a few people up the wrong
way at times in his career, which I think really influenced his
ability to get picked for Australia. I heard stories along the way,
particularly after his first Test in Perth, that people were saying
"he just hasn't got what it takes to be an international cricketer".
I don't know whether they were talking technically or about
how he was off the field. That perception of him ran through
Australian cricket.'*

By 2013, Australia was in no position to worry about those
perceptions anymore. What mattered to a new selection panel was
that Chris had exceptionally deep experience of playing in England.

*'Chris made his name for scoring runs around the world, and
in the end where the team was at, it was irresistible for the
selectors. He knew how to score runs and there's not many guys
nowadays who have an opportunity to play county cricket and
understand English conditions.'*

Among the roles Chris took on with the Australian side was to share his knowledge with others. Watson felt this effect when they were cast as opening batsmen together, and they struck up a rapport.

'I got to know Buck very well and absolutely loved his company on the field, because I knew he always knew the situation of the game, how he was going to play it to the best of his ability. I loved batting with him Where I was at in my career I felt he was able to really help me when I was batting, whereas most other people I batted with at that stage, because I was more senior, guys didn't really talk to me about my batting or about a bowler or how to approach a certain situation. Buck was able to do that.'

More widely valuable was a contribution to the side's culture. Ironically, given that earlier perception, the Australian team actually needed a social agent or two to help get the players more comfortable in the company of each other. In this, Chris served as an able lieutenant to new coach Darren Lehmann.

'What the team needed was to be able to socialise together. Whether you had a beer or not didn't matter, it was more actually getting to know each other and enjoying the privilege of doing what we were doing. Buck and Boof together was perfect because that's how both of those guys are, they've always played their cricket and lived their lives like that. Before that it had been like walking on eggshells, certainly no enjoyment off the field at all as individuals but also as a group.

'My favourite memory was after we won the Ashes in
Australia in Sydney, and seeing Buck enjoying that. As soon as
you'd walk into a bar or a club or whatever it is, it's just like this
energy comes out of him. He's very social, knows a lot of people
and certainly loves the dance floor. He's certainly got skills there.

'The other celebration I remember was we had a function
at Doc Brukner's place in Liverpool during the Ashes in 2013.
Everyone was trying to get Buck to dance because he's a decent
dancer and he thinks he's Michael Jackson. He had a beer in
his hand and everyone was telling him to dance. He thought "oh
well I need the floor to be slippery, otherwise I can't pull off my
moves". So on the floorboards of Doc's apartment he just poured
some beer on the floorboards to be able to make sure the dance
floor had the right quality to dance on, and then cut a few
moves. I'd never seen that before!'

TEST CRICKET'S TRUE toll didn't actually hit me until a
few days after the series in England was over. I had agreed to
go back to Middlesex for the last part of the domestic season,
thinking it would simply be a matter of fronting up again.
But after a day or two to relax, I was still feeling incredibly
drained, like I'd hit the wall, marathon style. In my first
match back against Surrey, teammate Dawid Malan hit one
to a deep mid-off with me at the non-striker's end and called
me through. Trying to run, I simply could not get out of first
gear and was run out easily – I was running slower than Boof
in his 100 metre sprint with Mark Richardson. Any other
day I would have been in by several yards.

Things picked up a little from there, but it was a real lesson in how much the pinnacle of the game really does take out of you. Apart from helping me know better how to handle it next time, this filled me with further admiration for the guys who had played 50 Tests and more. Coping with that cycle of heightened, adrenaline-driven performance for weeks, dropping right off and then coming up again, has to be a shredder of nerves as well as bodies. The only time I didn't feel this sense of exhaustion was after my final series, when it was as if I'd made a clean break from the cycle.

On my return home to Australia, the wheels were quickly rolling towards Brisbane. Darren had made a few changes to the team support staff, bringing in Craig McDermott to work with the bowlers and Damian Mednis as our strength and conditioning expert. The selectors were careful who they chose for a one-day tour of India, leaving David Warner and Steve Smith at home to play Shield cricket while Mitchell Johnson came home early. His work in the one-dayers against England after the Ashes, bowling fast and clearly troubling a few of their guys, had put him squarely at the centre of our plans for the summer.

I trained at the National Cricket Centre meanwhile, before we played two Sheffield Shield games. The second of these was against New South Wales at the MCG, where I battled to an ugly 88 before Davey and Steve both made much more entertaining hundreds. In the second innings Rob Quiney and I had a decent opening stand and this time I did get to a hundred, battling away again. Davey took great relish in light-heartedly sledging me as I struggled to hit the ball off the square at times, before both sides butted heads a bit when NSW declined to go after their second-innings target. We had a good competitive edge against each other, which was nice to take into Brisbane.

The main thing to me about the lead-up was how positive Darren was, even more so than usual. Mitch Johnson was bowling thunderbolts in the nets and practising bouncers against the top order. He was very scary in that situation, bowling bouncers that seemed to arrow in at your ribs, armpit and head – every ball he pitched up was almost cause for an audible sigh of relief. As batsmen we were all in a hurry to rotate out of his net. There were two Mitchell Johnsons to me: the one who got his arm up and wrist behind the ball and swing it late. And the Mitch with the arm low and slingy, which created another problem, as the ball skidded back into you on a shorter length. I felt it was important not to get too far across to his short ball, although that obviously meant the fuller deliveries became more dangerous.

For all his threat, we still felt that England were favourites, and we weren't sure if we were quite ready to beat them. That all changed in one moment. Day one had been difficult for us. I was out early to a Stuart Broad ball that climbed sharply at me, before Brad Haddin and Mitch got us out of trouble in the last session and helped us up to 295. During the innings break I was feeling as though we didn't have enough, because like a few others I could remember how England's batsmen had been so dominant in Australia three years before. With the exception of Boxing Day that summer, Australia's totals weren't completely terrible, but Alastair Cook, Jonathan

Trott and Kevin Pietersen had just bulldozed the bowlers. Those guys were all back again.

Ryan Harris was having none of that, and had Cook out with a good one early. But the instant in which I felt the whole series tilted was when Mitch bowled to Trott with a leg slip and a deep backward square leg. Up to that point his first five overs had gone for 26 and the rest of the script was anyone's guess. But Mitch's first ball was a short one right on the money that Trott played awkwardly with his gloves, and the first ball of the next over brought a glove down the leg side and into the gloves of 'Hadds'. This had all been a plan by Darren and Michael to Trott, glimpsed a little in the England one-dayers, and to see it work in the first innings of the series gave us all a huge lift. That was the moment we knew we were a really good chance, because when plans start coming together you gain so much belief. You see weaknesses in batsmen who'd previously hurt you, and your own confidence grows.

Not long after that, Pietersen tried to hook a bouncer from Mitch that was just too fast. We saw him react as if to say 'shit, that was quick', and though it didn't get him out, the effect was pretty clear. From there England's innings fell apart, and we won the match by all of 381 runs. All of a sudden, we were surging ... and singing. While we'd got close in England, because of where the side had come from in India, there was almost no belief in how to get over the line in a Test match. So to actually notch a win, and recognise that Mitch, Rhino, Peter Siddle and Nathan Lyon were a world-class attack, meant we weren't just in this series, but capable of dominating it.

Nathan's role was important as well, working in concert with the quicks and taking plenty of wickets along the way. Another memory of the Gabba is in the second innings, Matt Prior cutting an early boundary and saying something like 'get used to it'. Next over, of course, Nathan got him out for the second time in the match. All the bravado that England had built up over a few years, and brought with them to Australia, was just being washed away in the course of a single match. In the dressing rooms after, Nathan, who had inherited the position of songmaster for the singing of 'Underneath the Southern Cross', got to lead the singing for the first time – and I was singing it for the first time. There was a moment there when we looked around at each other all thinking the same thing: 'We've got these blokes.'

In Adelaide, Hadds followed up his 94 in Brisbane with a hundred alongside Michael Clarke, who had himself reached three figures alongside Davey Warner in the second innings in Brisbane. Hadds had a series almost as remarkable as Mitch, although in a strange way the misfortunes of the batting order may actually have favoured him. Quite often he came to the crease around the 40 to 50-over mark, which gave him that valuable 30 or 40 overs to bat against the older ball and set himself for when the second new ball came around. Sometimes No.6 or 7 can be very tricky, because suddenly you're up against a new ball late in the day. But the top order's misadventures helped Hadds in that regard, because those second 40 overs with an older ball in Australia is often the best time to bat.

For my part, I was intent on soaking up plenty of balls early even if I wasn't in the best scoring form. So after facing

81 balls in the second innings in Brisbane, I stayed out there for 167 in the first innings in Adelaide, 135 second innings in Perth, 171 and 155 in Melbourne, then 169 to round it off in the second innings in Sydney. The runs I made were useful, but in consistently taking the shine off the ball and hanging around I was doing the job I'd been chosen for. That, in turn, helped Hadds to strut his stuff down the order.

It was certainly more pleasant knowing I didn't have to deal with Mitch and company on the middle. The way Michael used the bowling attack was a really good lesson for me in terms of making the most of high pace. Mitch would only bowl three- or four-over spells, and Michael would make sure he kept him fresh enough for the arrival of the tail. At Somerset I've tried something similar with Jamie Overton, and on a couple of occasions seen a similar effect – you can just blow the opposition away and be batting before you know it. In the case of Mitch, new ball or old ball didn't really matter, as he showed to devastating effect in Adelaide.

Over the course of that Ashes series and the tour to South Africa that followed, Mitch reached a level of speed, accuracy and intimidation that I've never seen before or since. It was the difference between bowling very quick and absolute lightning, and it made plenty of great players look ordinary. The only player through this period who was able to play him with any consistency was AB de Villiers, which tells you something about his level of skill. But every other batsman struggled. Perhaps his most terrifying spells were at Centurion Park in South Africa on a pitch with pace and uneven bounce. In the first innings he got Graeme Smith,

Alviro Petersen and Faf du Plessis in quick succession, and in the huddle we were looking at each other thinking 'these guys are good players, and he's making them look poor'. I played with lots of exceptional players, but I've never seen a cricketer have a period as incredible as that.

When Mitch bowled Cook in Adelaide, it was symptomatic of the trouble I'd had in the nets. You'll often see a bowler get the ball swinging and maybe see it clip the outside of the off stump, as was the case when Rhino got Joe Root at Durham in 2013. But this one thudded right into the middle of the off stump, because a lot of guys, whether it was us in the nets or England's guys in the middle, were trying to cover for a short ball coming in at the body. That stayed with me, because it showed how his pace was affecting technical set-ups as well as minds. That was backed up when England folded in a flurry of hook shots to go 2–0 down.

That meant we needed only to win in Perth to regain the Ashes, and I gave us the worst possible start by running myself out in search of a single – my life in the West is seldom dull. It didn't help that Jimmy Anderson running me out in the second over of a match was perhaps one of the best pieces of fielding by a fast bowler in the history of the game.

I'd got to 11 in very good fashion, and walking off I realised I'd not only blown a perfect start on an easy pitch, I might well have blown my Test career. Immediately the scribes had a talking point and much was made of my scores – 1, 16, 72, 2, 11 – in this series. As the pressure built and my age kept getting mentioned, I realised my hope of playing a Boxing Day Test in front of my adopted home crowd could be shattered.

The evening of the second day happened to be the date of a big birthday party for my mother, Ros. She had flown back to Perth for the match, three months after moving east with Dad to run their new project, the Village Green Cricket Ground in Strath Creek, 100 kilometres north of Melbourne. A dozen of their closest friends were celebrating her birthday at a café in Claremont – all people I had known since I was a kid. By now I was in something of a funk, and a dinner party was the last thing I wanted. But I had to go. Within five minutes I had snapped at Dad, and for the first hour, I gave one-word answers. But my one-time babysitter Judy Thomson, whose four boys I had grown up with, kept chatting away to me, my brother David and wife Nikki were in great form too, and it was just good to see Mum enjoying herself – so much so that, eventually, I relaxed.

Yet going out to bat the next afternoon with a lead of 130, I still felt like I was batting for my Test career, and it wasn't pretty. Up the other end Davey was in great form, and I was able to ride along in his slipstream. By the time our 150 partnership came up – to which I had contributed 50 – my touch was back. Dad told me later that he and mum were in the airport terminal waiting to return to Melbourne as I came out to bat, and for the first time in my cricket career, he couldn't bring himself to watch, he was so nervous for me.

The next day Shane Watson and George Bailey took to the English bowling, George equalling the record of most runs scored off one over in a Test with 28 from Anderson. Setting England a target of 504, we eventually knocked them over for 353. Finally there was a highlight for me in front of the Perth crowd, as I sprinted and dived to my right to claim a catch at mid-off to put England nine down. We enjoyed it at the time, but even more so when the chance came for a re-enactment out on the ground after Nathan Lyon led us in the team song. A beer bottle replaced the ball, and this time the celebrations were showered in plenty of other beverages.

Before the match I'd arranged with 'Smudger', as we call Steve Smith, to travel down to the Raffles Hotel in Perth to have dinner with Sam Robson and Tom Scollay. 'Robbo' and Smudge had grown up a little together, and 'Scolls', Robbo and I had formed a very good friendship at Middlesex. Scolls had been a very good cricketer in his own right, but had found himself surplus to requirements at Middlesex. He's since become one of my best friends and he and his fiancée Becca Pink have stayed at my places in Melbourne and London.

Driving along on the way down, he let out all his frustrations and anxieties about the way his series was going, having not passed 50 in either of the first two Tests. He told me he felt like he might be dropped soon, as the most junior member of the top six, and was close to tears. I kept saying to him 'mate, honestly, they want you in the side. They see what you bring to the team, you're playing well. It'll happen for you. Don't worry.' After a chilled dinner, we drove back and spoke some more, and I was as pleased as anyone to see him get a very good hundred on day one to set up our victory.

We got into a tight huddle when Bails claimed the final catch to reclaim the Ashes, then spent a fair amount of time in the dressing room. That night the after-party was at Shane Warne's suite in the Burswood casino complex, and all the guys brought their partners or close friends – I brought my brother and his wife. Nikki had always felt that John Williamson's *True Blue* was a bit naff, but after we sang it together in a huge group she came to me and said 'Chris that was amazing, I take it back!' Later on the music took a turn into more upbeat territory, as we all fired up with the effects of plenty of celebratory beers. The boys dared me to bust a few moves, and I was quickly into it, challenging Davey in particular, to the amusement of all. After I'd settled down a bit, Warney came up to me and said 'mate, you can seriously dance, I'm so jealous!' He backed it up in commentary later on, calling me a cross between John Travolta and Michael Jackson. Cheers, Shane.

Boxing Day in Melbourne is a wonderful day on the cricket calendar, but it also comes with one of the toughest decisions any captain will make – bat or bowl? When we got to the ground, all indications were that Michael wanted to bat first, something I wasn't so sure about. Having played so often there for Victoria, I knew the drop-in wickets tended to start as puddings, slow seamers with tennis-ball bounce and difficulty for batsmen against disciplined bowling. In 2010, Andrew Strauss had sent Australia in on the advice of an ex-Bushranger in David Saker, and rolled us for 98.

But after that they flatten right out, and almost never offer any spin. I'd played in a Shield game where Queensland ran down around 400 against us and seen a very good spinner in Jon Holland just get monstered, because the ball would simply skid on. That was in my mind when I was stretching before play with Watto, when I told him 'I think we should be bowling here, the wicket's only going to get better'. He said 'go tell Michael', but because I was still somewhat unsure of my place in the side and didn't want to overstep the mark, I hesitated. So instead it was Shane who made the approach, before Michael came back to me.

'Do you reckon we should bowl?'

'Yes mate I do, every time we play here it's slow and hard for the first innings and a bit, but from there it'll just get easier.'

Michael did bowl, and we knocked England over for 255 early on day two. In reply we had a poor day with the bat, excepting an ugly 61 from yours truly, which included a hefty blow to the head from Broad. That blow drew blood, but weirdly I batted more fluently from that point, and was very annoyed to get out to a leading edge when I tried to work Tim Bresnan across the line. A few people thought I was trying to hit that one over the top. All I can say to that is they can't have watched me bat too often. From there Hadds came out and threw the bat without fear to squeak us past 200. At the break, Boof was again very positive, saying 'we've had a couple of bad days but that's ok, you're allowed to, I believe we can bounce back', which he tended to be in tough situations, rather than kicking the cat.

England started well, taking their lead over 100, but we hung in there, and as ever we had Mitch to thank for turning the tide. He had Cook lbw with a reversing ball, then threw down the stumps to run out Joe Root and get the crowd baying for more. In that environment the MCG can feel uniquely intimidating, and the roars kept coming as Nathan worked his way through their lower order and left us with 231 to win. Back out there batting, you could see English heads had dropped, and when they gave me a couple of lives it was another sign that their concentration just wasn't there any more.

On day four, Davey was out fairly early on, but with Watto at the other end we were quickly into stride. Before I knew it we were hurtling towards the target, playing our shots and having a whale of a time.

Overnight, the papers and the airwaves were full of stories about Australia's poor record in low run-chases – a disaster against South Africa and Damien Martyn's subsequent five-year exile from the Test team got plenty of mentions, as did the Botham/Willis English miracle in 1981 where we couldn't chase down much more than 100 at Headingley. And good reason, too – earlier in the year at both Trent Bridge and Durham our chase targets of over 300 had been whittled down to 230 via opening partnerships – the same as our target this time. Each time we had fallen away pretty badly.

I'd scored just one off 10 balls from Jimmy Anderson before I faced up to Stuart Broad for the fourth ball of the fourth over. He brought in a third slip and bowled a corker: just short of a length on off-stump it lifts and jags away – and I get a nick. I spin round to see it flying like a rocket – but bisecting the distance between new keeper Jonny Bairstow and first slip Alastair Cook. Bairstow doesn't move a muscle sideways, and at the last moment Cook shoves out a hand, which the ball hits before flying off to the boundary.

Broad's look is thunderous and he stomps back to his mark in that long-legged, idiosyncratic way that people love to imitate. I don't need to be a cricketing Einstein to guess what the next ball will be. It's short, quick and rising to head-height – but thankfully just outside off stump – and I'm ready. I try an uppercut – a shot I've never played before in a Test match – and hallelujah, I get it in the middle. Over the top of slips it flies, bounces once, and crashes into the fence. On any other ground it's six. The crowd roars – all 38,522 of them. It's got to be my day, I think.

But successful run-chases happen only when the top order holds onto its wickets. In experiencing lots of them over the years I know that to win, you also have to be bold. So I go for it, and the runs flow. Two things stick with me later. I hear that Kerry O'Keeffe in the ABC commentary box is on fire as he pronounces a personality switch has happened – someone who looks like Chris Rogers is playing like Davey Warner, while Warner is playing second fiddle, as Chris Rogers generally does. And that finds its way into our dressing room later, when Davey is called 'Buck' and I get 'Davey' …

The second thing is the astonished comment I get from my father. For years, he's tried to teach me how to late cut – and decided he was a complete failure. Today, it was my late cut that demoralised England – a third of my runs coming behind point. Like the uppercut, it's a shot I rarely play. Yes, I thick-edge them down there often, but late cut? Pretty rare.

There was another reason for my adventurousness: no more Graeme Swann, who had retired after Perth due to injury problems. When I heard that news, it was a moment where I thought, 'well the guy who keeps troubling me is gone, I could actually do all right here'. It freed me up even against other bowlers.

The hundred that resulted at the MCG was hugely satisfying, helping us to win from a poor position and keeping us on course for a 5–0 sweep. I wasn't happy to get out to Monty Panesar before we reached the target, but it was nice to get to walk off and take in the appreciation of the crowd, a bit like a footballer being subbed off late in a game where he's scored a hat-trick. The only source of deflation – and a minor one at that – was to be told I was man of the match and then hear it changed to Mitch. Who doesn't love a fast bowler?

By that stage we were all having so much fun, even as we moved on to Sydney for the fifth Test. The SCG pitch for the last game copped quite a bit of criticism, from Boof in particular, but I was prepared to wear the challenge because I just loved batting there, more than any other ground in the world. I can't put my finger on what it is exactly, but the feel of the venue, the old Members and Ladies Stands, the size of the outfield and the ground itself has always clicked with me. Perhaps it is something to do with being born in NSW, despite all the moves I made later on. To put together a chanceless hundred in the second innings there, striking at around 70 per hundred balls, was something of a batting peak. I'd gone from struggling early in the series to finding my very best rhythm.

In a way this was not surprising, as I'd always found myself improving as a series or season went on, working out how to deal with various bowlers and conditions. Added to that was the absence of Swann and the drift of the series towards us. It all made for a pretty joyous feeling. In the end we bowled England out so quickly on the third night that the official post-series party was to be held the following day, so we again spent plenty of time in the dressing room. After the presentation I rang Dad and found he was just about to board a bus heading for his original hometown of Gosford. He came back for the celebration, and thoroughly enjoyed a dressing room that, 55 years earlier, he had spent a season in as 12th man for NSW.

Not long after Dad arrived, Alex Kountouris, the long-term team physio suddenly appeared and loudly proclaimed: 'Chris Rogers, you are the greatest Test selection in the history of Australian cricket!' We both look a bit stunned. 'You've been selected at age 35 to open the batting for Australia and six months later you have scored back-to-back centuries at the Boxing Day MCG Test and the New Year SCG Test, as Australia whitewashes an Ashes series 5–nil. What a selection!' We all laugh of course at Alex being over the top. But I don't mind! Later, the guys ventured out to Kings Cross, still in its pre-lockout pomp. I had a great time with Watto in the outdoor area of a club called Goldfish, as a bunch of guys sang songs with us, and Hadds was flying too. Very happy memories.

The following day there were a few sore heads, as we were told we had to be on a bus for an afternoon party at a secret location. The bus ventured out of the city to Vaucluse Road, Vaucluse, for a party held at the private beachside compound of the Hemmes family, who own the Merivale portfolio of restaurants, bars and the like. No expense was spared for this event, which took a few of us out of the cricket world we were used to occupying and into the circles of the Sydney elite. As a guy who'd battled in domestic cricket for years and never seen the glitz of the IPL, it was certainly something to see. We were entertained by Rai Thistlethwayte, the singer from Thirsty Merc, who put on an absolutely brilliant set. Watto had a bit of a strum and a sing as well.

I had one obligation still hanging over me from Melbourne. For that game I'd won the team's own man of the match award, which came with a special jacket you had to wear that night. Your next task was to make a presentation to the team for the following match, after which you'd announce who had won the right to wear the jacket. Smudger had won it for Perth, and so after Melbourne chose to interview Sidds' partner Anna before presenting me with the jacket. At the end of the ceremony, Boof told me I would have to speak for seven minutes after Sydney. When I exclaimed 'but Smudger only spoke for five' he replied 'ok now it's nine minutes'. When I again complained, he shot back 'now it's 13 minutes, are you going to keep talking?' I didn't.

At the Hemmes' compound we gathered around a big pool area, the players, their partners and the staff. We'd already heard Darren and Michael speak, and I figured we were probably a bit over the speeches. So after a few initial thank yous I simply went around the team and asked each member what their best moment of the series had been, starting with my own – when we made it 5–0 in Sydney, I'd got into a tight hug with the two blokes I'd opened the batting with in the two series, Watto and Davey.

A few blokes were battling to get any words out, and I got down to Rhino and Smudger as the two contenders for the match award. I had to let Rhino down gently when I called him up, saying he'd missed out, and that led into my recalling the other moment I remembered most fondly: the conversation with Smudger in Perth before his hundred. It was great to reflect on how he'd progressed from the nervous, frustrated guy I'd shared a drive with, to the confident, visibly growing batsman who had made two of the very best hundreds of the series. Smudger then got up and spoke very emotionally about the whole experience, and how he'd never forget it. By now we'd gone for comfortably more than 13 minutes, but nobody cared. There are very few times in a cricket career when you get the chance to sit back and reflect like that, so everyone really enjoyed that night.

A lot of the guys were seeming to hit the wall by then, but I can't say I felt the same. The experience of playing in a winning Ashes team, after waiting so long for a chance, had been so invigorating that my energy felt almost endless. Later that night I ended up at a random house party, invited by an off-duty police officer, and didn't make it home until the not-so-early hours of Tuesday morning. This was how I wound up not making the team function at the Opera House on time, and unfortunately missed the Prime Minister Tony Abbott mentioning me by name at the official reception. I also missed a team message earlier on to say 'no sunglasses in photos', because there I was in all the shots, Ray-Bans wrapped around my tired eyes. Sidds coerced me into having a dance in front of the crowd, and the footage went everywhere. Perhaps the closest I'll get to celebrity.

I copped a hefty fine for all that. As Boof put it later, 'We don't want to fine you mate, but rules are rules.' This is true, but I can't say I felt too much regret. It was the time of our lives.

CHAPTER 12

RIDING THE ROLLERCOASTER

Johannesburg, Port Elizabeth, Cape Town,
Dubai, Abu Dhabi

WITH BELATED RECOGNITION and now a regular in the Australian Test team, Chris experienced a very different world. So too did his parents. Among the greatest changes for anyone close to an international cricketer is the fact that their innings are invariably available to follow on television or radio, when most first-class matches tend to require the refreshing of an online scorecard. At once they are also subject to instantaneous analysis and criticism, broadcast as far and wide as the pictures themselves.

More widely, Chris's relationship with his father had been evolving over the years, as other voices and influences broadened the way Chris looked at the game in general and batting in particular. John's opinions have always been strong, and he found his own perceptions of Australian cricket changing through his son's first-hand point of view.

'In terms of his relationships with other players, Chris was more guarded, but said enough for me to change long-held views – of Shane Watson especially, and also Brad Haddin and a few others. Chris does not like criticising others, particularly in public, and certainly became more guarded in his comments. For example I was quite critical of Michael Clarke's inconsistent form with the bat from the time Chris joined the team in 2013, but Chris would not agree and never criticised Clarke, which I admired in the end.

'I was confident I could give him good feedback at times. At other times I did feel I was out of my depth especially with the media scrutiny around the team. But twice in particular I got stuck in – once after being lbw in the first innings of the second Test in South Africa falling over and forgetting his long-held principles. He took both on board and fixed it in his own way.

'On a couple of other occasions I made strong suggestions to which he took exception and told me I was out of touch in no uncertain fashion – so I backed off quick smart, realising I was over-interfering and he was operating at a different, higher level. That was brought home to me when other email correspondents (non-first-class players) would make strong critical comments about some players that I knew, from Chris, were totally unjustified.'

A FEW PEOPLE have asked me how the Australian side managed to come off the high of the Ashes 5–0 and then back it up with such a strong display in South Africa a few months later. Well, it was clear to me that the team was motivated by the goal of becoming the No.1 Test team in the world, something within our grasp if we could win that series. This wasn't just a matter of prestige: due to the new wage structure brought in by Cricket Australia, there was a strong financial incentive for getting to the top. Beating England was an enormous relief and a great stepping stone, but we all knew there needed to be a follow-up.

Some of the guys in the team had played when we were No.1, from Michael and Watto to Hadds, Sidds and Mitch. They were all united in the desire to get back there and create their own legacy of success. The other thing on many minds was we now knew we had a bowling attack capable of going through any batting line-up in the world. Over the course of those matches against England we'd built up massive belief in our bowlers, in keeping with Boof's long-held view that taking 20 wickets was more important to Test match success than piling up mountains of runs. Make enough runs and the bowlers will do it for us.

Personally, my goals were more modest, but equally clear. Having got into the side and contributed to an Ashes win, I was still aware that as an older bloke I was playing from series to series. After Perth I thought I might be struggling to make the South Africa squad, and I remember Craig McDermott encouraging me that I'd get the runs I needed. Hundreds in Melbourne and Sydney helped me shore up my place.

I had got myself into the mindset that match by match I was simply trying to stay in the circus. I have to admit there was a financial incentive to this. Australian cricketers are so well paid that the goal went from staying in the side long enough to get an incremental contract, to staying there securely enough to get a full contract the season after the Ashes, for 2014–15, enough to help set me up for life after cricket. That decision would be made after South Africa. As useful as it can be to have goals, this stuff started to get increasingly into my head, to the point where it became almost too important. I was now riding a rollercoaster.

Up to that point all my international cricket experience had been in England and Australia, so it was refreshing, but also confronting at times, to get to South Africa. We started off in the town of Potchefstroom, which had been a successful base for previous Australian tours. It was heartland Afrikaner territory but also a university town, which made for a jarring mix at times. One night Davey and I tried a very rough-looking pub and after quickly vacating that premises and returning to the campus accommodation we noticed a university festival was kicking. They seemed like vastly different worlds to any I had known. In the end heavy rains flooded us out of there, and we retreated back to Johannesburg for an internal practice match.

The whiteboard in the dressing room had the words 'If your out, your out' written prominently, to try to get us into match mode. This was a source of some mirth when I pointed out to Darren that it should have been 'you're'. Watto half-jokingly suggested I should respect the coach a bit more, before Darren responded with a quite serious, 'No Shane, we can all get better!' Had to laugh at that one.

I found myself getting a good one early from Rhino, and then spent most of my day fielding while Hughesy and Moises

Henriques got runs, when neither looked likely to play in the Test. Another training session involved a centre-wicket session against Ryan, Mitch and Sidds all with new balls – I could tell this wasn't going to be an easy tour for the batsmen! Mitch bowled me with a full ball that was going to miss leg before swinging late and crashing into off. McDermott later told me that was as good a ball as he had seen.

I had an unofficial role as the team's distraction for David Warner. As you see when he is batting, he has so much energy and aggression. Sometimes that could throw the dressing room into chaos with a flurry of unwanted conversation, or barbs directed at a teammate for a seemingly minor reason. When we started batting together, he would make a habit of going hard at me in and out of the dressing room, and I'd deflect it, laugh it off or give it back to him. The rest of the team got a lot of humour out of that, but it also served the purpose of distracting him from everyone else. I was a bit of a lightning rod!

Much as I enjoyed the banter, at one point it did come to a head in South Africa, during the Centurion Test. While we were fielding, he yelled at me from across the field that I wasn't being vocal enough, a moment where I felt I had to draw the line. It was a windy day, so the fact I had been offering encouragement to our bowlers must have been lost on the breeze. So I stopped the game and yelled right back. The argument went back and forth for about 45 seconds, much to the bemusement of the batsmen and the amusement of everyone else. At the end of the day I went up to Davey and said, 'Right we've got to discuss this. I don't care who you are, you never yell at me in the middle of the game. If you've got a problem, come and say it to me in private.' Davey listened, never did again and we were the better for it.

Centurion is South Africa's Gabba – the wicket looked quite spicy, offering pace, seam and some variable bounce. This was my first encounter with Dale Steyn and Morne Morkel, and I walked away from it sore and sorry for a couple of low scores and a stinging blow to the shoulder. Smudger and Shaun Marsh, who'd come in for George Bailey, put together a tremendous partnership to give us a strong first innings, before Mitch, as mentioned earlier, took the Proteas apart. As well as Smudger played, I thought Shaun's innings was as good as any I'd ever seen, because he was in early at No.3 and batted right through the day against a moving, bouncing ball. In many ways we were perfect opposites: on SOS' best days no one could touch him, but on his worst he was the most straightforward of wickets. Meanwhile I would battle through, trying to keep the gap between best and worst as slim as possible.

At Centurion though, my Ashes rhythm had completely gone, and I found myself on the downward dive of the rollercoaster once more. As a result of my day-one dismissal by Morkel, I did some extra work on the bowling machine, with tennis balls pitched short and cranked up to 100mph. While it was meant to help my reactions, it didn't do wonders for my confidence as some balls flew off my gloves and others pinged me on the helmet. That intense approach had worked for me in the past, but this time I did not make many in the second innings before Steyn surprised me by going up a few gears and I played one onto the stumps. We won the Test by a huge margin, and stormed South Africa's Pretoria stronghold, but I felt increasingly shaky.

Alex Doolan had come in for an injured Watto and made attractive second-innings runs, meaning someone was going to have to make way whenever Shane was fit again. 'Dools' also took a couple of pretty staggering catches at short leg, leaving me wondering whether I would be surplus to requirements sooner rather than later. Due to our Ashes success I'd fallen into the habit of reading all the press reports on the series, forgetting that if you're not making runs you're probably better off sticking to the crossword.

I was starting to feel isolated, made worse by the fact that in South Africa I didn't have the networks of friends that I had in England and Australia, while most of the team went about their own lives or spent time with their partners. For the first time at international level I was feeling lonely, often eating alone. Port Elizabeth, venue for the second Test, was a sleepy seaside town, and having very little to do left me stuck in my drab hotel room a lot of the time. To be surrounded by so many people but to feel lonely was not something I'd experienced for a long time, and had me thinking this was why so many elite athletes settle down with partners at a relatively young age.

My mindset wasn't great, and when I was lbw to a Vernon Philander ball straightening down the line – usually a mode of dismissal I avoid – after South Africa made a big first-innings total at St George's Park, some panic started to set in. Thinking back to this time is strange, because with the perspective of distance I can see that I was still a key member of the side, and just needed to relax. But in those couple of days it was so difficult to get out of my head, thinking I was leaving the ground to go back to my room to have dinner on my own again and then I was going to get out cheaply again, and then I was going to be dropped and then I was going to miss out on a contract and then … who knows? Murphy's Law kicked in that night when I turned on the TV right on cue to hear a South African pundit demand that I be dropped. I nearly threw the remote at the TV. I had made two centuries in my last three Tests after all.

In the midst of this turmoil, I called Dad. 'I think I'm done,' I told him. 'This is not what it's all made out to be. I'm lonely, my cricket's not going well, I'm taking it too personally, and to be honest I think I'm going to be dropped after this game anyway.'

'Chris, just see how you go in the second innings,' he replied. 'Just see how it goes.'

'Dad, I'm actually hoping I nick off cheaply, they drop me, I get to go to Cape Town and relax, and then I'll finish up.'

'That's fine, whatever you think is best. But just try to go and enjoy yourself in the second dig, whatever it may be.'

Out of that conversation I decided not to hit any more balls in the nets, taking the opposite approach to what I'd tried so far on the tour. Davey and I walked out for the second innings needing the small matter of 448 to win, after we'd struggled in the first innings. Whether it was the match scenario, the conversation with Dad or the troubles of the previous few days, here was a moment when all that pressure seemed to fall from my shoulders. A bit like I'd discussed with Steve Sylvester before the Ashes the year before, I had basically accepted the possibility of failure, and so everything, even the survival of my first couple of balls, was a bonus.

Third ball Steyn pushed one and I middled one to the cover fence. More boundaries flowed from there against Philander, and before I knew it I had 20 in excellent time. So weirdly peaceful did I feel that one ball I felt certain Steyn was going to pitch short at me, and I consciously thought 'this is going to be short and I'm going to pull it for six'. I ended up being in position too early, and toed it for a one-bounce four to square leg. The game was feeling ridiculously simple, whereas a day or so earlier it had seemed fiendishly difficult. Davey and I had the 100 up inside 26 overs.

Morkel may have given me more problems, because I still didn't have an ideal method for handling his steep bounce. But this was where Davey's outrageous skill came to my rescue. Coming around the wicket, on an angle I found nearly impossible to score from, Morkel bowled two balls back of a length just outside off stump, and Davey flat-batted them through midwicket for boundaries. In response, Morkel went over the wicket to take it across Davey, who promptly leant back and slapped two boundaries through cover point. There was genius to that, shots I simply couldn't conceive of playing. Graeme Smith took Morkel off as a result, giving me more breathing room.

History shows it didn't stay as simple as that of course. Davey was winkled out by JP Duminy, and as they had done in the first innings, the South Africans started to get some prodigious reverse swing. Losing Davey, who had been skating the ball through the outfield, affected our momentum, and Dools and I made only another 16 runs in 76 balls before he was out. There was a lot of criticism of our new No.3 for not getting on with it, which I felt was quite harsh. Bunting the ball into a pretty abrasive square had got it nicely scuffed up for reverse swing. Alex was in his second Test match, fighting for his career, and to expect him to have come out and play with abandon was not realistic. However all of a sudden the ball started to boomerang, and when Dools was out you had new batsmen in against this movement: as tough a commission as you can get.

I've played in many games where reverse swing had played an important role, but the deadly, vicious balls Steyn was producing were something else indeed. He could hoop the ball into the right-hand batsmen and then get it to swing subtly away from them as well, but it was also the plans he was conjuring up. He set Clarke up beautifully before having him caught in the slips and then produced two deliveries to Smith and Haddin that would have knocked over most players in the world. It was pure skill out of the very top drawer, and the way he changed the game single-handedly was incredible to watch – even from the non-striker's end.

While the wickets were falling, my innings went into a second phase, where I reverted very much to survival mode, staying back in my crease and not committing until I could work out which way the ball was swinging. This was very similar to the way I handled James Anderson when he swung the ball both ways. One advantage of a swinging ball is that it can create new angles for you as a batsman, causing the ball to scuttle away into different corners of the field off your defensive bat and allowing you to scamper a single here and there – while also frustrating the bowler. I crawled my way through the 80s and 90s until Graeme Smith brought on Dean Elgar's slow left-armers with the light fading. A couple of boundaries got me to 98, and a couple off Philander brought three figures and plenty of emotion. With Shaun bagging a pair and Dools out twice cheaply, I was riding the rollercoaster back up again.

I ran myself out stupidly in the dying moments of day four trying to get myself to the danger end to protect the No.10, Sids, but I walked off with a level of serenity not felt in a long time. As much as I was gutted we'd lost a chance of salvaging a draw if rain had saved us on day five, I'm not afraid to say I was proud of myself, too. The constant knot in my stomach from the stress of poor performances had eased, and a century against such skilful bowlers with prodigious reverse swing – where all others failed – reaffirmed the belief from Sydney that I was adding value to the team.

That was when I went to Boof to say, 'Sorry mate, but I can't expend as much energy off the pitch as I have been doing in terms of hitting balls and training. I've got to find a way to keep an even keel.' He just said 'Yep, let's figure out what's best for you,' and from there I was able to find a better balance. I was probably the least of his worries at that point anyway, as no one apart from Davey and I had even made it into double figures in a bad defeat that threw the series back open.

At Newlands Michael won a hugely important toss, allowing us to bat first and to an extent neutralise the chance of South Africa getting more reverse swing. Davey had got in trouble for being outspoken on radio about certain work by the hosts to get the ball reversing, and there was plenty of niggle between the two sides. Whatever the truth of the matter, the exchanges certainly helped fire Davey up, and he rounded off an outstanding series with two of the best hundreds you're ever likely to see. I was very much the junior partner in stands of 65 and 123, as he drove Smith to distraction by manipulating the field in ways that reminded me a bit of Darren at his best. Whenever Davey retires, I think he'll look back on this series as close to his peak.

We all watched with some awe as well when Morkel worked Pup over and he refused to yield, going onto an excellent hundred of his own after a mini run of outs. We were all helped by the fact that Steyn had suffered a hamstring strain and was severely restricted when he did bowl. We were able to drive the game forward, but there would be times on the last afternoon when it looked like South Africa might scrape their way to a drawn series. Tempers frayed when an appeal for a catch against Philander was turned down, because the third umpire decided his glove wasn't on the bat handle when the ball hit him, and an open season of sledging between James Pattinson, Steyn and Michael followed.

In the end it took a superhuman effort from Rhino, basically on one leg, to get Steyn and the last man Morkel with a handful of overs to go. There's a fair chance the pain he pushed himself through that day was to catch up with him a year later, but that just goes to show how selfless Rhino was as a bowler and a teammate – perhaps the most generous to others that I've known. With the sun going down over Cape Town, we celebrated knowing we'd be going to No.1 when the fresh ICC rankings came out in April, with all the adulation and financial bonuses that came with it.

That night we enjoyed a dockside party, but celebrated separately from the South Africans, who were farewelling Smith. The other factor in this was how bad-tempered things had got on the field of play, a sign for both sides that we'd let things get out of hand. It was nice, though, to see the South African spinner Robin Peterson turn up for a drink later on in the evening. I'd spent the nights after the first two Tests in his company – after the second it was just the two of us, when despite a loss I had a sense of relief after forcing back my own demons – and it had been great to spend time with him in his homeland. Strangely enough he was as close a friend as I had on that tour, due to the fact we had become close during the 2010 season we'd spent playing for Derbyshire together.

Our team had to accept that the way we approached things in South Africa, while successful, had come at some cost to relations between the sides. I accepted this was the way the Australian side was most effective, but it wasn't really my game. Where some were spoiling for a fight, I liked to present as small a target as possible.

Returning to Middlesex once more a month or so later, I noticed a shift in my game that may have come partly from age, partly from the international experience. In the last week of April at Lord's, against a rampaging Yorkshire, I helped us overcome a bad first innings by racking up 241 not out, my highest ever score for Middlesex, to lead a successful chase for 472, the club's best ever fourth-innings pursuit at home. That was quite a moment, against a very good Yorkshire attack, and a bit like Port Elizabeth it was driven by a sense of freedom that only comes from accepting the possibility of failure. But it contrasted with numerous instances where I went through flat spots and runs of low scores, lacking my former consistency. While I'd been inspired to perform against Yorkshire, there were other days when that sort of focus didn't come to me as easily.

That innings demonstrated something else about playing in England as opposed to Australia. Apart from my 279 in 2006 for WA, none of my other really big hundreds came in Australia, and my top score for Victoria is only 159. English grounds are generally smaller and outfields much faster, particularly square where they have so many practice wickets. The weather is also less taxing, which means if you get into a rhythm there's a chance of batting for hours on end. While the ball will do less in Australia, the physical strain can be greater, with big, slow outfields meaning you have to actually run a far larger percentage of your score. Subconsciously, I occasionally felt myself switching off after getting to a hundred thinking 'my job's done, I've set the middle order up' and getting out. Victoria's captain Matthew Wade picked me up on this, and I tried to play it down, but I could feel the hunger fading.

Hot days and long innings were going to be a big part of Australia's next assignment. Going to the United Arab

Emirates in October to face Pakistan, who still could not play at home, I thought of it in two ways. The more positive view was that this would be a brilliant challenge, a chance to stretch myself in conditions I'd barely faced. But the other sensation was that you can't teach an old dog new tricks. As the series played out into a very heavy defeat, I wouldn't be the only one thinking along these lines.

In all honesty, this was a series I shouldn't have played in. Looking back, it would have been better for the selectors to choose someone else to partner Davey at the top of the order, and keep me on ice for the Ashes in England the following year. While I made a couple of starts in the first Test in Dubai, my struggles to score against the spinners did not help us get up any momentum at what should have been the easiest time to bat. There was a good argument, in fact, for playing Phillip Hughes ahead of me. While he did not have a great record against spin, the 2013 tour of India had taught him a few things, and he had the ability to slog sweep. Both Zulfiqar Babar and Yasir Shah would have been turning the ball into that shot.

There were bad signs when we were comfortably beaten by an invitational XI in our only warm-up game, though when Mitch and Sidds grabbed a couple of early wickets on day one in Dubai we thought that we'd just roll on. It was in this period that I dropped a catch at point, after swapping positions with Davey. I always found it tough to field square of the wicket, because my colour-blindness made it harder to catch the ball in flight as it changed direction. My preference has always been mid-off or cover, where I can watch the ball directly off the bat. At the time we didn't think it was going to matter all that much, but Younis Khan played an incredible, series-shaping innings and we were never ahead in the game again.

My pair of starts didn't look too bad on the scorecard, but being bowled twice on that surface was not a good look, and nor was my inability to put any pressure on their spinners. In the second Test in Abu Dhabi, their very shrewd captain Misbah ul-Haq elected to open the bowling with the off breaks of Mohammad Hafeez, who bowled flat and straight at the stumps. There was no pace on the ball, I had no ability to hit the ball over the top, and I was a reluctant sweeper at best. Once again we slid to defeat by a huge margin, Misbah putting the cherry on top of Pakistan's victory by equalling Viv Richards' fastest ever Test century, off 56 balls (since bettered by Kiwi Brendon McCullum, also against Australia).

I remember fielding at deep midwicket and watching one of his sixes off Nathan Lyon sail miles over my head, then going out to bat later in the day and not being able to get the ball off the square before I nudged a catch to leg slip. I came home knowing the difference between a very good player – as I had been – and a great one who could shape his game to all circumstances and all bowlers. In terms of how to play the conditions, these sorts of moments made it feel like we were a group of club players up against an international team. We may have been ranked No.1 in the world, but this was humbling.

On one level this was a useful reminder that the side did not compare to the great Australian teams of the early 2000s.

There was also a hard lesson for the players, coaching staff and selectors about working with the conditions, not against them, as we had done by trying Glenn Maxwell's death-or-glory approach at No.3 in Abu Dhabi, when what you really had to do was build big scores by turning the strike over and batting time – not to say I didn't agree with the decision at the time. After the series was over, we had a pretty frank discussion in the dressing room about how it had all unfolded. Something that stuck in my mind was one of the senior management guys rising up to say, 'The one thing I've learned from all my time over here is that you have to defend. You can't come over here and attack, you've got to stay in the game.' Wise words, but a lesson we had learnt too late.

That tour meant I was back at the bottom of the rollercoaster, unsure whether I'd be in the Test team for the first match against India, scheduled for the Gabba. The little bit of fortune I needed came via some outstanding bowling by Sidds in a Sheffield Shield match at Adelaide Oval, where he bowled great lines to Hughesy and got him cheaply in both innings, while I was able to go on to a hundred. The selectors' call to say I'd been picked for the Gabba arrived with the qualifier that I needed runs. In the last Shield match before we assembled, I was mentally preparing to ride the rollercoaster yet again. Then everything changed.

CHAPTER 13

A DEATH IN THE CRICKET FAMILY

Sydney, Adelaide

IT'S ALWAYS BEEN there. Whether right at the back of a cricketer's mind or pushed to the front when a batsman has been seriously injured by a projectile once described as 'half a house brick'. Great players and poor, young and old, nimble or clumsy, all have been aware that if a cricket ball hits, it has the potential to hurt and to break. Most have seen at least one instance of a bad injury, whether it be a deep cut above the eye, as Chris suffered at the hands of Mark Cleary in 2004, teeth knocked out or nose smashed in.

The worst that most contemplated was a broken jaw, as was the case with David Hookes when trying to hook Andy Roberts in World Series Cricket, or Geoff Lawson when trying to fend off Curtly Ambrose in a Test at the WACA Ground in 1988. Concussion, too, was a concern, as inflicted by Mitchell Johnson on Ryan McLaren at Centurion in early 2014, amid some of the more terrifying spells ever witnessed.

The possibility of *death* on the other hand, well that was something else entirely. It had happened though – Martin Bedkober when struck in the chest in Brisbane club cricket in 1975; Raman Lamba when suffering a blow to the temple while fielding in Bangladesh in 1998 – but the possibility still seemed remote.

Then it happened. At the SCG on 25 November 2014. To Phillip Hughes.

Sean Abbott bowled a bouncer that climbed slowly from a sluggish pitch, Hughes attempted to pull the ball fractionally before it arrived. Then there was the thud of ball into neck, the few deep breaths he took in an attempt to recover, and the lifeless collapse onto the pitch, face-forward, when the effect of a burst artery took its irreversible hold.

For a few moments no one quite knew what had happened. It looked bad. But how bad could it be? Batsmen had been felled before and resumed their innings after all. It was not until the SCG scoreboard showed a replay of the ghastly sequence that it was apparent this was worse than anything we had seen before. What followed was scene upon scene never meant to be glimpsed at a cricket match: the players' anguished cries for medical assistance, the first-aid work in the middle, then at the boundary's edge, the erection of a screen to shield Hughes from spectators, the arrival of ambulances and then a helicopter, the dash to a nearby hospital. The wait for positive news was interminable, and ultimately in vain. Two days later, Phillip was declared dead.

Players became grief counsellors or counselled. Coaches and administrators dealt in matters of life and death, not wins and losses. Cricket fans became vigil-keepers, and prayerful ones at that. In the space of 48 hours, all would become mourners. Peter Brukner, Australia's team doctor, remembers these awful days:

'On the night Phillip died, we had all been to see him, then held a press conference to talk about it. After that we all went to the bar at the SCG to have a drink and a chat and a cry in a lot of cases. I remember one of the players coming up to me that night and saying, "Doc, you've got to keep telling us it's a freakish incident and it's not going to happen again. Otherwise we can't get back out there." This was one of the more mature, sensible players saying this, so I was thinking this was going to be extremely hard to get through.

'So the next morning I got all the players together and talked them through things. I felt it was really important for them to understand everything that had happened, but also to really emphasise how freakish it was. It was similar to why I was part of the press conference the night before – I wanted to reassure every mum and dad out there that their kid wasn't going to die on Saturday when he goes out to play junior cricket.'

Cricket, after a while, did resume. Australia's Test series against India was reshuffled to begin in Adelaide rather than Brisbane, and players resolved to carry on, as Clarke exhorted them to in his emotive address at Hughes' Macksville funeral. But it resumed in a far different manner, with concern for the heads of the batsmen far more evident than ever before. Mitchell Johnson wept openly at Phillip's funeral, and was visibly distressed when he struck Virat Kohli in the helmet in Adelaide.

In the wake of Phillip's death, any knock to the head evoked memories of him lying motionless on the SCG turf. It is an image no cricketer will be able to shake for many a long year. In Shane Watson's words:

'You never contemplated that before. That's the very sad reality of the whole situation. After Hughesy passed away, anytime someone got hit and in not such a good area, that's what would flash through everyone's mind. You could see that with Buck, the thought that if I didn't have that extra protection there then what could have the consequences been?

'Everyone was affected by Hughesy's death in different ways ... but you could definitely tell Buck was really shaken up after he got hit at Lord's, and totally fair enough. Everyone even now is struggling to get their head around someone getting hit bad, because we all remember how horrendous that whole situation was.'

THE DAY PHILLIP Hughes was hit will never be forgotten by anyone connected to cricket. The initial news filtering through wasn't good, but it just couldn't be fathomed that the worst-case scenario would actually occur. What top-flight batsman hasn't been hit in the head? It's part of the job. You face fast bowlers who are trying to get you out by just about any means and this sometimes results in wearing one on the helmet.

I was sitting at home when I heard the news. A friend, Annie Hateley, who worked at Cricket Victoria, called me up to tell me. I didn't know what to do and sat on my couch trying to figure out how it was even possible. Annie, realising I was alone, came to offer her support. This was appreciated, but after a while all I wanted was to be alone.

Everyone reacts in different ways and unbeknown to me, all the Australian cricketers were making their way to Sydney. I didn't see how going to Sydney would help, when it seemed there were so many people there filtering in and out of the hospital. I'd never really had to deal with death before, apart from grandparents when their time had come, and how to cope with this disaster wasn't clear to me. The next day the call came asking if I'd made plans to go to Sydney, to which the reply was no. However, the team was being convened as the first Test in Brisbane against India was just around the corner. Advised to take cricket gear in case we had to fly on to Brisbane, I duly made my way to Sydney and the SCG.

It was an awful place to be, as grown men were crying openly and people could hardly speak. The team doctor Peter Brukner explained what happened and then questions were asked of team management as to what was to happen. The players were clearly not in the headspace to play cricket. The players' association, the ACA, discussed contingencies with Cricket Australia, who no doubt wanted business to continue due to advanced scheduling and keeping the Indian cricket board happy.

Eventually it was agreed to postpone the first Test, play it in Adelaide and fit in the Brisbane Test later in the summer. A number of players were privately unhappy and felt they were still far too raw to walk on to a cricket ground. I understood that I'd have to walk out there again, and while a little tentative now about the full ramifications of what a blow by a cricket ball could do, the show was going to go on.

Our first training session in Adelaide took place at Park 25 just outside the CBD. I walked with Brad Haddin from the hotel to the ground and Hadds was still very unsure that we should be playing so soon – it was a sombre conversation. I don't know why, but I seemed to be able to compartmentalise everything that had occurred and get on with the job at hand, which was facing cricket balls and trying to get my game in order for the match.

What was in the back of my mind though was this: if our scores had been reversed in the first round of Sheffield Shield matches when Phillip's South Australian side played my Victoria, it would have been him that would have been selected for the first Test and not me. I knew my time was coming to an end and that the selectors were desperately hoping Hughesy fulfilled his undoubted potential, but I had been hoping to put off my departure until after the Ashes the following winter.

My memory is often pretty poor and needed a lot of prompting for this book to be written, but I'll never forget that training session. The sight of Davey Warner walking out of his net after three or four slow throw downs from batting coach Michael Di Venuto to drop to his haunches and cry uncontrollably, and a fairly similar experience for Shane Watson, will live with me until the end of my days. Mitchell Johnson, who usually bowled almost as aggressively at his teammates as he did the opposition, could hardly let the ball go – and when he did accidentally bowl a shortish delivery, he was mortified. It wasn't just these three but a significant number of us who were struggling. It was an eerie scene. Cricket had changed.

I had first become aware of Phillip when he burst in to the New South Wales state side. The stories of his brilliant childhood hadn't reached a fellow left-handed opener in his 30s from another state, but it wasn't going to be long before seemingly everyone in the cricketing fraternity knew him. He did against my teams what he did to every opposition – and that was tally up big runs. I just couldn't work out how. We were almost the total opposite in style and everything I had worked at he seemingly went against.

I tried to get across into the line and score off the front foot and play as straight as I could and defend. He would stay leg side of the ball and slice everything through point, mainly off the back foot, and if you got a touch too straight he would whip it over square leg. It was infuriating and puzzling and astonishing all at the same time. How did he do it? Could I do the same? That last answer was no – he was just a freak with ridiculous talents and a thirst for runs I hadn't seen from a young player.

When the great Australian side started to break up through retirements, I'd been hopeful that my time would come, but one by one another opening batsman would stand in my way. I always felt that the door was still ajar though, as international success is exceptionally difficult. First Phil Jaques, then Simon Katich and then Shane Watson were taking an opener's place for the national side, but it wasn't until Hughesy got in and made those two sublime hundreds in the 2009 Durban Test against South Africa's vaunted attack that I thought my chance had finally gone.

I'd been hoping against hope that I'd get one more chance, but I'd seen Hughesy play, and while I knew there were some flaws in his game, his ability to find a way to score runs was as good as I'd seen. Given his youth, my time seemed to be up. Then, surprisingly to me, he was dropped from the team in England in 2013, and while I didn't agree with it, the door was ajar again.

The 2013 Ashes was my first close contact with Phillip. We'd been friendly previously, but given we were both trying to get into the Test team there was always going to be an underlying competitiveness between us, and we kept our distance. Then there was the fact that our ages were so different.

His 80 in the first innings of the first Test in Nottingham, batting at No.6, was arguably as good as any of his centuries for Australia, and we all felt like his time had come. But he was only given one more Test again before being dropped. You could see his confidence slipping away, even as he did his best not to show it. Outwardly he was still this jovial kid that smiled and spoke to everyone and anyone. He would come up to me and say, 'Buck, you're a legend mate, I love how you bat and your record is unbelievable.' I would smile and think either he was being cheeky or naive. But that was just Phillip being the great, supportive bloke he was. It took me a while to understand that.

After the 2013 Ashes we didn't have a lot to do with each other until the series in South Africa the next year, when he was once again in the squad as a reserve batsman. As I wrote earlier, it was a very lonely time for me as I was one of the few on tour without a partner – and Phillip was one of them. Slowly we began to hang out a little more.

The Aussie cricket circus continued on to the UAE to face Pakistan and the situation was replicated, and we spent more time in each other's company. Regrettably now, we mostly spoke of cricket and each other's situation. I kept telling him he was so close and that if he kept getting better and believing, when his time would come he would make it count, to which he would agree – but say not until I'd decided to finish, as Davey Warner's position was in no doubt. He even said he'd told his father he didn't want to replace me, as he felt I deserved the spot.

That was just the kind of person he was. When his death happened and the response worldwide was so incredible, it did not come as a surprise. Often in sport you have to be ruthless and you leave in your wake people who took exception to your treatment of them and I'm no different. Phillip was different – no one had a bad word to say about him. It was easy to see why. Every nice thing people said about him was true.

What blew me away most when I did hear people talking about him was just how little I knew about him. His family, his farming, his home town Macksville, his love of boxing and other interests – I hadn't talked with him enough about these things. This was probably because he was just happy sitting there listening and enjoying himself. He didn't want to talk about himself all the time. I came to respect him even more for it.

CHAPTER 14

PROTECTING THE HEAD

Adelaide, Brisbane, Dominica, Lord's

ALMOST IMMEDIATELY CHRIS Rogers had to confront his own fears over head injuries. Problems arose in the 2014 home Test series against India, then on the Caribbean tour that followed, and then the Ashes in England. He suffered multiple blows to the head – and although there were no fractures to the bones, his confidence was shattered. After struggling so long to get into the Australian team, an enforced retirement was suddenly on the horizon.

It was something he contemplated during this time more than once. At the Gabba he was struck on the head while fielding in the second Test. He spent quite some time in the company of team doctor Peter Brukner:

'At the Gabba Chris was very agitated. I assessed him and reassured him that he was ok, but when they came off at tea he was still really agitated. I said to the captain Steve Smith "you've got to get him out of there, otherwise he might walk away from

*the game". I spoke to the psychologist Michael Lloyd as well
about speaking with Chris and helping him to work through it so
he didn't do anything too drastic.'*

In the West Indies, Brukner found himself ruling Chris out of a Test match under Cricket Australia's recently instituted concussion policy. Then he was struck again in England, at Lord's.

*'I was somewhere else at the time he got hit [in the West Indies],
and it was mentioned to me "Buck's been hit on the helmet but
he's fine". The next morning he said he didn't feel great, a bit
fatigued, a bit sore. These were classic concussion symptoms.
Ultimately I ruled him out, and used that opportunity to talk to
the guys about what had happened and that I'd do the same
for any of them. As important as a Test match is, nothing should
take precedence over your health. Chris wasn't happy about it at
the time, but admitted to me a day or two later that it had been
the right decision. Originally we were going to have him back
ready in time for the second Test, but when he tried to step it up
he got his symptoms back.*

*'Lord's was bizarre. The inner-ear bruising is very
unusual, but his loss of balance was very scary. To be
telling me the Lord's Pavilion was moving, there was no
hesitation about getting him off the ground. This all took
place 24 hours after he had been hit, and I wasn't aware
of that occurring in concussion cases before. That's not the
way it works. I rang one of the concussion experts in Australia
to ask if he'd ever seen anything like it. He said "nope, think
about something else".'*

When Chris was struck on the second morning at Lord's he had already made a century. John and Ros were at the ground. John picks up the story:

'We head for the committee room, which is on the ground floor below the England dressing room and present our invitation. "I'm sorry sir, but I have it down that you are not due here till one o'clock." I point out my invitation says 10.30 and the attendant goes inside to check and returns to tell me that he has confirmed it is to be 1pm. Having orchestrated the invite myself, I back off. So what to do now? People have queued for hours for the Pavilion and there won't be a spare seat anywhere. So we head back across the Long Room and through a sea of heads, I see some disarray out on the field. Sightscreen problems I think.

'We head towards the library where a little back room has a TV set and suddenly we see Chris with helmet off and the doc Peter Brukner holding a bandage to the back of the head. Stunned, thoughts of his Caribbean concussion surface and we sit down quickly, but I can see he's still got hold of his bat and clearly he's going nowhere. Yes, first ball of the day, the lone other TV watcher confirms, he's been sconed. I'm feeling a bit toey, been tossed out of the committee room, my son's been floored on the pitch and I'm stuck out the back!

'I go upstairs to the dressing room and ask to see the doc, who comes out with a wary look. Just thought I'd ask, I tell Peter, and he relaxes and tells me that in getting knocked the helmet caused a cut behind the ear. Nothing serious he says.'

John and Ros had had a similar problem the day before when they tried to congratulate their son on his century. They ended up doing so, with a little help from Chris's boss at Middlesex, Angus Fraser, who recalls:

'One of the nice things when he got his hundred here, I came down and shook his hand in the Long Room as he walked off. At the end of the day's play his parents were down by the back of the Pavilion and the stewards wouldn't let them in, so I got them in to go to the dressing room to see him. They're obviously cricket mad, the family.'

IN THE LAST innings of the Adelaide Test that followed Phillip's passing I was fielding at cover when I ran at a ball that was bisecting myself and mid-off, where Michael Clarke was fielding. As he ran he suddenly winced in pain and pulled up with a significant hamstring strain. This would have serious consequences for me. But before I get to that, I must say the performances in that Test by those who were closest to Phillip – namely Michael himself, Steve Smith and Davey Warner – were truly phenomenal.

Vice-captain Brad Haddin immediately took over after Michael was led from the field, and his first direction was to ask me to call for short-leg gear – helmet, box and shin pads. A sinking feeling in my heart hit me straight away. Michael had not asked me to do this duty as Steve Smith and others had been put in there where their younger and faster reactions would be required. But Hadds felt Steve's

Tennis probably wasn't destined to be my favourite sport, as this shot of my racquet flying away shows. But sport was a big part of growing up.

The Australian Under 19 team at the 1996 Youth Series v New Zealand
BACK ROW: David Hussey, Lance Kahler, Don Nash, Matthew Innes, Nathan Bracken, Matthew Pascoe, Matthew Anderson, Bradley Haddin, Chris Rogers.
FRONT ROW: Christopher Davies, Paul Sutherland, Richard Done (Coach), Clinton Peake (Captain), Brian Taber (Manager), Matthew Bradley (Vice-Captain), Simon Dart.

RIGHT: A newspaper report showing Shaun Marsh, Scott Meuleman and me, all from Wesley, and all in the West Australian team in 2002, after I scored 101 for WA in March 2002.

LEFT: Getting one away against Andy Craddick of England in a WA v England tour match, at the WACA in October 2002. RIGHT: Hit at short leg playing for the WA Warriors in a match against the New South Wales Blues at Newcastle Oval in 2003. (GETTY IMAGES)

BELOW: Celebrating another ton on day 3 of a Pura Cup match between the Victorian Bushrangers and the Western Warriors at the Junction Oval in December 2004. (GETTY IMAGES)

RIGHT & BELOW: Playing for Leicestershire, and on the attack against Australia, on day 3 of a Tour match in Leicester, July 2005. Later the same day, a handshake from Michael Clarke upon reaching 200 against the Australians. (GETTY IMAGES)

FACING PAGE: Celebrating scoring a double hundred against Shane Warne in a Pura Cup match between WA and Victoria in October 2006. (GETTY IMAGES)

LEFT: With the trophy for State Player of the Year, presented at the Allan Border Medal night in February 2007. Big suit and all. (GETTY IMAGES)

BELOW: *Daily Telegraph* front page news on 16 January 2008.

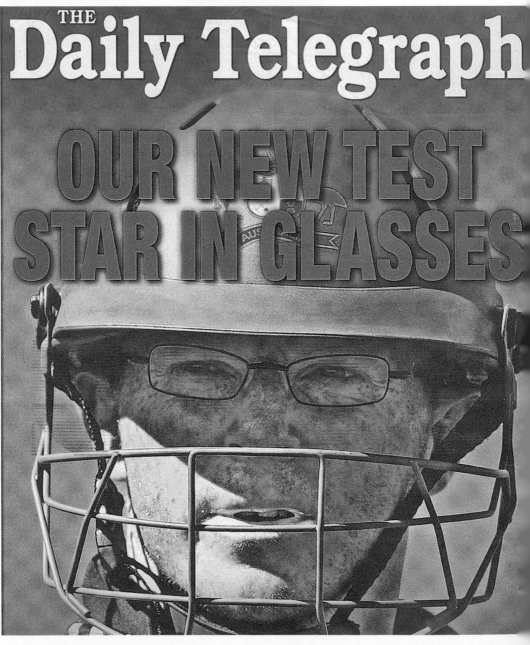

THE Daily Telegraph

OUR NEW TEST STAR IN GLASSES

ABOVE: Putting on my Baggy Green cap after it was presented to me by Justin Langer on 16 January 2008. (GETTY IMAGES)

LEFT: Getting used to the Australian set-up as I hit the nets for a training session in Perth, January 2008. (GETTY IMAGES)

RIGHT: Changing states led to a successful stint playing for Victoria in the Sheffield Shield. Here in a match against Queensland in February 2010. (GETTY IMAGES)

BELOW: Getting into a good stride for Derbyshire with the ball going to the boundary during a warm-up match between Derbyshire and Australia at the County Ground in July 2010. (GETTY IMAGES)

INSET: Celebrating the second division title after the LV County Championship match between Leicestershire and Middlesex at Grace Road in September 2011. (GETTY IMAGES)

ABOVE: Sums up my Thunder Big Bash League experience. I hit the ground after missing a catching chance during a BBL match between Sydney Thunder and the Adelaide Strikers in December 2012.
(GETTY IMAGES)

BELOW: At Lord's Cricket Ground the day the Ashes squad was announced, and I was included, in April 2013.
(GETTY IMAGES)

ABOVE: 50 in the second innings at Trent Bridge. Facing James Anderson of England on day 4 of the first Ashes Test match in July 2013. (GETTY IMAGES)

BELOW: A ton and a tear or two. Raising my bat as I leave the ground on 101 not out as bad light stopped play in the fourth Ashes Test match in August 2013. (GETTY IMAGES)

LEFT: Blood spilled on a difficult day after being struck on the head by a delivery from Stuart Broad during day 2 of the fourth Ashes Test in December 2013. (GETTY IMAGES)

BELOW: More enjoyable times two days later, a match-sealing 100 and a hug from Watto. (GETTY IMAGES)

BOTTOM: At 5–0 the Ashes had been won. Celebrations with Davey before the team song on 5 January 2014. (GETTY IMAGES)

RIGHT: Not much chance of positive press in the United Arab Emirites, and no runs either. BELOW: Pakistani bowler Imran Khan celebrates my dismissal on the second day of the second Test match in October 2014. (GETTY IMAGES)

BOTTOM: Missing 100 against India at the SCG, amid 7 consecutive Test 50s as I'm dismissed by Mohammed Shami on day 1 of the fourth Test match against India in January 2015. (GETTY IMAGES)

ABOVE: Michael Clarke, Darren Lehmann, team doctor Peter Brukner and I discuss ruling me out of the Dominica Test due to concussion in June 2015. (GETTY IMAGES)

BELOW: Arriving in the UK, Steve Smith feeds me a snag at the welcome BBQ in London in June 2015. A bit of fun before the Ashes. (GETTY IMAGES)

RIGHT: Hit on the helmet first ball of the morning by England's James Anderson on day 2 of the second Ashes Test in July 2015. (GETTY IMAGES)

BELOW: The pavilion was moving as Brad Haddin and David Warner checked I was OK during day 4 of the second Ashes Test. (GETTY IMAGES)

ABOVE: My last stand with Davey, walking from the ground at lunch, on day 1 of the fifth Ashes Test. (GETTY IMAGES)

BELOW: The presentation of my award for Australia's man of the series in August 2015. (GETTY IMAGES)

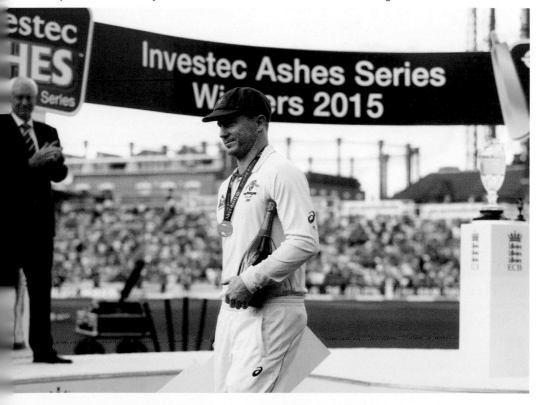

Above: Mum and Dad are my two greatest supporters.

Below: Captaining Somerset, during the County Championship Division One match between Somerset and Warwickshire in September 2016. (GETTY IMAGES)

exceptional fielding talents could be better utilised elsewhere and I was to take over.

I've always hated the position. I fielded there a lot as a younger player, particularly for Beau Casson. He mixed great deliveries with loose ones, meaning the short-leg could be peppered. During one match at Adelaide Oval for Western Australia, I was struck on the full on my ankle and the ball then ricocheted all the way to midwicket, who proceeded to take the catch. All the players ran to the fielder except for Beau, who ran straight to me, where I lay writhing in pain on the ground. After numerous blows, I started to dislike playing and would hardly speak when positioned close in.

It's a terrible spot to field and those who criticise these fielders would be better served to keep their mouth shut until they've experienced what it is like in there. The best ones are those who don't fear it and I wasn't one of them – Quiney is possibly the bravest I've seen. I did manage to take a catch in Adelaide when one popped up and practically landed in my hands, but I was hit when one of Rohit Sharma's fierce sweeps slammed hard into the side of my hip as I tried to take evasive action. Apart from the pain, I was beginning to panic. There was nothing I could have done to get out of the way and it was straight after Phillip's fatal blow. You would have to have nerves of steel or stupidity off the charts not to panic.

With the naming of Steve Smith as captain in Michael's absence for the next Test in Brisbane, the writing was on the wall. I was to be short-leg when one was needed. I didn't mind it so much for the pace bowlers, as ours were very quick and difficult to pull, but the Indian players were excellent players of spin and in particular good sweepers, which had me worried. The inevitable happened at the Gabba and once again the batsman was Rohit. He got every bit of a sweep and hit it uppishly. I was predicting what was coming and once again swivelled trying to present a smaller target. However my technique in doing this was terrible, and all I managed to do was present my back. The ball struck me flush on the back of the helmet, inches from where Phillip had been hit.

Team doctor Peter Brukner raced onto the field and almost in anger I pushed him away. I was furious and scared, but all I could think of was I had to get back in there and try to prove to teammates I wasn't a coward. I have no recollection of this, but Peter later said that I said to him 'Doc, I don't want to die.' It was how we were all feeling at the time.

After play the full understanding of what had happened hit me. My bad technique in evasion was down to a lack of courage. I had been lucky that more damage had not been done. While I tried not to show it, others could see just how upset I was. Team psychologist Michael Lloyd was the first to approach me and ask if I wanted to talk about it, so I invited him to my room, where I broke down. I had kept so much to myself throughout recent weeks, but the blow to the head had stirred something in me.

After talking to Michael, who was very supportive, the next contact was with Dad. I told him everything I was thinking and that it might be time to call it quits. As stated before, the lows are terrible, and what became consuming was a desire to get out of the bubble and live a more balanced life. Deep down, however, I knew I would fight on. I couldn't walk away and even though I considered it when Darren took me aside after the game and said I needed to be clear about whether I wanted to go on, I knew I would keep at it, otherwise I'd have felt a failure. It helped to contribute with the bat by getting the first two of seven consecutive half-centuries – and that the best two Tests of the Australian summer, in Melbourne and Sydney, were to come.

It was with relief that I wasn't asked to do short-leg after that, as Joe Burns was drafted in to the team and he took over the role. I was asked to do it in the Ashes series the following year but only for the quick bowlers – a good enough compromise.

However my days of being hit on the head weren't over.

Having been selected for the two-series squad to the Caribbean and then the United Kingdom, we travelled end of May. In a family mix-up, my sister had unknowingly scheduled her wedding for 30 May and it became evident I wasn't going to make it – another consequence of being a professional cricketer. Years before I missed my brother's wedding ceremony – but made it to the reception – as I was desperately trying to prove my position in the WA team at the time. His hunch that December 22 would not be a cricket day proved wrong, as we had a game scheduled to finish that day … in Adelaide.

In our warm-up week in Antigua I had made a paltry two in our only innings against a WICB Chairman's XI and was dismissed by one of the best diving catches I'd seen in the gully. The catcher was an unknown youngster called Carlos

Brathwaite, who wowed us all with his size and build. We then made our way to Dominica where the first Test was to be played and it was here I suffered another blow.

With the local groundsmen preparing the practice wickets so far out from the game, the first day of training proved to be lively. They were bouncing like tennis balls and I could not get a read on it as length balls were going through almost head high at times, not helped by the local net bowlers having a penchant for loving the short stuff. Finally I decided enough was enough and attempted a rare pull shot, but I was through the stroke too early and the ball cannoned in to the side of my helmet. Not thinking too much of it as it wasn't a particularly fast delivery, I carried on and was hit in the box next ball, sending me over the edge as I whacked the stumps out of the ground in a fit of petulant rage.

I've often told young players that getting mad in nets is pointless and counter-productive, so after picking the stumps up I chuckled to myself and took a deep breath and got on with it. The rest of the net was not too bad in the circumstances. Doc Brukner had seen me taking one on the helmet and after the net asked how I was, to which I replied fine, although a touch weird. I put that down to the raging heat, and having just spent 30 minutes in my gear and under a helmet. That night I started to feel a little fatigued so went to bed a little earlier than usual, still not thinking anything of it.

The next day we convened for training and the Doc asked to speak to me. His first question about my health elicited the response that I was 'just still feeling a little fatigued'. What happened next took me completely by surprise. He told me he was ruling me out of the Test as tiredness is an indicator of concussion – and therefore I wouldn't be able to play for at least six days. He then pulled over the captain and coach. While I half-heartedly tried to argue against the verdict, it was clear that once the doctor had said it, there was no way he could then let me play.

Initially the reaction was one of incredulity, as I'd been hit in the head numerous times before and this had never happened. I felt like I was a test case for the new concussion ruling. The last thing you want to do is miss a match and give another guy a chance to take your spot … especially when you are 36 years of age.

The next day I thought I'd train with the guys and maybe show Peter he'd misdiagnosed. After taking some diving catches from side to side amid some energetic fielding, all of a sudden my vision started to change. I felt this pressure inside my head and my vision started to narrow. Everything peripheral was blurred and it felt like I was looking down a tunnel from further back. Not only that but nausea started to rise – the possibility of throwing up was very real. Something was wrong and there was no denying it. Immediately I stopped and approached the doctor, who seemed very concerned, and sent me home to rest in my room with no light.

I'd been hit in the head many times and while I have no doubt I was concussed badly early in my career after Mark Cleary cleaned me up with a blow flush on my eye socket, since then I'd never worried too much when it happened and kept soldiering on. If anything, a blow by Stuart Broad in the

Boxing Day Ashes Test in 2013 seemed to sharpen my focus and helped me find rhythm.

This time was different. It had been such an innocuous blow and not even that fast, but something was very wrong. Trying hard to help out with 12th man duties, I tried staying at the ground during the Test but would get very tired very quickly and start to feel sick. The heat was oppressive and almost unavoidable so I would be sent home. I still remember walking through the streets of Dominica alone with Australian team training kit on, wondering what I was doing. Celebrations were had that Test after Adam Voges had played sublimely on debut but I wasn't allowed to drink, and it was the first time not being part of the team during my time with the Australian squad. While pleased for Vogesy, it was still a hollow feeling not being able to contribute.

The second Test was in Jamaica, where we were advised to stay in the hotel complex due to the danger of wandering off in what is a dangerous city. After about nine days off from training, I joined in for some light running with the guys in the first training session at the ground. Within five minutes, familiar sensations returned and once again my condition went south quickly. It seemed any time the brain was moved or bounced by exercise, I would deteriorate dramatically.

It was at this stage I started to become concerned. The doctor had suggested it would take a week or so to clear up, but the symptoms didn't seem to be abating. Querying the doctor about tests, he said there wasn't much point until we got to the UK, which made enough sense to me as once again I was ruled out of the upcoming Test and nothing could be done in the meantime. It was hard to shake the feeling that the symptoms were becoming permanent, in much the same way as when I had a bad back and couldn't move. The mind often deals in worst-case scenarios and mine was no different. It was a depressing time.

Speaking to my brother, he seemed to think being in the Caribbean was a lot of sitting on the beach relaxing, drinking rum and then the odd party in the evening. It was anything but, and being confined to a room was not how I'd envisioned a trip that used to be the envy of all professional cricketers.

Eventually the time came to travel to the UK for the Ashes, which was a relief. The chance to see a lot of friends and even family was a godsend. There was a lot of talk that Shaun Marsh would keep his spot at the top of the order after doing reasonably well in my absence. A few of us who hadn't played a lot of cricket travelled to the picturesque Isle of Wight just off the coast of Southampton for a friendly game – a match I'd been cleared for.

Driving down with Stuart Law from London while others were transported in a mini bus was a great opportunity to talk to a player I'd so admired. Still a little worried about concussion, I was nicked off by Ryan Harris for not many, which didn't help my frame of mind, but I managed to spend some time in the middle in the second innings. What was more pleasing was my confidence being slightly restored, even though the bowling wasn't anywhere near as fast as expected in the Test matches.

After a couple of warm-up games the selectors decided I was the man for the job, which came as a pleasant surprise, but I was also worried as the England fast bowling attack was not something to scoff at. Somehow I managed to get myself set in our first innings in Cardiff – the first Test – and was playing as well as I had for a long time. It was the introduction of Mark Wood that started to cause worries. 'Woody' had ridiculous athleticism and agility, which enabled a whippy action. Because of this he managed to get the odd ball to fly – without any noticeable difference in his bowling action, it would be considerably quicker. I couldn't get a feel for him and every now and again a ball would kick or fly past my head.

After fighting through these periods and continuing to tick the runs over, Stuart Broad joined in on the short-ball barrage and my heart started racing. It's easy for people to say fight hard and don't worry and toughen up but I couldn't shake the thought in the back of the mind that one was going to be too quick or awkward for me.

Getting into the 80s I started to play uncharacteristic shots and even top-edged a six off Broad – my only one in Test cricket. Then I tried to 'ramp' a couple of Broad's bouncers over the keeper unsuccessfully and then on 95 played a poor half-cut to Wood and edged behind. Michael Clarke was at the other end and I knew he was furious with me for my lack of discipline – but I had demons running through my thoughts. We lost the game and my dismissal was a key moment. A score of 150 instead of 95 might have been the difference in the result.

Heading to Lord's, there had been a lot of criticism in the media, including from the co-author of this book, Daniel Brettig. Our batsmen had been written off as performers only on home soil and it made me furious. I felt it was a bit premature, as the same journalists were the ones predicting an Australian victory in the series. After all, one bad game can happen. This along with the inspiration of playing at Lord's – and an easy paced surface with short square boundaries that deterred short-pitched bowling – combined for my best performance for Australia, the one time I batted a full day in a Test.

Going out to bat the next morning, my expectation was that a stiff Jimmy Anderson would serve up a nice loosener. But he isn't one of the best bowlers in the world for nothing and his first delivery was a surprisingly quick bouncer right at my head, which was too quick to evade in my slightly tired state. Turning my head, the ball clattered into the base of the back of the helmet, on the new stemguard protecting the neck that had been adapted since Phillip Hughes died.

I was very fortunate to be wearing it, as it took a fair portion of the impact. Even though I was able to carry on, the blow shook me badly and I knew my innings wouldn't last too long, as we were already in a very dominant position with a lot of batting to come. Choosing to be aggressive, I scored another 16 quickly before missing a fairly innocuous ball from Broad but I was satisfied – perhaps another sign that my time was coming to an end. (Steve Smith, by comparison, wasn't done and made a deserved double century.) After bowling out the English relatively cheaply we had the chance to bat for a second time at the end of day three. Davey and I had few alarms as we scored at a quick rate to be unbeaten at the end of the day with both of us in the 40s.

The next day was to be one of the weirdest experiences of my life. Starting once more I managed two very good shots in the first over and raced to 49. The next over, stationed at the non-striker's end, I watched as Davey had to deal with a Broad over. After the fourth ball, I turned back to walk into my crease and all of a sudden my eyesight started to bounce. Initially I wasn't concerned: sometimes this happens when you move your head too quickly and then it settles down.

However Broad bowled the next ball and it wasn't settling down. It was at this moment I became very worried. Everything seemed to be bouncing side to side and there was no way I could face Anderson while this was happening. Finally Broad finished his over and I could hardly stand. Davey immediately realised something was very wrong and told me to sit down and he called for the doctor.

It was my friend Darren Wates who later pointed out to me what had transpired between Davey and I as we waited for the doctor. He'd read Davey's comments in the media after Davey chatted to the press at the end of the day. As Davey kneeled behind me looking over my shoulder he asked what was wrong, to which I replied along the lines of 'Something's wrong with my eyes, mate. The Pavilion is moving.' Davey proceeded to look up at the pavilion, paused and then said, God bless him, 'No it's not.'

The doctor quickly realised I was in no state to continue and told me my innings was done and therefore, I knew, my Test match also. Sitting in the Pavilion and then on the balcony to be visible for friends and family I couldn't contact as we had no phones available – one of the rules to stop any possibility of match-fixing – the symptoms happened again that afternoon and again that night. On what turned out to be the last day of the Test as Australia ran through a dispirited England, I was getting an MRI on Harley Street in the city and by the time I'd returned I'd missed out on a lot of the celebrations as many friends, family and celebrities crammed into the change room to enjoy themselves.

Though I was originally scheduled to continue on with the Australian team, the doctor insisted I stay in London for more tests as the MRI hadn't indicated anything. A CT scan was next and once again it showed nothing, so eventually an ear specialist was recommended. It turned out I didn't have concussion at all, but instead bruising to the inner ear, although fascinatingly it was the opposite ear from the side that was struck, as the head was rocked to the side and some sort of reverberation had occurred.

It was a huge relief, as one more concussion would have been enough for me, even though I was desperate to keep going, particularly with the form I had. So despite some trepidation, I declared myself fit for Edgbaston, which turned out to be the quickest pitch of the series.

We batted first, and after lunch England came out breathing fire, particularly Steven Finn, who had been a teammate at Middlesex. I had pulled him before the break. He didn't like it and now bowled as quick as I'd seen him. His height and pace were difficult to manage. He bowled two bouncers that fizzed past my head. They were so quick I couldn't actually move to avoid them – it was just fortunate they were off target.

This was the innings when I knew my time was just about up.

Any thoughts of continuing in Test cricket after the Ashes were extinguished. I've heard people say that as you get older, you lose the ability to pick up the ball early, which is why the bowlers feel quicker. I don't necessarily disagree, but also feel the body loses its suppleness and can't quite physically react as quickly to move into position or out of position.

The feeling of being stuck as quick deliveries passed close by my head was enough to make me realise I had had my fair share of luck and that it was time to get out. It's not just the games – the nets can be even scarier, especially when it's Mitchell Johnson and Mitchell Starc bowling at you. I was all too aware what could happen following Phillip's passing. The growing fear in me was not subsiding. It was time to admit my age was becoming a factor. The next time I was hit might be one time too many.

CHAPTER 15

SWANSONG

Ashes 2015

TWO THINGS DOMINATED the weeks leading up to Australia's 2015 defence of the Ashes won so comprehensively at home 18 months before: hubris and tickets. The prevailing attitude of the touring side was summed up best by Steve Smith, in an interview with ESPNcricinfo: 'I can't wait to get over there and play another Ashes against England in their conditions after beating them so convincingly in Australia,' he said. 'If we continue to play the way we have been playing over the last 12 to 18 months, I don't think that they'll come close to us, to be honest.'

Other players weighed in with similar sentiments; journalists from both countries agreed. Curiously, the one dissenting voice was that of the former Australian paceman, then coach of Yorkshire, Jason Gillespie:

'England should look at Australia and go: "Hang on a minute, they've got a 37-year-old keeper [Brad Haddin]. They've got a 37-year-old opening batter [Chris Rogers], their captain

[Michael Clarke] has got a glass back and they've got a fast bowler – Ryan Harris – who's 35 years of age and who's got a dodgy knee". They're Dad's Army. I'd be thinking "let's keep them out in the field. Let's get them tired, they're old blokes. We can put these guys under pressure".'

For Chris, this pre-series period was complicated by the unravelling of a scheme to put together a tour group for the summer, in collaboration with fellow Australian and former Middlesex teammate, Tom Scollay. The idea was for a group pitched to a younger market than is usual, using some of Chris' knowledge of the pubs, clubs and restaurants of England as an itinerary that also featured time in the Mediterranean. Tickets to the Lord's Test were to be included, after Chris sought and received an allocation from Middlesex.

Unfortunately there is rather more to setting up an Ashes tour operation than simply acquiring tickets and putting up a website for 'Inside Edge Experience'. The tour group business is closely guarded by boards, venues and established operators, with resale of tickets outside official channels strictly prohibited. There was the further complication of Lord's being the domain not just of Middlesex but also the Marylebone Cricket Club, which quickly sought to protect its interests once the concept was publicised.

At training before Australia's first tour match against Kent in Canterbury, Chris clearly wanted to be talking about something else as he took his medicine. This was never more evident than when the experienced Australian news journalist Jacquelin Magnay pitched up with this question: 'This is something that could attract a year's jail in this country. Do you think someone should have flagged that up before now?' A stammering response was almost inevitable.

'Look in hindsight I've found out I should probably have gone in a different way,' Chris answered. 'But there was no intent to do anything other than start up a very small company and provide a good experience of London, which I've been lucky enough to spend some time in. The tickets have been refunded and no money has been exchanged with Middlesex, so hopefully no harm done. It was for a very small group of people and I went about it in what I thought was the right way, but it turned out it probably wasn't. I probably learned a lesson, but there was no intent to deceive or anything like that.'

The episode landed Middlesex in trouble with the MCC, and may have been a catalyst for examination of the role of the club's long-term chief executive Vinny Codrington, who departed by mutual consent some weeks later. Angus Fraser, the director of cricket, looks back upon the episode as a lesson learned for all concerned. As well, he is adamant it had no bearing on his decision to sign Adam Voges rather than Chris for 2016. As he says:

'It was an innocent, slightly naive cock-up. Chris had this idea, clubs sell corporate packages and he asked us to provide some tickets. The club were trying to look after him, it was Middlesex's cock-up, and that certainly didn't influence any decision I made [about 2016]. Middlesex messed that up because we shouldn't have done what we did. But it was done in a well-intentioned way, trying to help a Middlesex player out.'

'Innocent, slightly naive cock-up' is actually a reasonable description of how the 2015 Ashes would pan out for the Australians. While Chris managed to put together a strong final series, others were unable to do the same, as the 'Dad's Army' label ascribed by Gillespie started to stick. Ryan Harris, Michael Clarke, Brad Haddin and Shane Watson would all join Chris in Test match retirement by the end of the series.

There were to be mea culpas aplenty, not least by the selection chairman Rod Marsh, who had this to say at series' end:

> 'When we left Lord's [after the second Test] I thought "we will win the Ashes" because we'd played that badly at Cardiff, we played that well here, then we were just going to win. If that's complacency, then yes we were complacent. But I think we all thought we'd broken their back at Lord's with such an emphatic victory. Geez we were wrong. We were that wrong!'

The only source of consolation came from Chris' own performances, making him a rare batsman not only to finish a Test career on his terms, but to do so as his team's man of the series. As I wrote at the series' end for ESPNcricinfo: 'Rogers is leaving on top of his game … A concussion in the West Indies could have had a debilitating effect, as could the distraction of a mini-tour group scuppered by the MCC. But at Cardiff and Lord's, Rogers played a pair of terrific first innings, then shrugged off an inner-ear problem to contribute solidly over the final three. His final innings at The Oval was typical – a slogging knock to get the team past lunch and coax out David Warner's best performance of the series, setting up a win.'

AS EARLY AS 2014, the following year's Ashes series in England seemed like the right time to finish up – provided I could make it that far. I was realistic enough to understand that once we'd made our defence of the urn won at home, Darren and the selectors would be eager to move on to someone younger. I was also honest enough with myself to know that the scheduled series after that tour, against Bangladesh, New Zealand and the West Indies, would be good opportunities to blood younger players. It is my firm belief, as well, that if there is a younger player who can do the same job as an older counterpart, pick the young guy. Only stay with experience if you can see it will make a significant difference. After the Ashes were done, I knew my English wiles wouldn't matter so much.

A third factor came into my thinking as well. Being in the Australian team is a bubble existence, and after years of being outside it, I was looking for the right time to escape the environment. Don't get me wrong: I had some of the best moments of my life in the Australian side, and the validation of proving I could play at the highest level was something that I will always cherish. But it is such a highly competitive space, with constant travel and pressure, that not everyone can flourish in it forever. There was also a sense of isolation to it that I had not bargained for. Cricket becomes the be all and end all, less a game than a compulsion.

Add to this the physical toll of it all, whether it be keeping your body at the right pitch for training, or facing up to a quartet of fast and furious pacemen in the nets day after day – it all starts to wear. It is easy to underestimate the stress involved in going in to face Mitchell Johnson, Mitchell Starc, Josh Hazlewood or James Pattinson every week, merely as a preparatory exercise. Particularly after Hughesy, it was hard to avoid the sensation that you're one hit in the head away from serious injury or worse. So by the time of the fifth Test in Sydney in January 2015, a strong run of scores behind me, I set myself to have the best Ashes series possible, then call stumps.

We arrived in England with confidence as high as could be. This was summed up by Steve Smith's statement: 'If we continue to play the same way we've played over the last 12 to 18 months, I don't think they'll come close to us, to be honest.' The sense among a lot of the guys was exactly the same: that whatever the conditions or the opposition, we had more than enough firepower to knock England over. Given there was no Graeme Swann anymore, our fast bowlers were eager to bowl on the seaming pitches we expected, and the batsmen felt there was no challenge that could not be met with decisive stroke play and aggression. It was easy to get caught up in it all.

That being said, I had played enough in England to know that it could be a completely different ball game. The surfaces in 2013 had been dry and yet we still had our moments against the moving ball. Smudger was blooming into an absolute batting superstar, but I had no illusions about how difficult it might turn out to be, particularly against the new ball. I expected slow seamers that had the dual effect of not giving our quicks the pace and bounce they wanted, while at the same time helping the likes of James Anderson and Stuart Broad to pose very tough questions for our top six.

Another sign that things wouldn't be quite so straight-forward for us came during our warm-up matches against

Kent and Essex. During those games our bowlers were taking wickets, but we were going for four and five an over most of the time. The two Mitches were bowling so quick that a lot of the time you just needed to get a little bit of bat on ball and four runs were added on these smaller grounds and quick outfields. Daniel Bell-Drummond got a rapid hundred for Kent, and Tom Westley did similar for Essex. While captaining in England I've always felt that the key to bowling is to keep the runs under control. The Dukes ball and English pitches invariably have enough in them to create enough chances, but the question is whether you can prevent the scoreboard from getting out of hand until they arrive.

Our approach differed from this, but I was prepared to trust Michael and Darren, particularly given Darren's vast knowledge from his Yorkshire days. To an extent I suppose we were pushing the gamble button, because in Johnson and Starc we had two guys both capable of bowling a team out in the space of a session if they got it right. Our 'Plan A' was to be tossed out the window anyway when Rhino's battered right knee finally gave out in Essex, leading to a tearful retirement announcement during the game. To lose his skill and discipline before the series started was a massive blow, yet at the same time we didn't help ourselves through an apparent hesitance about playing Sidds. He was tough to face in the nets at Cardiff before the first Test, but never seemed to be in genuine contention.

The toss went Alastair Cook's way, setting us up for a hard task to win on a pitch that was somewhat dry but also two-paced. A lot was made of Hadds dropping Joe Root on the first morning, but the greater failure was our collective inability to go on from a bunch of starts when we batted. Compared to some of the pitches we played on in the latter part of the series, Cardiff was not difficult. And the wickets we lost as guys tried to dominate Moeen Ali's off-spin will always sit uncomfortably with Michael. We had entered the series with the attitude that we'd take him down and bring the quicks back, when in fact we should have been working him around and taking advantage of the loose balls he would invariably bowl. We corrected this approach for Lord's, but by then it had already played a large part in costing us the first Test.

Moeen's wickets were taken either side of my own dismissal, one that I still kick myself about. I'd played well to get into the 90s, but the speed of my scoring meant I almost got there before I realised. I have to admit that I simply got nervous, my heart rate went up and my demons came out. I remember Michael's obvious frustration at the non-striker's end; he knew an opportunity had got away from us on a sunny Welsh afternoon.

We copped a lot of grief after that match, largely to the effect that we couldn't play away from home. It was quite a turnabout from a lot that had been written before the series, and stung quite a few of us to want to prove them wrong. I had more motivation when Steve Waugh joined us before Lord's and told me 'mate, this is your ground, look forward to seeing you own it today'. Sometimes that sort of thing can add to the pressure you're already feeling, but this day it turned out to be true.

The lead-in to Lord's was affected by Hadds' withdrawal from the team because his daughter Mia was ill, but Michael then won the toss to give us first use of a pristine wicket.

Then came one of the great moments – walking through the Lord's Pavilion and out onto the ground to open the batting and take strike on the first morning of an Ashes Test at Lord's. The ground was full to bursting, and the egg-and-bacon ties and jackets were everywhere – the cream of England and the upholders of the game of cricket plus millions more watching prime time TV in Australia were looking on. The atmosphere was so fresh, so expectant, so electric.

One of the curious goals I had set myself but didn't tell too many people during the series was to not be dismissed while the England crowd sang 'Jerusalem'. Often this started just before the first ball of the innings and lasted for only a few deliveries. It was my first checkpoint. Lord's actually doesn't allow the song to be sung, but my first goal was still just to get through the first few balls.

This day I had a nervous moment as Anderson found excessive swing down the renowned Lord's slope – nerves took over and I swung wildly at it only to find a thick outside edge. Fortunately, Root and Ian Bell almost left it for each other and the ball flew away for a boundary. Immediately I decided to change my footwork and hang back so as not to go too hard at a full delivery again. Surprisingly though, Jimmy offered up another inviting fullish delivery and I creamed it through extra cover for four. This was among the best few shots I ever played.

Adam Voges told me later the Aussie blokes were in awe of that shot. Almost behind the bowler's arm, they saw the ball start outside leg stump, swing right across – and then saw me connect outside off stump, right in the middle, sending the ball racing to the boundary when generally most of my drives trickle over it. So that's 0/8 after the first over ... the tone was set.

What followed was one of the best days of my life. Davey squandered a good start, but Steve came to the crease and together we 'booked in'. This was a chance to make it count, and such chances don't come along all that often. Eventually we both were to reach triple figures moments apart. The pride of scoring hundreds at Lord's will last forever.

It took a long time for me to get used to batting at Lord's, with its slope, its practice wickets and other eccentricities, such as the minimal sightscreen in the Members Pavilion. But once I had gotten used to all these things, it became my favourite place to bat in England. You can work out so much about how the ball is going to behave before it is even delivered. A lot of balls are missing the stumps, the slope creates angles for you to work the ball around, and you can score mountains of runs square of the wicket by playing late. My knowledge and Smudger's talent made for a nice dynamic in the middle, and we more or less cruised right through the day to set the game up.

We played so well and so dominated the England attack that the English media condemned the Lord's pitch as far too placid. I can tell you it wasn't – Stuart Broad bowled a couple of really threatening spells. It was mainly that Steve and I both had a day out. An example was getting to my hundred. Jimmy Anderson had left a big gap at mid-on, so I'd decided the next time he pitched up I would flat-bat it through there. On the replay my normally vertical bat-swing has quite a tilt in it in order to manoeuvre the ball towards mid-on. That was a four I will always cherish.

Walking off the pitch that evening compared to any moment I'd had in cricket. This time I was looking straight at the Lord's members, and as I walked up the little rise to the gate, the whole pavilion of orange-and-yellow bedecked members are on their feet clapping. Many of them know me personally from Middlesex, and even though I'm part of the Aussie enemy they treat me as one of their own. And most of them would have remembered my heartbreak of the previous Lord's Test. As the passageway opened and Smudge and I walked through amidst continued clapping, there was Angus Fraser at the foot of the steps waiting to shake my hand.

Half an hour later Angus was to find my folks waiting outside, without the necessary tickets to enter the Pavilion. He simply waved them through. Sitting with them in the change rooms later, all my troubles and worries ebbed away – it was the best day of my cricketing life. From there we piled up a huge score, Smudger went on to a double hundred, and England's batsmen were worried out by the pace of Johnson, Starc and Hazlewood. It was almost as if we were back in Australia.

England, of course, took a tactical turn from there, serving up very grassy wickets and aiming to pick holes in our batting techniques. We had some internal issues around the decision to retain Peter Nevill as wicketkeeper in the third Test and in effect drop Hadds. While you could understand the desire to reward 'Nev' for an excellent debut, Hadds had been a central figure in the team for a long time, and to end his international career in slightly foggy circumstances did not sit right with everyone.

The Edgbaston pitch for the third Test was very green on day one, while also having some pace in it. We perhaps read it wrongly. Two days out, Michael said he'd never seen a pitch like it – there was nine millimetres of grass covering it and it had rained consistently for over a week. We were maybe spooked by the fact that all Test matches in England recently had been won by the team batting first.

Coming back from the inner-ear issue, I scratched out a 50 after we lost the toss, in conditions every bit as challenging as those we would face in Nottingham later on. Steven Finn came into England's team and found the rhythm he can occasionally conjure, bowling quick and moving the ball with bounce. I managed to get one of his deliveries away on the pull shot, before lunch, but after it he steamed in and took the wind out of my sails with a blow to the stomach. As I was gasping for air I thought I heard him exclaim 'Puss!' Finny followed up with a couple of searing bouncers, the ones that made it clear the end was near.

We were out for a mere 136, and once again could not control the scoreboard in conditions that were still very helpful for bowlers. Birmingham's crowd is the most vocal in England, and when we batted again it felt more cauldron than cricket ground when Finn bowled another very hostile spell to dismantle our second innings. They rounded on Mitch Johnson when we came out to defend a meagre target, giving him absolutely no respite throughout. While he smiled and played along for a while, you could tell it was wearing on him, even in the moment when he tried something different by bowling a ball from behind the umpire. I could feel him starting to think about retirement as well.

Broad got me lbw twice in this match from around the wicket, working on what he'd seen in Cardiff. Our battle was getting increasingly desperate for me, because I felt we both knew what the plan was – and that I wasn't equipped to deal with it. I spent a lot of my time leading into the fourth Test trying to figure out a way to cover his movement from around the wicket, straightening the ball to find or beat my outside edge. As a team our confidence had now taken a couple of blows. Lots of things were mounting up, from our unbalanced bowling attack and malfunctioning top order to the manner of Hadds' exit.

I twice had dinner with Hadds in Nottingham before the fourth Test. The first night he was very good about it all, saying he accepted they'd gone with Nev; that was the selectors call and that's fine. He admitted to being a bit frustrated with how it had happened, but stated that he didn't want to get in the way of the team's focus on winning the Ashes. When we dined again a couple of nights later, his mood had changed. Mia was again not in the best of health, and he asked what he should do. I just said, 'Go home, see your family, you know how important they are.' He went home after the fourth Test, ending an unhappy tour.

The Trent Bridge Test will forever be held up as one of Australia's worst cricketing disasters. And who started the ball rolling? Yours truly. One factor that is rarely mentioned is that we were playing on a newly laid pitch. A year previously, this particular strip of pitch had produced one of the most boring games of Test cricket ever – hardly a wicket fell over five days. So the decision was made to dig it up. (That strip, I'm told, happens to be the only one that the TV cameras can get right behind on top of the old, quaint and quite tiny Trent Bridge pavilion.) Not only had the pitch never been played on, there was more than seven millimetres of grass left on the pitch, as apparently decreed by the ECB.

What we needed at Trent Bridge was to win the toss and bowl, on a morning when a sprinkling of rain just added a bit of extra spice to the wicket in the half hour before play. As the scoreboard shows, we lost, and then just kept on losing! Anderson was out injured, and I faced up to Broad in the first over. For the series I had developed two trigger movements, one forward and one back, to deal with different bowling, often within the same innings. At Edgbaston I'd being going back to Broad and I felt that contributed to my two dismissals, so for Trent Bridge I decided to concentrate on getting forward to try to smother his swing and seam, a bit like covering a spinner's turn on a helpful pitch. Second ball I moved forward to do just that, and thought I had it covered. To my horror, I didn't hear the gentle thud of ball onto a defensive bat, but a sharper snick to Cook. I left the crease thinking 'What the hell happened there?' That sensation would run through the rest of the team.

There was plenty of analysis afterwards saying we were pushing too hard at the ball, but I can honestly say as someone who'd played a lot in England, I was trying to smother away movement I knew to be there. As Broad had got me lbw with a similar ball at Birmingham, I knew I couldn't just let these balls go. Sitting back in the dressing room and watching the carnage that followed, it genuinely felt like there was a wicket every ball. I had my head down, but I could hear appeal, after appeal, after appeal. It was extraordinary. If anyone needs reminding, we were out for 60. What's more, we all knew it meant the end of the series, and a few careers, in the most humiliating circumstances possible.

Broad was simply unplayable. He took five wickets in just 19 balls. Four deliveries went down leg side, there was one inside-edge and two were left outside of off stump. So 12 times our batsman played at his deliveries, seven times safely and five times we got nicks – almost 50 per cent.

In the time since, I've tried to figure out why things happened so dramatically, and I tend to think it was through a combination of leaping tennis-ball bounce at a pace where it was impossible to adjust – probably as a result of the extra moisture on the top from that rain. What was noticeable was that all the catches floated to the slips, who had lots of time to see them – even the one Stokes caught diving to his right. Clearly that means the ball had gripped on the pitch, deviated and then popped, to hit higher on the bat than expected. Tough conditions.

More definitive was the way we copped it from all angles afterwards. The worst piece I can remember was one by

News Limited columnist Rebecca Wilson, who essentially questioned us as blokes for getting out in that way. Yes, we were humiliated and yes, we could have planned better, but to have our humanity and character called into question – for issues largely of conditions and technique – was a bit much. It's a bit hard to show fighting spirit when you are never really in – I survived just two balls before being dismissed, Davey Warner one delivery, Steve Smith two, Shaun Marsh and Adam Voges three each. It's not like missing a mark early on in Aussie rules where you've got two hours to go. Or if you are aced in tennis first up, you've got a set or more to go. Once out in cricket, you are gone. No amount of fighting spirit or character will make any difference.

When Michael announced his retirement at the end of the game, *The Courier Mail* ran a front-page headline 'Loner to Loser', while having a bit each way on the back page of the same paper with the heading 'One of Our Greats'. I had to shake my head at that one. One of the effects this had on the guys was to cause them to retreat into their shells, and lose the gregariousness and goodwill that had carried us through a lot of the previous two years. One thing we had to acknowledge was that we had not adjusted well, mentally or technically, to the task in the second half of the series.

The scale of our defeat was shown by a few of the scenes in Northampton, where we had a tour match scheduled before the last Test at The Oval. Darren had told Michael to head straight to London and relax, while Hadds was on his way home to see his family. Josh was told he would be rested for The Oval, and I spent some time with Shaun Marsh after he asked me about finding the right technique for England – not that I felt in total command after Nottingham. Mitch Johnson and I also had some time off in London, but first we were part of a meeting in the middle of the outfield at the Northamptonshire County ground.

Sensing some lingering discontent over what had happened with Hadds, and also the composition of the team for Trent Bridge – Mitchell Marsh dropped for brother Shaun on match morning, Sidds left out again – Darren and Rod Marsh had a heart-to-heart with us. Essentially, Rod's message was 'like you guys, we're doing everything to the best of our ability. If we don't get it right we apologise, but we're trying just as hard as you'. In a way that was a good message to hear, because selection is a very difficult job that wins few plaudits from anyone. To hear how hard they were taking the defeat was a useful reminder that these guys weren't just toying with us.

All that was left was a final match at The Oval, which we wanted to win to farewell Michael, and also to give a far better account of ourselves than we had at Nottingham. England again had a grassy pitch prepared, and Pup lost the toss, but the combination of some smarter batting and a little less movement for the bowlers allowed Davey and I to get through the initial period that had so damaged us in the previous two Tests. The message to everyone had been to get out there and fight – a bit like a Justin Langer address – and I think that helped alter our mindset enough to do better. It didn't matter that we only had 19 on the board after the first 14 overs, the runs would come later, and they did.

My final innings had a few fitting aspects to it. I made 43, near enough to my Test average. I passed 2000 runs in Tests, ending on 2015, the year I retired. And I faced exactly 100 balls, a mark I always liked to reach as an opening batsman, because it meant that you'd done your job of seeing off the new ball and easing the path for the guys behind you. A last stand of 110 with Davey allowed Smudger and Vogesy to take advantage, and we rolled on to an innings victory, hollow as it inevitably felt for us. I wasn't keen for any sort of fanfare around my retirement, particularly next to Michael given the length of his career relative to mine, and was happy for him to get the full farewell treatment from England while I hung back.

For so much of our careers we were in vastly different orbits. One year I remember Victoria receiving a presentation from the Australian Cricketers Association, and among the 'wins' they spoke to us about was that the Australian captain's salary would go up by a significant amount as a result of him becoming a selector. I was at that stage on a minimum contract with the Bushrangers, and Michael's increase was about 10 times my entire salary from state cricket. As a bit of a joke I put up my hand and said, 'I'll be happy to be a selector for that money!' to laughter all round.

Michael was another person I had had little to do with until 2013. When I joined the side I could see that Michael, having led a very young side to obliteration in India, realised he needed some more senior players around him, to share the burdens of performance and leadership. Not only would this ease the pressure on him, but it would also give the younger guys in the squad a few more examples to follow. Anyone who has spent time playing alongside Michael has seen the intensity of his focus and his enormous capacity for hard work. It's not for everyone, and I think Michael and the side were feeling it by the time I arrived.

It had to help that I was arriving more or less free of any agendas, merely having the desire to do well. I hadn't been in India when things got so out of hand, and I also hadn't played for any length of time under Michael's predecessor, Ricky Ponting. Equally at my age I had absolutely no captaincy ambitions and was happy to help the team out in whatever way I could. This isn't to say I wasn't trying to assess how good he was up close, as I did with most guys I played under. Tactically I believe he was the best captain I had, particularly in terms of knowing how to win in Australia, and how to drive a game forward once you'd made a solid start. If I thought at times he over-attacked away from home, I could also see he was trying to push the team forward, and that's no bad thing.

Having said that, captains will also be aware that at times it is possible to feel a bit lost in it all. You can bluff your way through some of these passages – what did Richie Benaud say about captaincy being 90 per cent luck and 10 per cent skill? – but you might actually be hoping privately for someone to come up and offer a suggestion or two. I certainly got the sense that he was grateful for what I could offer. Michael joined us for the night out in at Bushwackers in Worcester and we enjoyed each other's company there, and over the course of the series he was happy to use quite a few of my suggestions for fields and other things. On one level that was surprising for such a tactical master, but it was a hallmark that in the middle he was always open to suggestions to pose a different question to the batsmen

A couple of times in 2013 he waked out to join me in a cricket cauldron. When Steven Finn was on a hat-trick at Trent Bridge then beat Pup's outside edge and off stump by a whisker, the roar was the loudest noise I'd ever heard. We walked down the wicket to each other with big smiles on our faces along the lines of 'welcome to the Ashes'. In Manchester, he came out after Usman's terrible caught behind decision and was clearly in a bit of shock at events. I had been batting in my happy zone, scoring freely, but I could see how distracted he was, looking at the umpires even as he was talking to me. All I could do was say 'Michael, look, we've got to get through this and get to lunch'. He snapped out of it and went on to make a terrific hundred, but at times we all need someone in our corner like that.

Over the years Michael has had more than his share of critics, and many have pointed to him being a selector as the wrong thing for Australian cricket. Some months after the series I heard from one quarter that he had wanted Hughesy to replace me for the 2014–15 India series, with the undertone that 'this guy doesn't want you in the side'. Many guys may have been wary upon hearing that, but after some thinking time I actually concluded I didn't have a problem with it. As long as a captain treats me well when I'm in the side, I can't have a problem if he has thoughts about going another way outside matches. Whenever we played together, he was nothing short of excellent to me.

While we weren't going to be taking the Ashes home, I was proud to be given Australia's player of the series award, chosen by England's coach Trevor Bayliss. It was an honour walking up onto the presentation dais to accept the award and say a few words. England had long been a second home for me and I wanted to show my appreciation. The crowd gave me a warm round of applause, and once again it seemed as if they were happy for me to be the only Australian to do well – so long as England won.

I had set myself for a big series, pretty much knowing it was going to be my last one, and to play as well as I had in any of my other Test encounters was a source of some satisfaction. This meant I was leaving the international game with a sense that I had got the best out of myself, even if 25 Tests was nothing next to the likes of Michael, Hadds, Watto, Rhino or Mitch, who were all retired, retiring or soon to do so.

The actual moment when I let the team know the end had come was a few days before The Oval Test, when I met them at the Royal Garden Hotel in Kensington after they got back from Northampton. The first guy I spoke to was Darren, who had been with me the whole of the way from his appointment two years before. We met across the road at The Goat pub for a beer, and I kicked things off with the words, 'Mate that's it for me, I'm done.' I was interested in what Boof's response would be, wondering whether he would say that because we were losing so many guys I might like to hang around. My mind was made up, but I was still curious. He just smiled and said, 'Well done mate.' Fair enough too.

CHAPTER 16

THE TECHNICAL GAME

MORE THAN ANY other bowler, Graeme Swann was Chris Rogers' nemesis. A method honed to deal with the new ball had something of a blind spot when it came to spin bowling. Partly, this was due to an upbringing on the hard, spin-impervious pitches of Western Australia, but even after a stint at Northamptonshire, Chris's commitment to solid defence while sweating on the bad ball met the stiffest challenge from Swann. By the time they met in the 2013 Ashes series, Swann was established as the world's pre-eminent spin bowler, combining sharp spin, canny variation and relentless accuracy. He tells how he went about tackling Chris:

'How it worked for us was that it was mainly the seamers who get plied with stats on how and where to bowl, where he normally gets out, if you bowl here this is how he plays. For me I'd just be asked "what do you want", and I used to look for three things. Whether a guy swept, whether a guy used his feet, and whether a guy looked to play you through straight

midwicket. They were the ones I looked for. As soon as I know that, then I sit down and think "right, how am I going to bowl at him". But with Buck it wasn't until we were actually playing in the [2013] Tests that I was learning on the go, because I certainly hadn't played against him when I was at a level when I knew where the ball was going all the time. I'd played against him years before when it was pot luck. I was always trying to get him to play across his front pad, because he defended, defended, defended. I'd bowl from wide of the stumps and drift It In, and like at Lord's either pitch just outside the stumps and come in on the inside edge for an lbw, or turn and go to slip. Otherwise I'd go slightly fuller and try to get him to hit to straight midwicket, which is a very hard shot to play on a turning pitch as they all were. He missed a straight one at Old Trafford, but he was a dogged bastard to bowl at.'

Chris endured the indignity of missing a high Swann full-toss at Lord's to be lbw, and in the second innings left an off-break that ran down the hill to hit off stump. Swann reckoned these to be mental, not technical, lapses.

'It was a massive Test match and we were playing some brilliant cricket at the time, and it was a ground I love bowling at, especially to lefties with that Nursery End, because one will run down the hill that you don't even expect to, and one will turn. I loved bowling at left-handers anyway because I always felt I'd get them out, and with that slope especially, I'd bowl there all year if they let me. Weirdly, that full toss I got him with at Lord's is still the worst bit of cricket that's ever been witnessed in the

Ashes, going back to 1880 or whenever – I mean it's horrific, dreadful ball, dreadful shot, dreadful decision, dreadful decision not to review, everything. That ball felt perfect out of my hand [but] I started getting trouble with feeling in my fingers, and during that game I got five in the first innings and genuinely say I was lucky.'

Even after that pair of dismissals, there was no sense among England's bowlers that they had Chris worked out. Fluent runs in the third Test at Old Trafford heightened the feeling, and led to a memorable duel over two innings in the next encounter at Durham.

'We had such good seamers in Jimmy and Broady with the new ball that every plan we had for all the Aussie batsmen was working an absolute charm. We knew exactly where to bowl early on, or after 40 overs with reverse we were getting them out. But with Buck our plans weren't working. So it was "Swanny you go after him, you go well against lefties, you go". It was a real battle. He was good for me as a bowler because he knew his limitations, you knew his limitations, but he wouldn't stray from it … He was so dogmatic in his approach and how he batted. He was a bloody hard bugger to shift.

'One thing that stands out to me from that whole Ashes was the Durham Test. Our bog standard plan [for the seamers] wasn't working because he was leaving the ball so well, and if he did nick it he plays with such good soft hands that it was going down. You can either say "God how lucky's this guy", which bowlers do, but when it's happening time and time again "well actually he knows what he's doing here".

'If you bowled 10 good balls to one of the other guys they'd try to come down the wicket or go at one hard. Whereas Buck wouldn't do that, he'd just sit and be patient. At Durham I was trying to get him to sweep it, and I kept saying "why don't you just sweep it, I've got no one out" because I knew he wasn't comfortable sweeping, and in the end he did. He just thought "sod this I'm going to do it" and he crunched it for four [to bring up his maiden Test century]. I remember thinking through gritted teeth "why did I say that for"...

'Because he was that bit older, and he hasn't got that arrogance or punchiness about him, just a good bloke who plays cricket, I really loved battling against him. He almost felt like one of ours because he'd played so much in England.

'In a weird way, you want to win the game, but you think if any of them are going to do it, I hope it's him rather than that other left-hander ... When he was batting you never begrudged him scoring runs. You wanted him to get out and you wanted England to be doing well, but it didn't hurt quite so much when he was doing well as opposed to some of the others, put it that way. To me he was the standout player in those Ashes series.'

I FACED SHAUN Tait in his first game for South Australia and I was his first wicket. He was fast and terrifying, with a muscular, awkward action that gave you a late sight of the ball. For a while I really struggled to face him, and he got me out six times in a row. But Shaun was a good lesson in terms of persistence and also problem-solving – once I figured out how to deal with him, he never dismissed me again.

The key to dealing with Shaun was to know that he basically only had three balls: one sliding across you on a length, a bouncer and an inswinging yorker. It was thus vital to be watching for the yorker, and to almost play French cricket so your front pad didn't get in the way of your bat. In response to Shaun's three balls, I had three shots: a square cut, a whip off the pads through square and a defensive block. He would bowl so quickly that sometimes the block was an effective scoring shot down the ground, but it definitely wasn't a drive.

How I learned to deal with Shaun was a good example of the way I looked at technique. It wasn't simply a case of finding your own method and sticking to it through thick and thin – I've never liked hearing a guy who gets out cheaply saying 'I was just playing my natural game'. Instead, I would constantly tinker with the way I batted, factoring in opponents, conditions and my own evolving skills. Equally, I looked closely at how the technical and the mental fed into one another: how guys who could play every shot in the book and look beautifully tight in defence were averaging in the mid-30s while my ugly 'cut and paste' method was allied to mental discipline and shot selection.

My tinkering ways started in the backyard. As a kid, Dad used to coach me by overloading me with information and leaving me to find what worked. To this day, I want to hear feedback from coaches and teammates, running through numerous options for how I could make adjustments here and there. Having listened to all that, I enjoy trying the possibilities and then narrowing it down to what I think will work best. That process didn't just take place in the nets. I can recall countless times when I would experiment with different methods within matches and innings, usually in an effort to feel comfortable because my previous set-up didn't sit right on the day.

As a young batsman, there can be days when you pick up the bat and it feels very natural in your hands. But on others you do the same and you may as well have tried to close your hands around a railway sleeper, so alien it can feel. Those days were always a cue for me to change it up, whether I'd adjust my grip on the bat, open or close my stance, raise my bat or keep it down. Most coaching manuals these days argue against this sort of thing, but I strongly believe that learning from mistakes and getting comfortable with making adjustments here and there are key factors in being a successful batsman. How do you know you have got the best approach unless you've exhausted the other options?

It wasn't until I got to Northamptonshire in 2006 that my technique settled down into something resembling what I used in Test matches. That year I struggled badly in the first part of the season, before being called up for Australia A duty in north Queensland and the Northern Territory. While it was a largely frustrating trip because I played very little cricket relative to the time I spent away from England, there was that clarifying conversation with selector David Boon that I mentioned earlier. 'Buck,' he told me, 'we look at you as someone who bats all day.' After that I made a couple of ugly half centuries for Australia A, but Boon's words meant I was less concerned with how I looked.

On my return to Northampton, I spent quite a lot of time with Lance Klusener. For most cricket followers, he's remembered as the axe-wielding all-rounder who bludgeoned his way to be the man of the tournament at the 1999 World Cup. But later in his career he completely reinvented himself as a thoughtful batsman, and in three years at Northants he made 3359 runs at 61.07, including 10 of his 21 first-class hundreds. A lot of our work together focused on spin, because the pitch at Northampton tended to favour spin, and also due to the fact that like me, Lance was both left-handed and hesitant about playing the sweep shot.

His method was all based around finding a defensive technique sturdy enough to wait until a spinner bowled a bad ball, without having to resort to a risky dance down the wicket or slog over the top to release the pressure. That made a lot of sense to me, not only against spin but against any bowler. Particularly as an opener, you've got to be able to work through the difficult passages to be there when the bad ball inevitably comes. 'Buck,' he said, 'no point being in the change room.'

That struck a chord with me and from then on I tried to grind out the spinners and make them get me out, as opposed to me finding a way to give them my wicket. Lance's release against the off spin going away from the left-hander was to roll the ball two pitches square of the wicket on either side and get off strike with a quick single. That tactic was one I adopted and would frustrate the bowler who wanted to build pressure on me. I have no doubt these lessons helped me enormously in my duels with Graeme Swann in the Ashes series during my Test career. Even though it constantly looked like I was losing the battle, I felt confident enough I had a defence and some sort of game plan against him.

Swann gave me very little peace in all the times he bowled to me. In part this was due to the fact that I'm neither strong enough nor nimble enough on my feet to dance down the wicket and hit over the top. Against a quality spinner that is vital, because you need to be able to push back fielders to create gaps for singles. Otherwise you can be tied down, because the loose ball isn't around the corner when a spinner is in command of his game. Swann would bowl good ball after good ball, pitching on the stumps from around the wicket and either hitting them or spinning sharply. That made the sweep shot dangerous, and nor was the cut shot particularly available.

About the only shot I could see regularly scoring with against Swann was driving him down the ground or through cover, but as I said I didn't have the strength or inclination to get down the pitch. I would watch David Warner play those shots numerous times against those same balls, and I know Huss was able to also. But for me it was a case of sitting back and admiring them while not letting myself think I could do the same. That left me simply trying to survive, waiting for the bad ball as Lance had counselled. Swann ensured I would be waiting a long time, and as each match went on he knew that he could just bowl at me without fear of being hit over his head.

This isn't to say I avoided trying to find ways of scoring. In between the dual Ashes series I did some work with

Dean Jones about getting down the pitch more often. But to have the courage to do that in a Test match is really hard, especially when your role in the side is to be the 'bat all day' opener. I have a vivid memory of watching the first Test in India in 2013 on TV, and seeing Ed Cowan run down the pitch to hit Ravi Ashwin for six. Trying it again soon after, he got nowhere near a higher, shorter ball from Ashwin and was stumped by miles. At the time I thought 'that's not your game', and had a similar feeling when it was me out there. Other guys in the order could go after Swann with success, so long as I sold my wicket dearly and wore the bowlers down.

One reason I was hesitant to get down the wicket was a sense that I wasn't always the greatest reader of a spinner's length. There were balls that I thought were short and ripe for the cut, but turned out to be flatter arm balls that skidded on in the direction of the stumps. As a younger player I was out a few times trying to pull a spinner and being hit on the back pad in front of the stumps. After that occurs a few times you lose your courage to take the risk. Shane Watson was someone who I'd see pull the spinners off the stumps and I'd admire the audacity of the shot. Ultimately I think my relative timidity against spin was drawn from an upbringing at the WACA Ground. You'd almost never see much in the way of rough, you could play against the spin with impunity, and so your tools to tackle a turning ball were affected. It wasn't until I went to Northampton and its spinning surface that I started to think more deeply about how to play spin, helped along by the wise guidance of Lance.

In my own way I worked out how to stop playing against the spin, trying to hit off-spinners towards cover, and working left-arm spinners through the leg side with my pads behind me as a second line of defence. I developed my own game, but never with the conviction or range to be able to take on the very best spin bowlers. That was to be exposed by Swann and also by Yasir Shah and Zulfiqar Babar in the UAE against Pakistan. Where Lance and I decided to wait for the bad ball, we were fine at first-class level for the most part, but the best spin bowlers in Tests don't give you that leeway.

Funnily enough, it was actually Shane Warne who encouraged me to keep going down that path. Shane was bowling for Victoria when I made my 279 for WA in 2006 on a flat deck in Perth. After the innings he offered a kind word about it in the lunch room, and in reply I asked him about talking a bit more after the game. In the rooms a couple of days later, he called me over to chat, and very generously answered my questions.

'Do you think I handled you ok?'

'Good mate. If that's your game, just be patient and don't get out.'

Simple stuff maybe, but with that I had confirmation that I'd found the right game for me, even though it wasn't the usual Australian method for handling spin.

The other thing I took from Lance was how he set up. His front foot pointed towards the bowler, something I also noticed about Sachin Tendulkar whenever he drove the ball. Because I'm bow-legged and almost pigeon-toed, I could find it difficult to turn my hips and get my foot down the wicket.

Often I would shape to drive and my front foot would be headed towards point, which makes it difficult to bend your knee down the line of the ball and create the right shape for the shot.

It took a while for Lance's style to feel right, but once it did I enjoyed the most fruitful period of my life, in which I averaged over 80 for almost a year. When Lance and I spoke about it, he asked me where I wanted my feet to be when I hit the ball. When I said down the wicket, he said 'why don't you just start with your feet in that position?' That also made a lot of sense, because it was working backwards from my finishing position to where I would be when the bowler delivered. It also served to simplify my movement – why worry about how to get into that position when I could already be there, waiting, and giving myself so much more time to actually play the shot?

This conversation grew in part out of the work I'd already done with Paul Nixon before my double hundred against the Australians in 2005, getting my weight and head moving towards mid-on or at least straight down the pitch, rather than across the crease. Opening up my front foot in order to be able to get my weight moving straight through my front knee was a natural extension of that, and the two ideas have been at the forefront of my way of dealing with new-ball bowlers ever since. I know it's far from the most aesthetically pleasing technique, but it worked for me, and got me making a nice straight line back down the wicket to meet the bowler. Most of that came from Lance and Paul.

Another element of my game was learning to play the ball late, something derived in large part from watching Justin

Langer at close quarters. If a fast bowler got too straight, he'd let the ball travel all the way under his eyes before rolling it down to fine leg. When they angled it across him, he would seldom fail to get the ball down to third man along the ground, meaning a cheap boundary or at the very least an easy single. Countless bowlers, captains and slip fielders would get frustrated by this and rant about how lucky he was, but it was all very deliberate, and something I picked up on.

Once again, this worked nicely in concert with another idea, this time from Dad. We talked a lot about swing patterns, and his belief that you should always finish a shot with your hands high, almost as though you've rolled the ball down the face of the bat. I've seen so many batsmen who virtually jab at the ball rather than stroking it, which only serves to give the ball momentum. What that tends to mean is that if the ball moves and catches the edge, it's going to fly at catchable height, as it did too often during the 2015 Ashes series.

By contrast, if your hands are finishing high, it should follow logically that the ball will be going down – far less likely to offer a catch. Interestingly given our earlier conversation, high hands at the finish was something I noticed about David Boon when he was such a reliable top order batsman for Australia. Add to that some softer hands and an angled bat, a sort of a delayed use of your wrists, and the chance of an airy edge is greatly reduced. This was what I spoke about quite extensively with Shaun Marsh after the Trent Bridge Test of that 2015 Ashes series, and something he used to good effect to help Australia win the first day/night Test against New Zealand later that same year.

The best way I found to develop those soft, high hands was lots of throw-downs with tennis balls, where I taught myself to play with a slower motion through the ball and make softer contact. Otherwise the balls would fly in the air and not into the ground. Part of this stemmed from knowing that I didn't have the power to muscle my way out of tough situations, or 'put the pressure back on the bowler' as it is often referred to. Instead I needed to find ways to get through those spells via defence and thinking. Now every batsman is going to hear the phrase 'use soft hands' a heap of times as they're growing up, but it's not as easy as saying it. The adrenaline pumping through you in the middle is such that you see so many guys trying to hit the cover off the ball, when what you should be doing is starting softly and moving up through the gears.

At Victoria, Greg Shipperd would talk a lot about the three paces of batting. Your first 15 to 20 runs should be about getting in tight with your defence, being solid and taking few risks. Next you should be trying to work the ball around more, finding gaps in the field and working the strike over. Get through that phase and then you can expand your game and hit the boundaries. That message resonated with me because it spoke to finding a mentality where you focused first on defence, then accumulation, and then attack. As an opener in particular you need a defence you can rely on, and it is often dangerous to be thinking about going after the bowlers early.

Over the course of the Test matches I played, a few duels stick in the mind. For England, James Anderson and Stuart

Broad posed very tough and different questions, before Swann followed them up with off spin of the highest class. Against South Africa, Dale Steyn and Morne Morkel also offered sharp contrasts, high skills and a considerable intimidation factor. I'll break down what I was trying to do against each bowler, and how I adjusted my methods depending upon what they were offering up.

Anderson's skill levels were outstanding, and as a classical new-ball swing and seam bowler he was in many ways the ideal test of an opening batsman. As mentioned before, a lot of my technical base was built up around how to combat the early movement of the ball, and making sure I didn't get tangled into a position where I was playing around a planted front foot and susceptible to lbw. Against Anderson, I actually found that his technical perfection worked in my favour. Because he got the seam in great position almost every time, I had a relatively good idea of which way it was going to swing. Other clues included whether his action was getting a little more side-on (inswing to the left-hander) or front-on (away swing). A lot has been made of his 'wobble ball' with a splayed seam, but he only very occasionally used that against me.

That being said, a swinging ball is still an enormous challenge, and if your technique isn't shaped the right way to cope it will only be a matter of time before Anderson gets you, particularly as he can move it both ways. This was another area where I was able to find a bit of an edge, because my positioning was neutral enough to be able to cope with both. A lot of batsmen with more attractive techniques than me will be nicely set-up to handle inswing, or outswing, but not many are able to handle both. A bit like when dealing with reverse swing, it's vital that you shorten your stride moving forward and be prepared for the ball to go either way.

If you show Anderson a desire to commit early, he will be all over you, using whatever combination he thinks best to set you up for the wicket ball. Most often he would drag guys across the crease with away swing before an inswinger or cutter would seek the stumps. To tackle that, I would hang back, watch the ball extremely closely and just try to play it as late as I could. I'll be the first to admit that this doesn't look pretty, but it worked for me. After Anderson got me twice in the Trent Bridge Test in 2013, he only dismissed me once more in the remaining 12 matches we played against each other.

In contrast, I found Broad to be more difficult as our Ashes battles went on. Where Anderson was highly consistent, Broad could have days and spells where it just wasn't working for him. Lacking rhythm, he would either float the ball up to the bat or drop short and I would feel I could get him. But on other days he would just be so good, finding the most awkward length and line that made the most of his height and pace. In addition to this, he worked out in the 2015 series that he was most dangerous to me when going around the wicket and moving the ball away from me through the air. That was extremely challenging, and required me to find another technical way to counter him. Essentially I found myself going back and playing as late as I could, and if the ball moved away I would simply hope to miss it while covering my pads and stumps.

That realisation hit me after the first over of the Trent Bridge Test, when I walked out thinking my best method was to get forward as much as possible and try to cover the movement. But with the help of some tennis ball bounce from a fresh pitch, Broad got enough movement to find the edge. At the time, as I have said, I genuinely thought I had it covered, played it perfectly and was surprised to hear the snick and be caught behind. Replays made it look as though I was pushing out in front of myself, but this was a product of my desire to try to get to the ball before it moved too far – a bit like trying to get to a spinner before the ball turns too far. So for the final Test at The Oval I elected to go back, and played him more effectively. The series was gone by then of course.

Overall, Broad at his best was as difficult as any bowler I faced. The other thing he could do quite often was seam the ball in the opposite direction to the way it was swinging. Get that right and it is next to impossible to deal with, no matter what technical preparation you've made.

At times I felt similarly helpless facing up to Morne Morkel in South Africa. Because he is so tall his trajectory was unlike just about anyone else I faced. A lot of bowlers around the world are tall, but because they have a long bowling stride the ball isn't actually leaving their hand at too great a height. Morkel on the other hand delivered at close to his full height. In the 2014 Centurion Test, he struck me on the shoulder from a delivery that I tried to duck. Still smarting from the blow, I tried to stand up and ride the bounce of a similar delivery next ball, and gloved it to backward short-leg. That worried me, because I felt as though neither option worked.

However after that initial experience, I figured out that every dangerous ball from him was going to be somewhere between my stomach and my head. My response was to stand as tall as I could at the crease with my hands up high, almost as though I was setting up like a baseball hitter. I didn't want my hands coming up to meet the ball, reasoning that this could only increase the risk of a glove popping up to short-leg or slips. Instead I wanted my hands up as high as I could, so I could be coming down on the ball. That worked better for me, as I made runs in the second and third Tests, albeit on pitches that didn't offer quite the same level of bounce.

During that series I felt Dale Steyn was a little way short of his peak, certainly at Centurion. He bowled some brilliant spells of reverse swing in Port Elizabeth, but his pace was not as slippery as I'd perhaps expected. Additionally he has always tended to bowl quite full, and with my technique based on tackling a swinging ball I was more comfortable dealing with that. Nevertheless, he still had the ability of a great bowler, specifically the knack of producing a brilliant, wicket-taking ball out of nowhere. You might be cruising along, thinking yourself to be in control, and all of a sudden he'd conjure a ball slightly faster or moving more than the rest, and even if it didn't dismiss you, the dynamics would change.

One of the underlying points I think all this demonstrates is that there is no *one* technique that works, no single approach superior to all the rest. I disagree, for instance, with the recent view that all batsmen should be tapping the bat before delivery. Batting is about figuring out a way that works best for you, whether it is standing up like Joe Root, Jonny

Bairstow, AB de Villiers or Mike Hussey, or tapping the bat like Mark Waugh. It is a matter of personal preference, and then you work out all the other components of your game from there.

That applies as much to the decisions you make as to the way you equip yourself. A batsman is often described as making a technical or shot selection error, but to me they are one and the same. When I hear someone has a good technique because they can hit a pretty cover drive, I maintain that any player who tries that pretty cover drive against a good length ball that's nipping away is more than likely to nick it. To me, the best players are where they are because they'll choose to leave those balls, and use their cover drive, whether it be pretty or ugly, when it's there's to hit. That's as much technique as the shape of the shot itself.

A lot of the guys I competed with as a younger player looked great when they were going well. They'd make a hundred and coaches, selectors and media would fawn over them, saying how great they could be. But that same player would then get out cheaply in innings that followed and find himself under pressure. To get out of that they'd conjure another hundred, and the same judges would exclaim 'oh he's worked it out now, watch him go', only for the pattern to repeat. To me a key to averaging 50 isn't making lots of hundreds, but fighting it out on the days when you're not in good rhythm. It might mean the difference between making five and 25, and helping your team. A lot of coaches and observers will criticise the batsman who makes a start and gets out. But if that player has actually fought it out for a couple of hours despite his own lack of touch, he's in turn made life easier for the next man.

Let me say, never would I try to model a player's technique completely on mine. For one thing, I've seen a couple of youngsters who look like they've done this, and I've never seen anything uglier. However I do believe that a lot of the individual parts of my game can work for others, as they've been picked up along the way through the lessons of experience. Find out what your strengths and scoring areas are, and then build a technique around that.

CHAPTER 17

TEAMMATES AND COACHES

SAM ROBSON IS 11 years younger than Chris, which qualifies as a generation gap in a cricket dressing room, yet they have a relationship that runs deep, starting with their fathers, who played together in similar circumstances. When John Rogers moved to the University of New South Wales grade club he was already a player of some note and experience, having played for NSW in addition to many years with St George. It was there he met Jim Robson, 13 years his junior and eager to learn. The pair struck up a friendship based upon the older man's tutelage, and remain close to this day.

Sam was similarly youthful when Chris arrived at Middlesex in 2011, having worked his way into the first team after making the move from Sydney in 2008. He had played Under 19s for Australia and has now played seven Tests for England. Thanks to their fathers' friendship, Sam already knew John Rogers, and that connection helped as the pair found themselves cast as opening partners for Middlesex, and neighbours in West Hampstead. Just as Robson was looking for a mentor, so was Chris seeking friends in a new city. As Sam tells it:

'On the field he trained hard and he was all about saying you switch on and focus when you're there to train or to play. But he also focused on living in a good nearby location in West Hampstead, getting everyone to socialise together after games and making a point of celebrating success. If you won he was a big one for everyone getting out together and enjoying the good moments. Similarly when there were individual milestones he wanted everyone to acknowledge that. So he brought the guys together.

'A lot of that stemmed from the fact he liked going out himself, and that suited him, but it actually was what we needed as well.

'It helped as well that he liked talking about cricket. So even when we were away from the game, at dinner or socialising we'd talk about the game. For some of the young blokes at Middlesex that was big, hearing him talk about players he played with and against, some of the great Australian or English players, talking about when he did well or what he picked up from them. It seems like an obvious thing within a team to talk about the game together, but it doesn't always happen naturally. Someone's got to get it rolling.'

Robson and Rogers contrasted, being right and left-handed, young and not so young, but they shared a desire to defend their wicket and a willingness to tough it out against the new ball. Both men had set themselves up as first-class players, lacking the desire to mutate their games for Twenty20. And when Sam was selected for England, he could tap into Chris's experience.

'As a batter he looks at things quite technically. The other thing was that as batting has got more aggressive through T20 and other factors, you hear coaches and players say "it's all about looking to score, all about being aggressive and positive and taking it to the bowlers". But Chris came from the other direction. He said to me one day "basically batting is about not getting out". If you say that in the wrong environment now, it could be perceived as being negative thinking. But it was refreshing to hear that and be secure in the idea that I could base my game around staying at the crease. He reassured me that it still worked.

'Something that was very impressive about him then and in 2012 in particular, was that … he still had the determination to succeed, and went out there each day with a focus and a desire to do the very best he could for the team. To churn out a hundred at Derby when no one was watching, or at an out ground in Uxbridge in front of 500 people. He set high standards and kept living up to them even when it didn't look like he'd play Test cricket again. It showed great professionalism and hunger for the game and I think that rubbed off on the rest of us. He had a good impact on us because we saw a professional cricketer who'd played for 15 years, scored all these runs, played Test cricket, but even then he was working on his game and fiddling around to try to get himself in the best position for *that next innings. Also it stood out how much as an overseas player he cared not only about his own performance but also the team. Buck really wanted the team to do well, to celebrate when we did win but also at the end of a bad day to be gutted and take it like someone who had always been at Middlesex.*

'He rarely had really poor games either. Of course there would be games where he didn't get hundreds, but there were very few where he'd not get at least a start in either innings. A big mantra of his was even if you're not at your best, get stuck in and make some sort of contribution, whether it be 17 and 24 or whatever it was.

'He'd experienced it [Test cricket] in Ashes series, so he could talk to me about the pressure and all that goes with playing at international level – it is very different to first-class level. At times you might be playing the same bowlers or the same grounds, but all the other stimuli and things going on around it are different. He's the sort of guy who even now whether you have a good week or a bad week he'll be in touch.'

I'VE ALWAYS ADMIRED those players who have been one-club, one-state cricketers. There are numerous players like that in Australia, where the geography dictates that a professional cricketer can't just quit and go work for someone else just around the corner. England, with three times as many professional domestic teams in one-sixtieth the space, is a different matter.

As a teammate of Marcus Trescothick in 2016, I was in awe of him and his steadfast attachment to Somerset Cricket

Club – helps when you have a stand named after you! But still it's all he ever wanted and to send him out a Championship winner before he retired would cap a remarkable career. He still is the only player I've ever met who doesn't ever want it to rain and put his feet up in the change room. He wants to milk every last moment he has playing.

My career followed a vastly different path. Circumstance dictated certainly, but it is also a reflection of my personality. Being easily bored and chasing new challenges have been life-long characteristics. At times I've wanted a more settled life, but those periods have unfortunately been fleeting – just two Australian winters in the past 20 years is proof of this.

After backing myself into a corner in Western Australia and realising I didn't fit, I made the move to Victoria. For quite a while I was bitter I had to leave family and friends, but no longer. Playing for five counties – Leicestershire, Northamptonshire, Derbyshire, Middlesex and Somerset – is less surprising I believe. With an allowance now only one overseas player per county side, these roles are highly sought after and moving clubs to find a better 'fit' happens. Sometimes counties want an overseas bowler, or a Championship style player, or a white-ball specialist.

Combined with Australian representation – WA, Victoria, Sydney Thunder and of course Australia – I've played for nine professional sides. That in itself, I've realised, is a phenomenal statistic in my career. Most play for one or two. And that's not even counting five Leagues sides in England and five district clubs in Australia. With all that comes numerous teammates, coaches, mentors and different cultures – and I loved these new experiences.

Many times I've played in sides that had bitter rivalries with certain opposition and even refused to socialise together in the belief the competing players are 'ordinary blokes'. Victoria had a reputation for being that side in Australia. Tough, often nasty, on the field and uncompromising, the side had a stigma of being one to avoid hanging out with. Moving to and playing with Victoria reinforced my belief that every side has its good blokes, provided you make the effort to find them.

But to play with so many teammates and under so many coaches had a far greater impact for me. Impressionable and slightly needy, I've experienced so much from so many ... good and bad.

Initial experiences with WA were not some of my most enjoyable and no doubt I needed a firm hand and a few rockets but also perhaps an arm around my shoulder every now and again and better direction. Returning from England to the Western Australia team as a 23-year-old and finally starting to perform, I found two senior characters at the opposite end of the spectrum in terms of personality.

Justin Langer was and always has been all business – the utter professional. His day didn't end at stumps. As a player he was driven to perfection and it was incredible to watch him up close – but also not something I could emulate. I have no doubt it's why he managed to play 100 Tests and was an integral part of one of the best sides to ever grace a cricket field.

One evening after an interstate game for WA, I got back to my hotel room quite late in the knowledge we had an early wake-up call the next morning. Among my thoughts was the need to pack my bags before departure, and how little sleep I was bound to get. But when I looked around the room in half darkness, I realised it had already been packed. Lying on the other bed, sound asleep, was Justin. This episode summed him up in a lot of ways – JL had an amazing capacity to be understanding, considerate and helpful. He also had a hard and ruthless streak – if you stepped too far out of line you knew you were going to get nailed.

Murray Goodwin, the ex-Zimbabwe international, was another constant in the side. Both he and JL had fantastic careers but went about things very differently. 'Muzz' was very professional in his training and to have the career he had proves he worked hard too – but he definitely had a wild side. He proved to me alcohol wasn't the devil if you combined it with hard work when you had to. Apart from calling everyone 'chum' (a trait I often copy) he had a catchphrase … 'Just enjoy'. It was his way of saying that the journey can be fun and doesn't have to be all business.

There's a legend – which I believe Steve Waugh started and which I've repeated in a few speeches – about Muzz meeting the Queen. The story goes that all 12 sides of the 1999 World Cup were to meet the Queen and Prince Philip at Buckingham Palace. Somewhat of a logistical nightmare, it was decided the teams would be divided into two rooms.

Muzz, being a social butterfly, entered the 'other' room to speak to a few of the Australian players and in mid-conversation the doors were shut, barring him from the Zimbabwean players. Trying to find a way out with no success, he eventually stood at the end of the West Indian line. As captain Brian Lara introduced the Queen to his players and as he got towards the end of the line and it went something like Curtly Ambrose (6 foot 7), Courtney Walsh (6 foot 6) then 'aah Murray Goodwin' (5 foot 9).

The Queen didn't bat an eyelid, but Prince Philip took one look at the blond Murray and said 'you don't look much like a West Indian', to which Muzz replied without missing a beat, 'Nah ... but I wish I was hung like one!' Allegedly Prince Philip thought it was one of the funnier things he'd heard.

To be under the influence of these two was a huge eye-opener for me. It taught me that there isn't one secret formula you have to follow to achieve your dreams. The one constant was they both worked hard, although it is hard to match JL's work ethic.

Batting with these two was very different as well. Murray was a very relaxed and often funny person at the crease and when I was set in my innings I would often like this approach. Yes, switch on when about to face the delivery, but between overs the conversation would often wander. Towards the latter half of my career that has mostly been my method. I found it hard to be intense all the time and often it would burn too much energy.

Justin was all intensity and it would drag you along if you could use it. I must admit I loved it at the time. Often Justin and I would be at loggerheads about various issues surrounding the side, but when it came to batting, I've never enjoyed batting with someone as much. He would get himself so worked up it would become infectious and inspire me.

Two vivid memories stick out. The first was the time the former Test off-spinner Dan Cullen sledged him at the WACA. They had history on the field and Dan could get very fiery himself. Apparently he was told not to sledge JL but couldn't help himself – and a relatively calm Justin saw red and returned serve at Cullen. Then the next ball he launched him over mid-on into the stand and again the next ball. Then with mid-on being sent back to the fence Justin went again but it bounced short of the fielder. At the end of the over we met in the middle of the pitch and Justin was furious. He was frothing at the mouth and telling me he wanted to take Cullen down. It was incredible the intensity he could find. The story of his first century for WA, in the 1992 Sheffield Shield final, is still told. He was battered from head to toe but refused to yield and I've always admired that story.

The other time was playing against a strong NSW side that featured the Waugh brothers, Michael Slater, Stuart MacGill, Stuart Clark, Nathan Bracken and others. We watched helplessly as Slater flayed us to all corners of the WACA in compiling a brilliant double-century. When our time to bat came we were knocked over for just over an embarrassing 100 and immediately sent back in.

Justin had been furious and gave us an unbelievable dressing down and told us we needed to 'fight'. He must have used that word at least 10 times and it stuck with me. We went out to bat a second time and I was on a pair. JL took strike and first ball hit Nathan Bracken over his head for a one-bounce four. That was the last thing I'd expected, but I realised it was game on and we weren't going to lie down. Justin didn't last too long but he had set the standard and Marcus North and I ended up putting on 369 for the fourth wicket.

I'd taken forever to get to 20 as I was inspired and determined to fight every ball and not give my wicket away, but once that mark was passed batting became a lot easier. It wasn't until I was 194 that I gave it away, the best innings of my life against a world-class attack. The experience made me realise if I was going to make it I had to emulate Justin's mindset when it came to batting.

He often spoke about perfection when playing, which wasn't about averaging 100 but instead about getting yourself into the exact same mindset every time you went out to bat. That's essential for an opener as every time you go out the score is 0–0. Yes the situation of the game might be different but often it's about doing the same job over and over again.

We ended up doing a lot of work together and Justin was always positive. He used to say he wished he could have my stance, but sometimes I thought he was humouring me. Who wants to stand like they look like they are sitting on a horse? He always wanted feedback too. When I threw to him often I'd suggest something and he would lap it up. It was great to see a player such as himself wanting to improve. If he thought I'd seen something different or needed work, he would demand I say it and I've always wanted that in my own game. I don't have to listen to advice, but equally it will make me think and perhaps find my own solution.

Justin did have a few curious tics, and one that used to make me laugh was when we'd walk to the crease at the beginning of an innings and take guard. He would then walk all the way to the other end of the pitch where he'd ask his partner if he was ready. A friend told me Langer was asked about this in a question-and-answer evening and he said that Matthew Hayden and Michael Hussey would both be pumped and say something like 'yeah, come on, let's do this,' while I would not say a thing and just nod my head almost dismissively.

There were some things he did that inspired me, but being asked if I was ready to go at the beginning of an innings didn't. I'm not sure why. It was a bit like when I played for Australia. I didn't feel the need to touch the flag as I walked out to bat or bleed 'green and gold' to show I was giving anything less than my best.

The next big influence on my career was an English wicketkeeper. Paul Nixon was someone I didn't know a lot about apart from being a chirpy menace behind the stumps I'd encountered in county cricket in 2004 when playing for Derbyshire against Leicestershire.

The next season on a short stint with Leicestershire he became my favourite teammate. As mentioned previously, he took me aside on a bus trip back from Somerset to Leicester and told me we would be working all week leading up to the county's tour game against Australia.

The following year when I'd been signed unseen by Kepler Wessels at Northamptonshire I found myself out of form due to some extraordinary spinning wickets that didn't suit me at all. Northamptonshire is one of Leicestershire's neighbours and main rivals, but I received a call from 'Nicho' asking me how I was going and if I wanted to do some work with him. I jumped at the chance.

Next day I drove up to Leicester where he threw me balls at the county ground nets while the second team trained. Even now I still can't believe that. For an opposition player to help out a rival's overseas player is incredible, but just showed the measure of the man. He didn't care what people thought. He wanted to help a fellow professional and friend. I've never forgotten that.

It was at this stage I was starting to drift away from using my father as coach. Not because I had stopped believing his theories and style had merit, but to become a better all-round player. It had become clear to me that my technique had been honed on fast, bouncy wickets and was not suited to slow seaming wickets or spin-friendly ones.

Lance Klusener was also a teammate, who taught me a few things, as I have written. Lance is a remarkable man. Despite his reputation of being a big South African slogger, I found him to be extremely thoughtful, perceptive and inspiring. His weight at the 1999 World Cup was around 100 kilos but by the time I played with him he had shredded himself to 78 kilos and exceptionally fit. The fact Klusener and Nixon were constant tinkerers of their techniques reinforced my belief that the best players kept improving on their game even during the season.

It was at this stage I think I settled on a workable technique. Often I would discuss it with teammates I later encountered such as David Hussey, Andrew McDonald and Marcus Trescothick, but by then I was a senior player and started to give back, while teammates figured they didn't need to help me. Coaches, however, were still having a large influence.

My first taste of a coach in professional cricket was Wayne Clark, who oversaw a highly talented Western Australia side and did it fantastically. When you have the sort of squad he did, actual technical coaching is secondary to team- and man-management. Wayne or 'Dunny' as he was known, managed to get all these guys to pull together and go in one direction, which wouldn't have been easy at times, especially with quite a few having an eye on national selection.

When the inevitable breakup of that side happened, due to retirement, national selection or injury, Wayne found himself with a much inferior side and perhaps found other skills were needed, which proved difficult for him initially I believe. Personally I hadn't had much to do with him apart from being rightfully disciplined by him at one stage. I'll never forget him verbally abusing me following a beach fitness session where I was trailing badly and opted for the hard sand near the water. It was a lesson learnt.

He was then released around 2002–03 and Mike Veletta took over for two years before Dunny returned for a second stint. It was then that Wayne became quite influential on me. By this stage I was one of the better performers in the side and Dunny and I quickly built up a close relationship.

He much preferred dealing with self-sufficient players who thought for themselves and found a squad who, while talented, kept making the same mistakes. Because of this he gave me a certain amount of freedom to work things out and encouraged me to be myself.

His son Michael had tried his hand at Aussie Rules Football and had been contracted at the Fremantle Dockers then Collingwood before turning his hand to cricket. He became a very good left-arm swing bowler who, despite being exceptionally fit, found his body and in particular his back, unable to cope with the demands of bowling. But for a while Murray, Michael and I were very close and performing well.

It helped my relationship with Wayne and he became a supporter of mine, often pushing and challenging me to set my goals higher. The Australian side was almost unbeatable at this stage and I felt there was no room for me so did not dare to dream but instead settled into a routine of enjoying life and scoring runs.

To have a coach who has such belief in you, even when you don't, acts as such a spur and my performances only got better. Wayne and Justin often didn't see eye to eye, as Wayne liked a more laid back approach without the intense pressure that can come from trying too hard; I enjoyed his approach and vice-versa. He also made me feel completely at ease in the change room and would tell me that what I was bringing to the side in terms of my personality was excellent. It was refreshing after feeling outside of the group initially.

I found Wayne to be a fantastic man manager but he couldn't get the most out of the group, which seemed to lack direction and needed a tighter fist to guide them, as well as constant attention. It was a shame he was moved on for a second time, as he had the best intentions and genuinely wanted everyone to do well, especially me. Unfortunately the playing group made mistake after mistake and Wayne fell victim. His mode of coaching though has always stuck with me and I took a lot from how he operated.

Mike 'Waggy' Veletta's selection as coach in between Wayne's two stints initially filled me with dread. In a grade game at the end of the previous season, with rumours of him taking over rife, he sledged me mercilessly and smirked at me, daring me to throw down the stumps, which I did – only for him to get an overthrow.

He proceeded to tell me he wouldn't be contracting me shortly after his appointment and I was thrown into the wilderness. With plans to return to university and give up on my cricketing dreams, I was completely surprised when the WACA did a 180-degree turn and offered me the last contract.

In a strange way, it was thanks to Waggy. Brendon Julian was frustrated with Waggy's iron fist and opted for retirement, where his personality ensured success. With almost no one else to contract and forced to sign someone, I got lucky. What followed was two years of game development for which I will be forever grateful. Being an opener, Waggy saw me as a pet project and his technical coaching I found to be brilliant.

He helped my game rise considerably and it was in his first year as coach I became a permanent fixture of the four-day side. It was only at this stage I felt my spot wasn't in jeopardy, which made playing even more enjoyable. Waggy was exceptionally supportive to me, but was meanwhile losing the dressing room much as he'd lost BJ.

He had played with a high level of intensity and I daresay he had a fear of failure, which seemed to emanate from him and started to affect the players, who weren't used to such a stressful environment. Quite simply Waggy was desperate to succeed, but almost too desperate. The players started to get jittery in his presence, and consequently mistakes followed.

My last season for the Warriors came in 2007. The big signing in the off-season was coach Tom Moody, who had been a legend as a player for the state and had built an impressive CV coaching Worcestershire and more notably Sri Lanka.

I got off to a shaky start with Tom. Days after returning home a team-building exercise was scheduled in the hills past Gosnells, outside of Perth. I managed to get lost driving to the event and turned up late – not a good first impression. I was left a little frustrated by the day that took place. While Tom had the best intentions, it turned into a bit of a joke.

For each team exercise we had to do things like erect an imaginary doorway out of equipment provided and find objects in a treasure hunt, to which points were attached. In the end we accrued a combined points tally of around 1.3 million. The organiser said it was a record and that he had no doubt we would have a very successful season. We didn't. It felt like a waste of time and corny.

Tom wasn't to know that beforehand though and he quickly made his presence felt – hard not to when you're over two metres tall with a personality to match. I'd started to struggle with bowlers attacking me from around the wicket and Tom helped me tirelessly, throwing balls from that angle at a time before the whirler (or dog-stick) was introduced.

My issues started to appear when it became apparent Tom was, it seemed, backing Shaun Marsh and Luke Pomersbach unconditionally. Both had been reprimanded the previous year under Wayne Clark's leadership, and were given a clean slate under Tom. When Luke was picked out of the crowd to represent Australia in a T20 game at the WACA when Brad Hodge picked up a late injury, he was in Perth only because a misdemeanour had kept him from travelling interstate with the WA team. The decision to allow Luke to play was green-lit by the WACA and in particular Tom, but it rankled with senior players. The following week Tom met with nine of the squad's senior players in the middle of the WACA Ground and stated his case. He said he felt as a new coach everyone was to start afresh and that it was too good an opportunity to deny a young player – both very good points. However all nine players expressed their disapproval and felt it was time Luke was dealt a harsh lesson, as he seemed to be being rewarded for mistakes and a bad precedent was being set.

I think how I would I have handled that situation as a new coach, and empathise with Tom, as I think I might have done the same. But the players were becoming increasingly worried for Luke and disappointed he was letting the team down. On a personal note I started to feel a shift in the team dynamic and felt I was being slightly sidelined. My place in the one-day side was lost and young players who hadn't really earned their spot were leapfrogging me. These kids were very talented but didn't quite have the mental capabilities as yet.

Over coffee I expressed my concerns to Tom and said picking people on talent alone was dangerous in my opinion.

I felt my South Perth teammate Darren Wates (a lawyer as well) should be in the side, as while he might not be the best player he would make good decisions under pressure. I recalled the time he and Kade Harvey (a chemist) won us a one-day title with the bat from a seemingly lost position against Queensland at the Gabba.

The meeting didn't really work out as I hoped and I left it feeling deflated and seeing the writing on the wall. Tom had every right to try to develop the vast talent Western Australia provided on the cricket field, but I think a better balance could have been struck and people like Darren would have provided leadership and guidance to help that talent.

Tom only had the one contract with the Warriors and I feel a few of the players he backed let him down, which was disappointing as he gave them every opportunity to succeed. To be fair to Tom, I'm not sure anyone would have found the task of leading that side easy. While talented, the players kept making the same mistakes and when I spoke to the Vic boys about the Warriors, they just felt a few of the players would crack under any pressure.

Years later I worked with Tom in the commentary box and I think we both regret what happened and get on well now. Sometimes you just don't see eye-to-eye about philosophy and approach and it was a good lesson to learn. What became clear was that as a player, if you try to fight management, 99 times out of 100 you'll end up losing out and that I did.

I agreed in March to sign for Victoria and would relocate there at the end of September after another season in the UK. This time with Derbyshire after the England Cricket Board had changed the rules on overseas signings, making it possible for clubs to only sign one for red-ball cricket. Northampton had opted for Johan van der Wath, as he was a fantastic cricketer and exceptional with the ball.

John Morris was my new coach and it quickly became apparent we would get on well. 'Animal' as he was known was the other person in the plane with David Gower when they flew a Tiger Moth over a game they were playing in between England and Queensland. John had already scored a hundred in the match so when Gower suggested it he was very much up for it. I noticed quickly John had a huge love for life and I loved being in his company, although I gave him a bit of a fright early.

I met a friend for a quiet beer on almost my first Sunday there. Knowing I wasn't going to be drinking much, I opted to drive. Parking on a fairly busy road in the middle of town I left it on a slight slope. After returning from the pub I walked to where the car was meant to be only to find empty space. Panicking, I came to the conclusion it had been stolen.

Not knowing what to do, I called John as I didn't know anyone in the Derbyshire offices particularly well. He told me to go home and he'd try to sort it as he knew a local copper. Next morning I woke to the ringing of my phone. It was John telling me I must have left the handbrake off and it rolled and had to be towed to the impound. I felt a prize idiot, but John could only see the funny side of it.

John had signed the ex-England international Rikki Clarke as captain but it became clear early that the two didn't particularly get on and there were some fundamental differences in their approach. Rikki's performances started to drop away and at one stage he dropped himself and I stood in as captain. The following game we were playing on our outground Chesterfield and it looked like a very green wicket, so Rikki was reselected as his bowling would be required.

The twelfth man wasn't named until just before the warm-up began and when Rikki realised who he was to replace he became very agitated and felt the other player didn't deserve to be dropped. What followed was an argument between captain and coach that lasted about 15 minutes before John approached me with a wry smile to tell me I was to captain and could I do the toss. It was how my captaincy started, as Rikki and John fell out and Rikki wasn't to play for Derbyshire again. He relocated to Warwickshire, where he has been excellent.

As coach of a small club in county cricket, the coach has a lot of responsibility. Not only does he have to coach, but he is often director of cricket, scout, psychologist and father figure. I loved John's approach, which was typically Australian – hard but fair. I'll never forget a phone call I received relatively early on from him out of the blue solely to tell me I was doing a great job and to keep going. Naturally I'd been praised before, but this was the first time a coach had called just for the purpose of saying well done. It's always stuck with me.

Equally he would ring players to tell them they weren't pulling their weight and improvement was needed. I respected John for this, but it turned out not everyone did. The problem with small counties is that they have lower budgets and therefore can't afford the top-class players. As the saying goes, if you pay peanuts you get monkeys and this is what Derbyshire often had.

Some players would perform badly and we'd lose and John would be on their cases. Instead of taking responsibility, the same players would then look for excuses, culture being the main one. I heard from a few that the reason they weren't scoring more runs or taking wickets was the bad culture. What horse shit, I thought. Myself, Wayne Madsen and Chesney Hughes could perform. Why wasn't the bad culture stopping that?

Culture is one of those elusive terms in cricket. How do you get a winning culture? By winning. It's the chicken and egg question ... which comes first?

Basically players couldn't handle the pressure and blamed everything else than themselves. I learnt a lot in my time under John. It was about the time I was starting to properly mature and John showed me it was fine to enjoy life and play good cricket. I had three very good years at Derby and a lot was down to his guidance. After three years though the bright lights of London beckoned. I felt the time was right to leave and I told John I wanted to play for Middlesex, a team that was underperforming but had a lot of potential and a home ground at Lord's.

The second year of my stint with Derby, we almost got promoted to the top division but with Middlesex nine wickets down, a bad umpiring call cost us a win and we had to settle for a draw. Tim Murtagh was the batsman and he confessed to me the following year he should have been given out. That cost us a chance of promotion, which was a shame as we fell away the next year and I felt I had taken the team as far as it could go under my leadership. I was holding the team together with my runs and felt the players had become a little too reliant on me and needed to step up with more responsibility.

John understood my feelings and credit to him he didn't stand in my way. He was disappointed as I was 'his man' so to speak, but he wanted me to be happy. I saw how he dealt with people, particularly Graham Wagg who had a tough time at one stage and how John made the club stand by 'Waggy'. He was a man of his word and that was unbreakable.

For my four years at Middlesex I came under the guidance of Richard Scott and Angus Fraser. Angus was a legend for Middlesex and England and as director of cricket he was charged with getting Middlesex back to where it belonged – successful in the first division. He made a couple of signings to offset the departure of Owais Shah and brought in myself and Corey Collymore, two older guys to help with leadership.

Initially I found Angus a little hard to read. He is your typical English, dour, dull man with hunched shoulders. But I quickly began to realise this was just a front and he is in fact a witty, intelligent and warm character. As director of cricket he didn't get involved with the day-to-day running of the team, but instead oversaw the whole operation. That didn't stop him bowling to us in the nets off about 18 yards. Even over 50 he was still a handful. Unfortunately that came to an end when he decided to run the London marathon and his back said, 'Enough!'

Angus sorted out my accommodation every year and always looked after me. He didn't delegate any responsibility when I asked for things and I came to think of him as one of the best people I've met in cricket. He also liked my approach and wanted the players to be closer as a team.

Richard Scott acted as first team coach and as captain I had to work hard side by side with him. He was fantastic. My problem as captain is I can be too demonstrative and the players notice it. While it shows that I'm deeply invested in the game it also can have the effect of showing teammates when I'm disappointed with them.

As years have gone by I have improved in this but I'll never completely shake it. What Scotty brought was complete calmness and consistency. Even when things weren't going our way, he remained just the same, and I admired him for it. At times there were murmurings that players wanted more from him, but he was always first there throwing balls to guys at 9 am on the morning of matches, so I couldn't understand those sentiments.

It was fantastic to see someone be so calm even when his career could be on the line. I could only admire him for it. Now with Middlesex one of the best teams in the country, I have no doubt it has a lot to do with Scotty's unflinching patience and calmness.

In County cricket I've come to understand that consistency from a coach is almost the most important quality. Technical coaching is important no doubt, but with such a high volume of games and results that are always going to fluctuate, it is important to keep an even keel. The coaches who go up and down and enforce naughty boy nets quickly lose the players. No one is perfect, but players need to have their feet kept on the ground when they are doing well and made to feel it's ok even when they lose. Seems pretty simple, but it's hard to do when the pressure comes on.

It's been fantastic consequently to work with Matt Maynard at Somerset. At a club with supporters who are as passionate as I've seen and quite outspoken when performances are bad, it's been incredible to see him deal with criticism. I can get quite prickly when I feel some views are ignorant and negative, but he takes it all in his stride and that allows the players to feel safe.

It seems as if Matt will be my last coach and if that's the case then I'm happy. A fantastic man, he's been dealt his fair share of bad fortune in his life but is always happy and positive. As a coach I admire him for many qualities and am trying to learn as much from him as I can before I hope to get into coaching.

I've taken a lot from every coach I've worked with but have saved the best two for last. I touched on Greg Shipperd earlier – he and Darren Lehmann are clearly the finest coaches I've worked with. Up until playing for Victoria I mainly encountered 'feel' coaches – those who liked to manage players and felt the best way of getting the best out of the team was verbal communication. That's fine, but it was my experiences with Shipperd that showed the value of preparation and analysis.

It was around mid to late 2000s that the 'cricstat' technology was coming into vogue. This enabled widespread information and footage of all teams and cricketers, letting players watch all their innings as well as study the opposition. 'Shippy' took this to another level. The day before a game after training or the morning of the game we would convene in the 'war room' at the MCG if it was a home game, or the change room when away, and the white board would be literally covered in notes.

Shippy's design was three columns. He would have our general goals throughout the match – or 'KPIs' as they get referenced to these days. Then the opposition list with notes on strengths and weaknesses, and then finally our list with notable recent history, such as if a couple of players had combined for 100-run partnerships a number of times lately.

With this would be a folder of 22 sheets for each player to take with him, showing all the statistics for the opposition and us with dismissal types as well as wagon wheels etc. Not only would Shippy have this prepared pre-game but what also became very apparent was the preparation he must have done every night of the game in the lead-up to team talks in the morning. These meetings can be monotonous and thus counter-productive, but often Shippy would change the style to get his point across – whether it be an assistant coach to talk or each player to speak about something he had noticed, until Shippy got to the point he wanted to discuss.

This type of coaching is becoming more common, but Shippy still sets the standard for preparation in my opinion. It's not surprising considering he is brimming with intelligence, wants to stay in the background and is solely occupied with improving his charges. It's a style I see in

England's Australian-born coach Trevor Bayliss now. From what I've heard he is exceptional as well.

Shippy's only weakness was the intensity he could bring to the group when things didn't go well. He wasn't averse to spraying a player if he felt that player had played irresponsibly. However I never experienced one of these. I think Shippy saw how hard I fought every time I went out and every time I did play a poor shot he would give me the benefit of the doubt, as he knew it was out of character. Generally the younger players copped his wrath, but that was a part of their development.

In my last year playing for Western Australia, in the last match before the final, Matthew Wade was dismissed playing a reverse sweep which cost Victoria their last chance of winning the game and a home final. 'Wadey', I later heard, was given a severe tongue lashing from the coach and was promptly replaced by Adam Crosthwaite for the final. It was a massive lesson for Wadey and he came back better than ever. He has arguably been Victoria's best player over the past five years and has even ascended to the captaincy.

The old school, in-your-face approach worked in Victoria where it felt like cricket was being played in an Aussie Rules style of take no prisoners – I can tell you all the Bushrangers fancied themselves as an AFL prospect if only cricket hadn't got in the way. It is still the most unique place to play cricket in Australia. The grade cricket is fierce and the sledging worse – I was sledged by a 17-year-old debutant in my first grade game for Essendon. Also it is the only place in the world I've heard where the players ask 'How did you "go" out' rather than 'How did you "get" out.'

But Shippy read the cards well and his style was fantastic and a reason why Victoria was always so competitive and successful. When he was moved on, coinciding with my last year playing for Victoria, privately I could see he was disappointed. Despite how good he was, I agreed it was time for the Bushrangers to have a new approach. The next coach could be rubbish, but the point was some of the players had only ever experienced one style of first-class coaching and needed a different approach to help in their adaptability if they wanted to progress higher.

From my own experience it has been a blessing to experience so many styles and pick and choose what works. Hopefully I can use that in the future.

That brings me to my Australian coach Darren Lehmann. I actually experienced three national coaches – Tim Nielsen, Mickey Arthur and Lehmann, but I only played one match under Tim and none under Mickey, who, as I recounted earlier, was fired before the 2013 Ashes got underway.

Sometimes coaches can get too technical and KPIs and the like take over, to the point that the off-field work such as training and behaviour become even more important than the actual matches. With Boof, the desire to let the players express themselves has returned. It's a fine line between being prepared and being over-informed.

Another quality Boof possessed was common sense. The 2013 Ashes tour was a time when some relationships had become a little strained. I remember one day a senior player was disappointed with something fairly insignificant and started to say something to the coach that perhaps could've become an issue. But Darren just said in an even voice, 'Hey, no problem, don't worry, I'll take care of it,' which resolved an issue that could've easily grown legs.

Boof also had complete conviction about the style he wanted his sides to play. It would be a high-intensity approach where attack and aggression were applauded. Sledging, if done in the right manner, was fine and bowling short at the tail became common practice and a statement of intent. I had no interest in playing this way, as my game was built on defence and making the target on my back as small as possible. This worked well when batting with Davey Warner, as often the opposition focused their attention on him and I slid under the radar in accumulating scores.

But what that approach did achieve was to give the players clear direction. All players are gifted with different talents. My best talent was my mind and how I problem-solved, as I wasn't that gifted with physical talents and could definitely not hit the ball as well as some. Other players though didn't quite have the same mental skills – what Darren did was give that to them. By having a clear approach, the players had to think less and just follow a formula. It sometimes came unstuck, particularly abroad, but it was a wonderful tactic and the players responded to it.

I'll always remember how Darren would respond to bad days or Test matches. He would be completely upbeat and positive and remind the players it's just a game and that they would be better next time. This style is very uncommon and is only shown by coaches who are completely confident in themselves. Those who are not will often rant and rave after poor performances and even call for naughty boy nets. Darren was the opposite and I can say it was a godsend. The players are under enough pressure and know when they have had a poor game. The odd spray might be applicable, but what the players need is support. It's why coaches in football codes so often criticise the referee. They are trying to deflect blame from the players.

Simplicity and direction is what makes Lehmann stand out, and while that seems like pretty simple, surprisingly it's not. Darren has as good a grip on the intricacies of the game and the tactics required as I've ever witnessed. He also understands what the players are going through, having played at the highest level. While this is not essential, it has to help when an international coach understands how difficult that 'bubble' environment is.

It's been one of the real fortunes of my long and well-travelled career that I've experienced so many coaches. While some are better than others, every one of them has had a significant effect on my outlook and personality and if the day comes when I join them in the coaching trade, hopefully I can influence others in the right manner.

CHAPTER 18

LESSONS

SOMETIMES YOU MISS the story. It could be argued Australia's selectors missed the story with Chris. Washington political reporters missed the story with Watergate – two metro reporters broke that one. And this reporter missed Chris Rogers' story first time around – he made plenty of runs against South Australia, where I was based, but I never asked to speak to him. When he made his Test debut at the WACA Ground in January 2008, I felt like many others that he was merely keeping the seat warm for a week. For five years it looked that way.

By 2012 I had learnt, and watched Middlesex at Lord's as Chris took the visitors for 173 at a helluva lick. He had clearly progressed as a batsman and a leader from the man I had seen at the Adelaide Oval; after play I spoke to him about his worries that he would soon be cut by Victoria. So I'll quote him in his own book:

'I know there's a big push for the youth and the old guys are kind of being pushed through the back door. I still think I can give

something to Victoria … But I must admit I do love it over here. I do love the county system and the emphasis it still has on the longer version – maybe my future's over here. I understand there's a lot of pressure at home, Victoria already have quite a few experienced guys, so you've got to have that balance and bring the young players through … I don't hit the ball as far as most of the guys, but I think if you can use your brain and manipulate the ball then there's still a role to be had … My goal was always to play Test cricket so that's why I set myself to play the longer version.'

That post-play interview at Lord's evolved into a catch-up for dinner later in the week, and regular conversations since. I was thus able to watch Chris closely as he kept his Victoria contract, peeled off a trio of Shield hundreds in the next home season, and won his Test call-up.

Equally, I discovered the multiple dimensions of the man. His analytical, even bookish approach to the game contrasted with a mischievous, fun-loving streak away from the field. There were harder sides too, an occasionally caustic tongue and strong opinions. But most of all, there was an infectious sociability that was refreshing to me in addition to many others: Chris was invariably up for a coffee or a meal whenever we found ourselves in the same town, and equally happy to introduce me to his friends and family.

Most of the time, Chris and I kept at arm's length during international series, apart from the odd conversation, but the 2015 Ashes was an exception, when I was not enjoying the experience, dealing with weight issues and the aftermath of a violent mugging in the preceding tour of the West Indies. Chris was the one person who spoke to me, clear-eyed and forcefully, about needing to look after myself, even though he was wrapped up in the final chapter of his own international career, and in the harshest of cricket spotlights.

A similar tale can be told by Paul Sealey, a friend Chris met through the Prahran cricket club after his move from Perth to Melbourne in 2008. At the time Chris was playing for Essendon, but Sealey saw a side of the man that transcended links to the cricket team of the moment. He also saw a very funny byproduct of publicity.

'He was playing for Essendon, but as it transpired he basically socialised and hung out with us [at Prahran] most of the time. At the Victoria awards night after that first year he won the Bill Lawry Medal and at the presentation all the district clubs were there, including Essendon. But when he got up to speak, he actually thanked the Prahran boys because we gave him a bit of a social outlet in Melbourne! He went on to play for Prahran, and that was where our connection sprang from.

'[One night] we were near Chapel Street when we were about to go out to dinner, and he was taking out some money from a Commonwealth Bank ATM. They are sponsors of the Australian cricket team, so there was a photo of him on the ATM itself when he was drawing cash out. He was so excited about it and so keen to tell us all that he walked away and left his money there. The cash was never seen again, but at least we all knew about the photo!'

BEING FORTUNATE ENOUGH to have spent nearly 20 years as a professional cricketer, a number of these in recent times as captain, taught me a lot about fitting into a team and how to get the best out of myself. With that I've come to have certain beliefs about fundamental principles it takes to achieve success. Others may have different views, but generally I believe they will be similar ideals delivered through different words.

BALANCE

Perhaps the greatest lesson I've learned is that cricket can consume you. A game that should be simple is often so complicated it becomes ridiculously difficult. Every now and again you see batsmen mouth to themselves 'watch the ball' as a bowler is running in. Why would a player say this when surely it should be a given? Often it's because there are so many things going through the brain that this most important requirement takes a back seat.

Such thoughts aren't confined to the cricket field. Sleepless nights are common for cricketers. If you speak to any batsman, ask them if they have had the nightmare they can't get ready quick enough to go out to bat and are timed out. I'll be surprised if they answer 'no'.

Maybe the worst part about living as a cricketer is that your performance on the ground invariably dictates how happy you are off it. I'll never forget Michael Hill of Victoria having a three-week purple patch and his enormous relief and happiness after he'd scored a century and we'd won a Sheffield Shield match against Queensland. 'Hilly' had been fighting for his chance for a number of years and his celebrations were impressive, but as harsh as it seemed that night I felt the need to tell him that he only did his job and to keep his feet on the ground.

Unfortunately for him he fell away in the last two Shield matches of that year for four single-figure scores and the word was he was back at rock bottom mentally. Similarly, after scoring two consecutive centuries in Tests in the Ashes in Melbourne and Sydney I thought I was invincible. Three innings later I was sitting in my hotel room in Port Elizabeth contemplating retirement.

The only way to get things in perspective is to find balance in your life. Whether that be study, work or travel, something is required. I look at Ryan Carters, formerly of Victoria and now New South Wales and Sydney Thunder, with a lot of admiration. He has started his own charity called Batting for Change, a tremendous initiative that has given him direction and responsibility away from the game.

Darren Wates studied and practised law throughout his brief professional career. While those demands may be a little excessive, cricket was never going to be the be all and end all for him, which meant that every opportunity that came his way was greeted with enthusiasm and joy – not always the case for others.

I was fortunate enough to complete a journalism degree while trying to break in to the WA side, for which I'm grateful. Since securing my first county contract and playing back-to-back seasons in Australia and England, I've found it very difficult to do any such further development and have had to find balance elsewhere.

After last year's Ashes I travelled with Peter Siddle and his girlfriend Anna Weatherlake to Spain for a wedding. It's no surprise Sidds is one of the happiest and friendliest teammates I've had. His love of life is almost second to none and the amount of hobbies and passions he has is impressive. Whether it be his veganism, commercial ventures, dogs, hats, watches, fishing, the North Melbourne football club, American sport and a lot more ... seems to be you name it, he knows about it.

Once cricket takes over, you enter dangerous territory. Yes, focus is key, but the ability to switch on *and* off is imperative. A lot of the battle is won off the ground. If you can walk out on to the ground confident and relaxed, the chances of success are far higher.

IF YOU ARE NOT GIVING, YOU ARE TAKING

Captaining sides has taught me a lot about leadership. In cricket the easiest place to lead from is the front. To stand in front of a group and demand excellence is so much easier when you are doing it yourself. No doubt this is fundamental in most industries, but cricket is full of statistics and individual battles and everyone knows the score.

But still, this only works if you are a positive influence on the group and teammates want to perform for you. Too often I have seen the culture of cricket clubs when only two or three players are creating drama. The issues are usually around money, not enough opportunity or excuses for why they aren't performing.

At Derbyshire, a couple of players blamed the coach and the culture of the club as reasons for why they weren't performing. As I said earlier, why then were some succeeding? Winning breeds a winning culture and it takes individuals to put aside issues and not complain.

In a team environment, the players who do not help provide a happy vibe and try to undermine management are not needed – even if they are the best player in the team or the next superstar. A key element to this is enjoying the success of others in the team, rather than ruminating on what it means for you. If you cannot bring yourself to do that, then you should perhaps find another occupation – more on that later.

ONE STEP BACK – TWO STEPS FORWARD

Having a father who played first-class cricket is a fortune most other cricketers didn't have and having high-quality coaching day to day was no doubt the making of me. For all his qualities, Dad still had weaknesses. His style of coaching these days would be frowned upon, yet I'm still to be convinced about the new wave of coaching.

Dad would overload me with information. One moment he would be telling me to get my front elbow higher, the next to get a bigger stride in as I play a drive, the next to get my eyes further across into line with the ball. Often this overload would leave me bewildered, trying to process so many things at once. But this style helped me become an effective problem-solver.

In the end, something Dad would say would click, the focus would sharpen on that, and I would work it out for myself. Towards the middle of my career I pulled away from Dad to get a wider grasp, but often would return to him when in need. He would say a few things and the cycle would start again – one thing would resonate with me and everything else would fall into place.

These days it's felt the best way to coach is to ask players how they feel, to speak to them about game awareness and try to coach them in reading the game. That's all fine, but often I see these kids having no technique to actually play certain shots. This can be anyone from a 17-year-old to someone nearing the end of their career.

I've always been a tinkerer. There were times as a young player playing club cricket in my early 20s when in the first session of a match the bat would feel like a railway sleeper, so uncomfortable it felt. As bowlers were running in I would be fiddling with my grip or changing my stance from ball to ball. Often I would battle to lunch then come out to play afterwards, and all of a sudden the bat would feel like it was an extension of my body. Often it was a case of trying something that would feel alien but then become second nature – one step back, then two steps forward.

In my experience the best players are never satisfied and are always searching for something better. I've spoken to some players who say they do all their technical work in the pre-season and then don't change at all during the season. I find this both fascinating and naive. What happens if you have a form slump? How will you ever get to where you want to be if you don't use all your time to improve?

While I acknowledge this can create over-complication, if you keep striving slowly it will become clearer. I've tried most technical styles and discarded most of them, but I know now what works best for me – yet it's still a work in progress.

Justin Langer was fantastic in wanting to soak up every bit of help he could get and sometimes in our one-on-one sessions where we threw balls to each other I would give him more advice than he would me – such was his open-mindedness.

Marcus Trescothick has had a wonderful career but even now I see him wanting to try new things and he is in his forties. Ricky Ponting is one of the best batsmen to walk the planet and a freakish talent, but the stories of his work ethic are legendary. It was clear at the end of his career he was trying to adapt his footwork to combat being dismissed lbw.

Davey Warner in the 2015 Ashes on UK soil realised England had tactics for him and he immediately went about adapting his game in the conditions to combat them – this from a player who is thought to be completely instinctive. Steve Smith decided to emulate how AB de Villiers moved a long away across his crease to the offside and found it worked for him.

If it's good enough for these guys to tinker, then why aren't we challenging the techniques of the younger players more? The best players constantly evolve, even if change does not always bring immediate success.

CONSISTENCY

I've played with a number of players who can make batting look easy when they are in form. Fine, but the problem comes when judges see one innings and immediately proclaim them as the next world-beater. Cricket is about being consistent – there is no point being brilliant one day and rubbish the next three or four. No doubt there is a place for match-winners, but consistency is what helps cricket sides.

Michael Hussey would often talk to me when we were opening the batting together about 'batting time', so we were doing a job for the next batsmen to come in. The longer a team's innings goes, the more tired bowlers get – and then batting gets easier. Huss's motto was to bat for time every chance he got and do a job for the team. That was why he became a superstar and so valuable to every side he played in.

Often I hear coaches saying when a batsman gets in to go 'big'. This new term of 'daddy hundreds' grates with me – it is a stupid term, like 'going forward'. (Is it people trying to sound knowledgeable when they aren't?) It's great to have one player get a big score, but why should so much pressure be put on one or two players? For me, if everyone contributes regularly then the team will perform.

Shaun Marsh was the most talented junior I saw and his hundred as a 19-year-old at Newcastle, against a full-strength NSW with Steve Waugh at the helm, was incredible. Good enough for Waugh to claim it was one of the best innings he'd seen by a young player for a long time. Immediately Shaun was fast-tracked, but his performances were anything but consistent and it took him a number of years before he did find consistency.

The same was the case with Usman Khawaja, who had sublime gifts as a youngster and was in the Australian side early, but wasn't quite ready. His game wasn't yet three-dimensional and he didn't yet have the skills to be consistent.

As a selector, consistency would be a major factor for me. Look at the overall, not merely the evidence of the eyes on a given day.

GOOD SIDES CELEBRATE WITH EACH OTHER

In a day and age where professionalism is greater than ever in sport, with cricket no exception, finding opportunities to enjoy each other's success and to celebrate victories is still essential.

Cricket is a team game played out through individual battles. Yes, batting partners can help each other in rotating the strike or taking the majority of certain bowlers for each other, and bowlers need fielders to take catches for them, but in general it's about delivering your own personal skill. Yet it's a team game and sides succeed only if they have a common goal. Teammates don't have to get on, but they should be heading in the same direction and be prepared to be happy for each other.

The best sides I've been a part of loved playing with each other and would fight for each other. When I first played for Middlesex we had a lot of initial success in winning the second division of the County championship and finishing third the following year in the first division. Often after games all the players and partners would convene in a pub and have a fantastic time.

Durham always seem to over-perform and the fact they are the most remote side doesn't surprise me. There is a certain 'us against them' mentality that carries them through the inevitable tough times. While the Victoria side I joined had rather large divisions, there was still the same kind of adversarial attitude that had come from those guys sticking together through thick and thin – most noticeably the passing of David Hookes – and of a culture where each player was pushing others to attain higher honours.

ENJOY YOURSELF

Perhaps I over-indulged in this theory as a youngster, but I worked out quickly that if I wasn't enjoying it, a career as a professional was never going to eventuate. As touched on elsewhere, the game can become overbearing, and the pressure too much. I never once considered cricket to be work. Yes, it paid the bills, but I never said to family or friends that I was going to 'work' that day. It was always about going to 'play'.

The life of a professional cricketer can arguably be one of the best of all sports. International travel plus being a part of a team isn't that common, at least for the amount of time cricketers do it. These opportunities are unlikely to come around again and while I'd like to think I gave everything when I trained and played, I made sure I had a lot of fun doing it and it was never a hardship.

Murray Goodwin taught me this and I am grateful he was one of my early influences. In the end cricket is just a game and should be treated as such. His catchphrase 'just enjoy chum' is one I've never tired of using.

CHAPTER 19

FINAL THOUGHTS IN THE MIDDLE

AT ONE STAGE writing this book I spoke to my co-author Daniel Brettig about not wanting to sound like I was a party boy who didn't care about my cricket – I did. Cricket is a unique game in that it can last four or five days with long periods of idleness where you are left alone with your thoughts. It can often be these thoughts that define us.

Having played against England's Nick Compton and seen how good he is at County level, it came as a surprise when he wasn't quite as successful as he should have been in Test matches. By no means is he on his own though. Mark Ramprakash was widely regarded as the best batsman of his generation in the UK, but he couldn't achieve consistent success at the highest level that his talent demanded.

After playing for so long I suspect I know why. Cricketers, like golfers, play the game between their ears. The new formats (one-day matches and Twenty20) call for more instinctive play, but often the longer version is a battle of the mind, particularly for batsmen. Make one mistake and you can be out and under pressure the next time you go out to bat.

The players who are most successful find a mental state and approach that works for them. Sitting in a hotel room contemplating whether one more low score can mean the end of an international career, and therefore failure in the eyes of family and friends, can be soul-destroying.

I worked out quickly that if I lived and breathed cricket it got the better of me, and failure followed. I needed to be a free spirit and enjoy myself. Averaging 50 wherever I went seemed to justify this, but when people said to me I could have averaged 60 if I was more driven and more professional, I thought 'Bullshit!' More likely the average would have dropped to 40 or 35 or lower. That approach was tried and tested and it left me feeling empty, bored and frustrated.

I wish I'd been a lot smarter about how I went about things when younger, and been less influential on others who couldn't operate the same way I did. But equally I needed an outlet – it gave me balance. Balance to train hard and to enjoy myself. When I played for Australia at 35 I went against my method and started hitting more balls than ever. It had the opposite effect to the one intended. My game and swing became too rigid and I was gripping the handle as if trying to choke the life out of it – a sure path to failure.

That's not to say I didn't work hard on my game. The days of hitting for an hour every day down the local nets or in the backyard with Dad, and the constant deep inner desire to get better, were imperative in my development. Darren Lehmann is an example of someone who succeeded through a similar approach, and even now I look at Glenn Maxwell and his need to be doing other things, not just sitting in his room thinking about the game.

Of course there are numerous examples of guys who have dedicated themselves completely, like Justin Langer – while we had the same approach on the field, we were vastly different characters off it.

Often pre-game meetings would fill me with terror as I was shown clips of opposition bowlers taking wickets; thoughts of inferiority would take over. My best skill was problem-solving and often I could walk out without a lot of preparation, quickly sum up conditions and bowling styles, and go about my batting. That enabled me to spend less of my time away from the game thinking about it. Spending time with family friends was often far more helpful than sitting at home alone, contemplating what was to take place the next day.

That being said, I'd like to think I've grown and matured. Even at 30 when I debuted for Australia, there was a lot of naivety. I see how driven younger players are these days and can only admire them. To watch how Steve Smith, Davey Warner, Josh Hazlewood, Peter Handscomb, Marcus Stoinis and numerous others (Phillip Hughes was definitely in this group) chase their dreams is incredible.

But then the opportunities offered to these guys are so much more than were about when I was their age. There was no Twenty20, I wasn't getting into the national one-day side and the Australian Test side at the time was arguably the best team that will ever walk the planet. Opportunities were scarce.

Being a professional cricketer travelling from Australia to the UK every six months was a wonderful life and the chances to enjoy myself were fantastic. Often I look at other players and question whether they will get to the end of their careers and look back and wonder whether they actually enjoyed it. A lot of players put far too much pressure on themselves; others seemed to blame everything else *but* themselves and were inherently bitter.

I look back and think yes, I could have done so many things better and might have played more for Australia, but I loved the career I had, and to be someone else just to please others didn't sit well with me. To have a brief but very enjoyable stint with Australia right at the end and to go out on my own terms was such a great feeling.

Any feelings of bitterness have long disappeared and the friendships I have made over nearly a 20-year career in cricket are among the strongest relationships I have.

Apart from my best mate Shaun Doherty, whose wedding I was best man at, just about all my closest friends have been met though cricket one way or another. Guys like Darren Wates, Chas Keogh, Sam Robson, Tom Scollay, Ben Chapman, Phil Watkinson among others have cricket backgrounds, and while I've looked to further my horizons since finishing with the Australian and Victoria teams, it's not surprising, seeing as my life has never been too far away from a cricket pitch.

As mentioned elsewhere, going to a new team always provided at least 10 friends. Perhaps my greatest bit of fortune was coming across such a great bunch of blokes at Prahran Cricket Club in Melbourne – they looked after me and made my time there as good as any I can remember. Paul Sealey, a diminutive opening bowler with a gigantic heart, and Adam Bull, a fellow opening batsman albeit with a very different style, even took the time to do a stocktake of my apartment when I belatedly decided to rent it out for a period I was in the UK. Those two, along with Chris Williamson, Sam Coates, Steven De Bolfo, James Wild and a host more from Prahran showed me just how good Melbourne could be, particularly Saturday nights on Chapel Street and Sunday afternoons at the College Lawn Hotel.

This wouldn't have happened if I had been too blinkered in my approach to realise that friendships were more important than the cricket.

A few people have spoken to me about my career being a story of resilience. I'm not truly sure about that. Perhaps resilience is a by-product of something else. When I was being overlooked for the Australia opening position for others who often had inferior domestic records, I was naturally disappointed, but never had thoughts of 'if I continued to score more runs than anyone else they'd have to pick me'. In fact it was probably the opposite. Many times I confided in family that I was never going to be picked and for them to give up hope, like I had.

What I did have though was a competitive spirit. Breaking tennis racquets as a 12-year-old showed how much I hated to lose and while I fine-tuned that trait, it was what kept pushing me – I just wanted to do as well as I could every time I went out to play. That seems cliched but I've witnessed many batsmen who have opted out when the conditions got tough and saved their efforts for when it was easier.

Often it's actually the fear of failure that drives us. Looking back over these pages, it's as if I was on the verge of throwing in the towel myself every time the going got tough playing for Australia. Living in the bubble of an international cricket side can do that to you. You ride a rollercoaster not experienced before. The best moments like, the Ashes wins in Perth, Melbourne, Sydney and Lord's, and the Cape Town victory to decide that series, are moments that will stay with me forever. So will the moments of supreme loneliness and failure and those feelings that it was all too much.

After retiring and commentating, it is so much easier to have perspective. It's just a game that goes on and on and new players emerge and new matches are played. But when you're in the midst of it and living and breathing cricket at grounds and hotels, it's easy to get lost in the supposed importance of it all. For the most part I felt I dealt with it well, but I think I would've enjoyed it all the more if I'd accepted the possibility of failure, as psychologist Steven Sylvester taught.

The players I've come to admire the most are those who have had long international careers, like Ricky Ponting, Steve Waugh, Allan Border, Michael Clarke and a number of others. To constantly put themselves out there and to fight every time on centre stage over years and years is an incredible achievement. Often it's why these guys have no difficulty in later life as their constant desire to be the best pushes them.

Captaining Somerset has been an eye-opener. I thought I would have more perspective and enjoy it more, but the pressure of captaincy and to avoid being the first Somerset captain to have them relegated has meant I've been lost in the moment too often. The constant pressure has been building. Sometimes I yearn for an easy life under the radar, away from the spotlight and the possibility of being critiqued by Joe Bloggs, but then I realise it probably wouldn't satisfy. Whether this is unhealthy I'm yet to fully comprehend, but it will be interesting to embark upon life after playing and find out where that leaves me.

In my mind I was never the most gifted player, with flaws in my game and my personality. But I look back and remember the naive, tiny, impressionable kid who started out playing for Western Australia and find it hard to believe what he was able to achieve. The stuff of his dreams.

CHRIS ROGERS

Born: 31 August 1977
Height: 1.77m
Left hand batsman

Was one of five Wisden Cricketers of the year 2014
Won the Keith Miller Medal as Australia's player of the series in 2015 Ashes

CHRIS ROGERS all CRICKET

	M	I	NO	RUNS	HS	AVGE	100	50	CT
Tests	25	48	1	2015	173	42.87	5	14	15
First Class Matches	311	551	39	25175	319	49.17	74	121	244
Sheffield Shield	120	214	13	9917	279	49.34	33	42	90
List A	167	160	15	5346	140	36.86	5	36	74
Aust Domestic One Day	73	71	6	2226	140	34.25	2	13	31
All Twenty20 Matches	43	37	1	627	58	17.41	0	3	22

Bowling in all Cricket

	Overs	Runs	Wkt	Avge	SR	Best	5i	10w
First Class Matches	41.2	137	1	137.00	248.0	1–16	0	0
Sheffield Shield	7.4	46	0					
List A	4	26	2	13.00	12.0	2–22	0	0

No bowling in Tests, Aust Domestic One Day or Twenty20

TEST MATCH BATTING FOR AUSTRALIA

Opponent

	M	I	NO	RUNS	HS	AVGE	100	50	CT
v India 2007–08	1	2	0	19	15	9.50	0	0	1
in England 2013	5	9	0	367	110	40.78	1	2	4
v England 2013–14	5	10	0	463	119	46.30	2	3	4
in South Africa 2013–14	3	6	0	181	107	30.17	1	0	0
v Pakistan (in UAE) 2014–15	2	4	0	88	43	22.00	0	0	2
v India 2014–15	4	8	0	417	95	52.13	0	6	2
in England 2015	5	9	1	480	173	60.00	1	3	1
Total	25	48	1	2015	173	42.87	5	14	14

BUCKING THE TREND

Test Batting home v away

	M	I	NO	RUNS	HS	AVGE	100	50	CT
Home	10	20	0	899	119	44.95	2	9	7
Away	15	28	1	1116	173	41.33	3	5	7
Total	25	48	1	2015	173	42.87	5	14	14

Batting in each inning

	M	I	NO	RUNS	HS	AVGE	100	50
First innings		25	0	1064	173	42.56	2	8
Second innings		23	1	951	119	43.23	3	6
Total	25	48	1	2015	173	42.87	5	14

Test Result batting

	M	I	NO	RUNS	HS	AVGE	100	50
Wins	11	21	1	937	173	46.85	3	5
Losses	10	20	0	682	110	34.10	2	4
Draws	4	7	0	396	95	56.57	0	5
Total	25	48	1	2015	173	42.87	5	14

By Opponent

	M	I	NO	RUNS	HS	AVGE	100	50	CT
England	15	28	1	1310	173	48.52	4	8	9
India	5	10	0	436	95	43.60	0	6	3
Pakistan	2	4	0	88	43	22.00	0	0	2
South Africa	3	6	0	181	107	30.17	1	0	0
Total	25	48	1	2015	173	42.87	5	14	14

Bowlers who dismissed Rogers most: SCJ Broad (Eng) 8, GP Swann (Eng) 7, JM Anderson (Eng) 3

Test Hundreds (5)

	Venue	Runs	Balls	4s	6s	Match Result
v England 2013	Durham	110	250	14	0	Lost
v England 2013–14	Melbourne	116	155	13	0	Won
v England 2013–14	Sydney	119	169	15	0	Won
v South Africa 2013–14	Port Elizabeth	107	237	12	0	Lost
v England 2015	Lord's	173	300	28	0	Won

STATISTICS

FIRST CLASS CAREER

	M	I	NO	RUNS	HS	AVGE	100	50	CT
Test Cricket	25	48	1	2015	173	42.87	5	14	14
Sheffield Shield	120	214	13	9917	279	49.34	33	42	90
England County Championship	142	248	24	11756	248*	52.90	33	56	126
Australia A	7	13	0	372	70	28.61	0	5	2
For Australia on overseas tours	4	7	0	285	84	40.71	0	2	2
Marylebone Cricket Club	1	2	0	19	18	9.50	0	0	0
Other First class cricket	12	19	1	811	319	45.06	3	2	10
Total	311	551	39	25175	319	49.17	74	121	244

BATTING IN SHEFFIELD SHIELD CRICKET
Season by Season

	M	I	NO	RUNS	HS	AVGE	100	50	CT
1998–99 (WA)	3	5	0	83	36	16.60	0	0	3
1999–2000 (WA)	3	5	0	36	20	7.20	0	0	2
2001–02 (WA)	4	7	2	411	102*	82.20	2	2	5
2002–03 (WA)	10	17	1	745	194	46.56	2	4	10
2003–04 (WA)	8	16	1	864	142	57.60	4	3	8
2004–05 (WA)	8	15	0	645	153	43.00	1	3	10
2005–06 (WA)	10	20	1	794	161	41.79	2	4	12
2006–07 (WA)	10	17	0	1202	279	70.71	3	7	10
2007–08 (WA)	9	17	0	744	166	43.76	3	2	5
2008–09 (Vic)	11	19	3	1195	159	74.69	5	5	9
2009–10 (Vic)	9	15	2	641	149	49.31	2	2	4
2010–11 (Vic)	4	8	0	218	73	27.25	0	1	2
2011–12 (Vic)	10	19	0	781	124	41.11	3	4	3
2012–13 (Vic)	10	17	2	742	131	49.47	3	1	5
2013–14 (Vic)	3	6	0	297	117	49.50	1	1	1
2014–15 (Vic)	8	11	1	519	112	51.90	2	3	1
Total	120	214	13	9917	279	49.34	33	42	90

Bowlers dismissed most by: SR Clark (NSW) 8, BW Hilfenhaus (Tas) 7, SW Tait (SA) 7

Shield Cricket for each State

	M	I	NO	RUNS	HS	AVGE	100	50	CT
For Western Australia	65	119	5	5524	279	48.46	17	25	65
For Victoria	55	95	8	4393	159	50.49	16	17	25
Total	120	214	13	9917	279	49.34	33	42	90

Chris Rogers in Australian Domestic One Day Cricket

Season by Season

	M	I	NO	RUNS	HS	AVGE	100	50	CT
1998–99 (WA)	1	1	1	19	19*	–	0	0	0
2001–02 (WA)	4	4	0	100	39	25.00	0	0	0
2002–03(WA)	11	10	1	327	67	36.33	0	3	6
2003–04 (WA)	9	9	2	272	117*	38.86	1	1	3
2004–05 (WA)	4	4	0	68	43	17.00	0	0	3
2005–06 (WA)	8	8	1	259	72	37.00	0	2	3
2006–07 (WA)	6	5	0	100	46	20.00	0	0	5
2007–08 (WA)	2	2	0	30	18	15.00	0	0	1
2008–09 (Vic)	10	10	0	448	75	44.80	0	5	4
2009–10 (Vic)	10	10	0	342	140	34.20	1	0	5
2010–11 (Vic)	1	1	0	1	1	1.00	0	0	0
2011–12 (Vic)	1	1	0	31	31	31.00	0	0	0
2012–13 (Vic)	6	6	1	229	64*	45.80	0	2	1
Total	73	71	6	2226	140	34.25	2	13	31

Bowlers dismissed most by: SR Clark (NSW) 4, GJ Denton (Vic, Tas) 3, JR Hopes (Qld) 3

Batting in English County Championship Matches

Season by Season

	M	I	NO	RUNS	HS	AVGE	100	50	CT
2004 (Derbyshire)	6	11	2	498	156	55.33	1	3	6
2005 (Leicestershire)	2	4	0	176	93	44.00	0	1	4
2006 (Northamptonshire)	13	22	2	1352	319	67.60	4	5	11
2007 (Northamptonshire)	7	13	1	264	69	22.00	0	3	10
2008 (Derbyshire)	14	24	2	1232	248*	56.00	3	8	13
2009 (Derbyshire)	13	21	1	1461	222	73.05	6	4	21
2010 (Derbyshire)	15	27	3	1285	200	53.54	4	5	19
2011 (Middlesex)	15	25	3	1286	148	58.45	4	6	6
2012 (Middlesex)	16	29	2	1086	173	40.22	3	6	7
2013 (Middlesex)	12	22	3	1068	214	56.21	3	6	11
2014 (Middlesex)	15	28	4	1333	241*	55.54	4	4	10
2016 (Somerset)	14	22	1	715	109	35.05	1	5	8
Total	142	248	24	11756	248*	52.90	33	56	126

BATTING
Chris Rogers First Class Centuries (74)

	Score	How Out	Fielder	Bowler	Match	Season
1	101*				Western Australia v South Australia	2001–02
2	102*				Western Australia v South Australia	2001–02
3	110*				Western Australia v South Australia	2002–03
4	194	c	DE Bollinger	MJ Clarke	Western Australia v New South Wales	2002–03
5	103	c	AB McDonald	AB McDonald	Western Australia v Victoria	2003–04
6	120	c	DG Wright	AG Downton	Western Australia v Tasmania	2003–04
7	142	b		SR Clark	Western Australia v New South Wales	2003–04
8	119*				Western Australia v Queensland	2003–04
9	156	c	A Pratt	LE Plunkett	Derbyshire v Durham	2004
10	153	b		IJ Harvey	Western Australia v Victoria	2004–05
11	209	c	RT Ponting	SCG MacGill	Leicestershire v Australians	2005
12	161	c	SCG MacGill	SR Clark	Western Australia v New South Wales	2005–06
13	135	lbw		BW Hilfenhaus	Western Australia v Tasmania	2005–06
14	319	st	SJ Adshead	CG Taylor	Northamptonshire v Gloucestershire	2006
15	112	ro			Northamptonshire v Derbyshire	2006
16	128	b		ID Blackwell	Northamptonshire v Somerset	2006
17	222*				Northamptonshire v Somerset	2006
18	279	c	LR Mash	CL White	Western Australia v Victoria	2006–07
19	152	c	DJ Marsh	BG Drew	Western Australia v Tasmania	2006–07
20	110	c	DJ Harris	DJ Cullen	Western Australia v South Australia	2006–07
21	138	c	CJ Huntington	FB Baker	Northamptonshire v Cambridge Uni CCE	2007
22	123	c	SG Clingeleffer	LR Butterworth	Western Australia v Tasmania	2007–08
23	116	lbw		CP Simpson	Western Australia v Queensland	2007–08
24	166	c	CL White	BE McGain	Western Australia v Victoria	2007–08
25	114	c	MJ North	MJ North	Derbyshire v Gloucestershire	2008
26	118	c	AJ Hall	JF Brown	Derbyshire v Northamptonshire	2008
27	101	c	Mushfiqur Rahim	Rubel Hossain	Derbyshire v Bangladesh A	2008
28	248*				Derbyshire v Warwickshire	2008
29	159	c	PJ Forrest	NM Hauritz	Victoria v New South Wales	2008–09
30	115	c	L Ronchi	SJ Magoffin	Victoria v Western Australia	2008–09
31	147*				Victoria v Western Australia	2008–09
32	123	c	A Symonds	CP Simpson	Victoria v Queensland	2008–09
33	105	c	RA Broad	DJ Doran	Victoria v Queensland	2008–09
34	104	lbw		J Lewis	Derbyshire v Gloucestershire	2009
35	107	st	GO Jones	JC Tredwell	Derbyshire v Kent	2009
36	163	c	JWA Taylor	WA White	Derbyshire v Leicestershire	2009

	Score	How Out	Fielder	Bowler	Match	Season
37	208	lbw		A Khan	Derbyshire v Kent	2009
38	112*				Derbyshire v Middlesex	2009
39	222	c	DD Masters	GR Napier	Derbyshire v Essex	2009
40	149	c	AW O'Brien	DT Christian	Victoria v South Australia	2009–10
41	110	c	DC Bandy	AC Voges	Victoria v Western Australia	2009–10
42	200	lbw		GJ Batty	Derbyshire v Surrey	2010
43	140*				Derbyshire v Surrey	2010
44	141	lbw		JD Middlebrook	Derbyshire v Northamptonshire	2010
45	115	c	JN Batty	GM Hussain	Derbyshire v Gloucestershire	2010
46	125	c	AN Petersen	JAR Harris	Middlesex v Glamorgan	2011
47	148	b		DA Payne	Middlesex v Gloucestershire	2011
48	145	lbw		RA White	Middlesex v Northamptonshire	2011
49	121	c	MA Wallace	WT Owen	Middlesex v Glamorgan	2011
50	106	c	MC Henriques	SM Katich	Victoria v New South Wales	2011–12
51	118	c	TIF Triffitt	JM Bird	Victoria v Tasmania	2011–12
52	124	b		MA Beer	Victoria v Western Australia	2011–12
53	138*	no			Middlesex v Lancashire	2012
54	173	c	AV Suppiah	PD Trego	Middlesex v Somerset	2012
55	109	c	V Chopra	WB Rankin	Middlesex v Warwickshire	2012
56	125	c	DG Dawson	MA Starc	Victoria v New South Wales	2012–13
57	131	lbw		CJ Sayers	Victoria v South Australia	2012–13
58	101	c	CJ Gannon	JR Hopes	Victoria v Queensland	2012–13
59	214	b		GJ Batty	Middlesex v Surrey	2013
60	184	c	MH Yardy	SJ Magoffin	Middlesex v Sussex	2013
61	110	c	MJ Prior	GP Swann	Australia v England	2013
62	108	c	LJ Fletcher	AR Adams	Middlesex v Nottinghamshire	2013
63	117	c	SA Abbott	NM Lyon	Victoria v New South Wales	2013–14
64	116	c	JM Bairstow	MS Panesar	Australia v England	2013–14
65	119	c	SG Borthwick	SG Borthwick	Australia v England	2013–14
66	107		run out		Australia v South Africa	2013–14
67	241*				Middlesex v Yorkshire	2014
68	106	b		MNW Spriegel	Middlesex v Northamptonshire	2014
69	180	c	JWA Taylor	AR Adams	Middlesex v Nottinghamshire	2014
70	203*				Middlesex v Somerset	2014
71	107	c	PJ Hughes	JM Mennie	Victoria v South Australia	2014–15
72	112	lbw		AC Agar	Victoria v Western Australia	2014–15
73	173	b		SCJ Broad	Australia v England	2015
74	109	c	JA Simpson	TJ Murtagh	Somerset v Middlesex	2016

Acknowledgements

I'd like to thank my family first and foremost.

Dad pushed me, but always in a good way. His motto 'if you're not doing the work, Chris, someone else is' stuck with me. He was my biggest supporter, even when things seemed hopeless, and I can't imagine how I would've developed if not for him. Mum was always there providing balance to my often impulsive ways. The fact that she finds it too nerve-racking to watch me bat has always made me smile. She taught me the value of sticking at it; without that I would never have realised the highs I experienced.

My elder sister, Gillian, and my brother, David, often joked I was the favourite – no doubt it might have seemed that way, but they never begrudged me, even when I had to miss their weddings for cricket – something I'll always regret. To their spouses, Simon and Nikki, and to my nephews, Tom, Orson and Gulliver, and niece Bailey: I look forward to spending more time with you.

I couldn't have asked for a more supportive family, including the extended one: the children of Dad's late brother, Derek – Matt, Sally and Cathy; Dad's sister's family, the Giffords – Aunty Jude, Giffo, Helen, Bronwyn and Alison; and the family of Mum's brother, Rod Horn – wife Toni and children Peta, John and Ebony.

Huge thanks to so many I've been lucky enough to be coached by and to have played with.

Darren Wates, Phil Watkinson, Mike Paine, Chas Keogh, Charlie Burke, Toby Adams and Hugh Brown from Perth left big impressions on me and will always remain close friends.

Thanks to my best mate Shaun Doherty for everything. Being asked to be his best man was a very proud moment – I was slightly emotional at 2 am in Shaka Zulu in Camden, London.

John Morris, Angus Fraser, Greg Shipperd and Matt Maynard all took punts on me as a player and now their friendships mean a lot to me. Simon Helmot threw thousands of balls to me when I came to Melbourne and never complained once. His limitless enthusiasm is infectious.

Thanks to all the amateur clubs I played at in England, in particular North Devon, Exeter and Wellington, where I had fantastic times and made lifelong friends. Colin Payne at North Devon was like another father, while Frank Biederman and Lee Hart have been like brothers. Terry and Sharon O'Connor from Wellington have travelled the world to watch me play.

Melville, South Perth and University of WA clubs in Perth all gave me strong support, as did Essendon and Prahran in Melbourne. I'd very much like to thank Prahran, whose players made me feel so welcome, making Melbourne one of the best places on the planet for me.

The Warriors, such as Steve Magoffin, Ben Edmondson, Adam Voges, Marcus North, Ryan Campbell, Kade Harvey and Jo Angel, all made a difference. While I had to work for it, they gave me great support.

The Bushrangers were fantastic. I can't speak highly enough of Dave Hussey, Andrew McDonald, Brad Hodge,

Cam White, Damien Wright, Pete Handscomb, Aaron Finch, Dirk Nannes, Matty Wade and Bob Quiney. Those years winning titles with these guys were as good as any.

To all the guys who spoke in this book – Angus, Sam Robson, Graeme Swann, Steven Sylvester, Shane Watson, Peter Brukner and Paul Sealey – thank you for your time and kind words. Also Shippy for the foreword. Without your support, I'd have never played more than one game for Australia.

As for the Aussies, Darren Lehmann told me one of the best moments he's had in coaching was telling me I was to play in the First Ashes Test in 2013. I'll never forget that. Boof pushed me and supported me in equal measure, embracing my boisterous and fun-loving outlook. For that I am grateful, as it's the only way I could have succeeded.

To Michael Clarke, I was a little wary to begin with, but you had nothing but support for me and laughed at my (bad) jokes and made me feel at home. Hadds, Watto and Smudger all looked out for me, as did the support staff, in particular Peter Brukner, Alex Kountouris, Damian Mednis, Michael Di Venuto, Michael Lloyd and Dene Hills, whose use of my look-alike in team meetings always brought the house down. Davey Warner took a while to get used to, but he's got a heart of gold and always keeps in touch. Peter Siddle was the best to me, always there to put an arm around me when things were bad or when I'd done well. I have nothing but respect for him and his partner, Anna, and their passion for life.

I have deliberately not mentioned too much about my personal life in these pages, but to Kate, Kerry, Emma, Lucy and Sandra – I know I'm not perfect, but you all changed me for the better.

As for this book, I never really considered writing one, but my old agent, Rick Olarenshaw, was a believer, so thank you for your support and friendship. Also thanks to Pam Brewster and Michael Epis at Hardie Grant Publishing, who surprised me with their enthusiasm.

Lastly to Dan, my co-author … I've been fortunate enough to meet many fine journalists through cricket and had no hesitation asking Dan to help me. Apart from being a very skilled writer and award-winning author, he perhaps has a few similarities to me. While not always a natural fit with the players, he is a genuine guy who cares. Our friendship has been tested, but the more I got to know Dan, the more I saw those similarities – a little self-conscious and eager for approval, but also unwilling to back down and prepared to call a spade a spade. For that I have a lot of respect.

No doubt I've forgotten a few. I've been very fortunate to have an enjoyable career and, as so many past cricketers have said, it's all about the friendships you've made. In that sense I've been even more fortunate.

Chris Rogers,
Taunton, August 2016

I was very glad to get the call from Chris to help tell the story of his career and at the same time look into some of the areas of Australian cricket I'd not been able to get at when writing *Whitewash to Whitewash*.

Spending time with Chris as he played for Somerset was vital, which would not have been possible without the generosity of many, not least Brendan Cowell and Steve Cannane, a pair of tremendously giving hosts.

Thanks also to Clare Skinner and Neil Robinson at the MCC, who kindly let me use the Lord's library as a writing and researching base camp, while also offering good counsel and companionship. So too Sam Collins, Jon Hotten, Will Macpherson, Vithusan Ehantharajah, Melinda Farrell, Jonathan Liew, Joe Barton, Isabelle Westbury, Scyld Berry, Wayne Palmer, Mark Gallagher, Rob Wynn Jones, Jonny O'Hara, Sara-Jane Stone and the indefatigable Adam Collins.

At Hardie Grant, Pam Brewster has been an excellent and attentive publisher, keeping her composure even as the manuscript was a little slow to arrive. Michael Epis provided a high-quality editing job and lively email correspondence.

John and Ros Rogers opened up their cricket ground home, The Village Green, for an enjoyable visit and book-shaping discussion, while their photos, clippings and memories added just the right amount of anecdotal pepper.

At once subject and co-author, Chris has been unfailingly helpful, energetic and insightful. The care and attention to detail he has shown mirrors the fastidious nature of his batting, while he has also offered up the sort of frankness so rare in the airbrushed sporting world. His memory is better than he thought it was!

Daniel Brettig,
Melbourne, August 2016